18

Values and Development in Southeast Asia

Values and Development in Southeast Asia

JOHN CLAMMER

Pelanduk
Publications
www.pelanduk.com

Published by
Pelanduk Publications (M) Sdn Bhd
(Co. No. 113307-W)
12 Jalan SS13/3E
Subang Jaya Industrial Estate
47500 Subang Jaya
Selangor Darul Ehsan, Malaysia

Address all correspondence to
Pelanduk Publications (M) Sdn Bhd
P.O. Box 8265, 46785 Kelana Jaya
Selangor Darul Ehsan, Malaysia

Check out our website at *www.pelanduk.com*
e-mail: *mypp@tm.net.my*

1st printing 1996
2nd printing 2000

Perpustakaan Negara Malaysia   Cataloguing-in-Publication Data

Clammer, John
Values and development in Southeast Asia / John Clammer.
Includes index.
ISBN 967-978-568-8
1. Asia, Southeastern—Cultural policy. 2. Social change—Asia, Southeastern. 3. Asia, Southeastern—Social conditions. 4. Asia, Southeastern—Economic conditions. 5. Asia, Southeastern—Intellectual life. 6. Asia, Southeastern—Politics and government. I. Title.

Printed in Malaysia by
Academe Art & Printing Services Sdn Bhd

CONTENTS

ABOUT THE AUTHOR

Dr John Clammer is presently Professor of Comparative Sociology and Asian Studies at Sophia University in Tokyo, Japan.

A graduate of Oxford University, Clammer's previous positions include teaching positions in the Centre for Southeast Asian Studies at the University of Hull and at the Department of Sociology of the National University of Singapore, and visiting positions at the Institute of Southeast Asian Studies, Singapore; the Centre for Southeast Asian Studies at the University of Kent; the Asia Research Centre at Murdoch University; and the Institute of Oriental Cultures at Tokyo University.

Clammer's interests include the sociology of religion, ethnicity and social change in Southeast and East Asia, and he has published widely on these topics, including books on the Peranakan Chinese communities of Malaysia and Singapore, on ideology and religion in Singapore and on the political economy of Southeast Asia.

ACKNOWLEDGEMENT

This book evolved in the course of my teaching and research on issues related to the sociology and anthropology of development at the National University of Singapore and at Sophia University, Tokyo. Chapters 2-5 and 8 emerged out of seminars in the Advanced Management Development Programme at Sophia University and I would like to thank my colleagues there and especially Radha Sinha and Yoshino Kosaku for their encouragement and critical feedback. Chapter 6 began as part of a collective project directed by Grant Evans whose detailed criticisms greatly shaped the final version. The other chapters grew out of work undertaken at the National University of Singapore and the stimulation of former colleagues at the Department of Sociology there is acknowledged. Wazir Jahan Karim of Universiti Sains Malaysia inspired Chapter 10 and has been a constant source of intellectual friendship and support. Last but not least, thanks to Chikako for her help with word processing, critiques of my writing and perceptive observations on many of the issues discussed in this book.

Chapter 1

CULTURAL ANALYSIS AND THE PROBLEMS OF DEVELOPMENT IN SOUTHEAST ASIA

Despite decades of economic growth in Southeast Asia many of the classical problems of "development" have not disappeared. At the practical level poverty continues to be a major problem, uncontrolled urban growth leads to immense stress for city dwellers and to great strain on national infrastructures, and high growth itself leads to the pollution and destruction of the natural environment and to the promotion of consumption as a way of life. At the theoretical level there are likewise many unresolved questions: of the relationship between economic growth and social change, of the place of religion and systems of values in determining the direction that development should take and of the possible foundations of local models of change and development different from those of the already developed West or Japan.

Many answers have been proposed to these questions and a number of methodologies formulated in attempts to define the issues of development in terms of local political or ethnic conditions (Mahathir 1970), of indigenous religious traditions and especially Buddhism in Thailand (Sulak 1992), Islam in Malaysia (Jomo 1993) and Catholicism in the Philippines, or of the connections between local cultures and planned social and economic change (Dove 1988). Others have attempted to explore these questions historically through the analysis of indigenous social movements themselves, often religious in inspiration (e.g. Ileto 1989) through the way in which images of Asian society have been constructed, especially through colonialism, and then used to justify unequal patterns of development (Said 1985; Alatas 1977a), or through the social roles of particular strategic groups such as indigenous intellectuals which have played a key part in formulating thinking about change and the ideological conditions which lead to the production of particular models of society (Alatas 1977b).

Common to many of these approaches, and especially those that have emerged within Southeast Asia itself, has been a preoccupation with issues of values. This preoccupation has appeared in a number of forms: concern with religion in its relationship to development, deepening interest in what has come to be called "sustainable development", increased interest in ecology and the question of what kind of society and economy ecological responsibility implies, concern with the meaning of the term "development" itself and engagement with theoretical debates mainly coming from the West about the concept of modernity and of its possible successor—post-modernity—and the vital question of whether these large scale historical movements, which have in complex and sometimes indirect ways influenced most parts of Asia (Clammer 1995), have led to increased human emancipation or increased entrapment within what Weber called the "Iron Cage" of rationalised, bureaucratised and managerialised modern societies.

In all of these approaches there is the recognition of the fact that all development or concepts of development must include at their core the human dimension. All development worthy of the name must in other words be in the interests of human beings, their fundamental needs and their self-fulfilment. While economic growth may be part of the total package of development, it cannot be the whole. Economics, indeed, from this point of view, is subordinate to other objectives: sustainable change, cultural development, modification of social structures in more humane directions and the recognition of the fact that values (whether expressed in religion, in indigenous agricultural or ecological practices or through more diffuse cultural forms) are not just "related" to development or somehow need to be taken into account in formulating economic or social policies, but in reality are true and integral development in themselves or at the very least are the basis for any such development. Values on this view are foundational, not derivative.

To some people this view will be contentious and so it is necessary at the outset to establish some premises on which this position can be justified. The starting point must be the view that it is necessary to examine the nature, rate, direction and constraints on social, economic and political change in Southeast Asia in the context of specific historical patterns discernible in the pasts of the individual societies of the region. At the same time as the specificities of individual societies are respected, there are also broad principles of analysis and of relatively recent historical experience (for example, colonialism and postcolonialism, increased contact and influence from Japan rather than directly from the West) that make comparative analysis and generalisations both possible and necessary. There are indeed patterns of social transformation in Southeast Asia that are unique in certain important respects, but many are also part of larger global changes. These two levels are not contradictory, but can be treated together within a unified model that grapples with what I see as being a major theoretical gap in conventional forms of analysis—the linkages between the level of political economy and the level of culture (Clammer 1985).

Many studies of Southeast Asian social transformation that have come from the "development studies" perspective (and especially those of a Marxist or neo-Marxist persuasion) have seriously neglected the dimension of cultural history. Those approaches that do stress such factors (such as the sinological or history of religious traditions), on the other hand, largely ignore the economic, political or even social structural questions. Both approaches offer important but incomplete versions of reality, and a more accurate model for exploring social change requires as its theoretical core a synthesis of political economy and cultural analysis. This requires a methodology that we still have to largely create and this book represents a step in this direction.

Currently, there are four major competing paradigms. The first of these is the Marxist approach, stressing the primacy of economics and the methodology and assumptions of historical materialism, class analysis, imperialism and in the current context in Asia, the new international division of labour. While many attempts have been made to relate Marxism to the analysis of Asian societies (e.g. Banerjee 1985) the fact remains that Marxism is weak in its treatment of culture and even weaker in its empirical treatment of religion as a social phenomenon. The second is the empirico-historical approach, stressing actual historical case studies and using these to build large scale theories of social transformation. This approach is exemplified in the work of individuals such as Max Weber, Barrington Moore, Edward Said, Ferdinand Braudel and Perry Anderson. The third is the sociology of development approach, using such concepts as peripheral capitalism, world system, dependency and specific localised expressions of these with reference to factors such as gender, ethnicity and the "informal sector". Out of this approach has emerged the "culture and development" methodology. The fourth represents a constellation of theories coming out of debates about postmodernism, contemporary cultural theory, social movements theory, critical theory and postcolonial theory. All of these approaches, which in practice overlap and draw on each other, provide many of the elements of a vocabulary of social transformation. The acid test however in this context is the extent to which they genuinely explain Southeast Asian social realities.

Here, a number of preliminary points need to be made initially. We are in this text using the term "Southeast Asia". It would be quite possible, but probably rather fruitless, to spend time here debating the precise geographical boundaries of Southeast Asia. These questions do indeed have their place, but mainly because they actually pose political and cultural rather than really geographical questions: who defines the boundaries of the region, what power relationships are revealed by this process of naming, categorising and excluding? A better approach might be to accept, at least provisionally, the more or less conventional geographical boundaries as a creation of the modern world system and then to raise other questions about what these geographical categories reveal. And they do reveal a number of things: not only colonial images of spatial boundaries, but also images that are not primarily economic or political on the surface (although they may also have these dimensions) such as ideas about "race" and especially about religion and also about culture and language. Parts of Southeast Asia which are clearly separated and even antagonistic politically may in fact be deeply linked ethnolinguistically for instance.

But while culture, and with it values, needs to be reintroduced into the discussion of development in Southeast Asia, it is also very necessary to avoid the pitfalls of culturalism. The concept of "culture" is often used as an explanation of last resort: if nothing else works, then try "culture". In fact culture itself needs defining, not only in an abstract anthropological sense but also in terms of how the concept is used in specific local contexts, and needs to be subject to critical appraisal since cultural arguments can as well be used to promote bondage as to promote liberation. It is exactly here that the notion of culture needs to be related to economic, social and political processes: how is it produced, reproduced and consumed? By whom and in whose interests? Does it liberate or produce subtle and hard to recognise bonds—does it for example through mechanisms of socialisation reproduce gender and class inequalities? Culture is clearly two-faced: it is both the necessary vehicle for personal and collective identity and it can also oppress and distort true humanity, as commentators on mass culture like Adorno have argued.

Having said this, several examples of the role of cultural analysis in the definition of social formations and in the explanation of their transformations come to mind. An obvious one is religion—a vital and major force throughout Southeast Asia, but with many diverse articulations with ethnicity, economic structures, ideologies, gender relations and images of nature. The religions of Asia themselves, their socio-political implications and the intellectual models needed to understand them are often at radical variance from their Western counterparts. But at least religion has a major place in the scholarship of both modern and historical Asia, but the same cannot be said for many other dimensions of culture such as literature, the material arts, ideas of selfhood, ecological practices, images of the body or indigenous technology, to name a few of the most important. Culture in turn is related to sociology—to kinship and family, for instance—and forms the central theme in the sociologies of knowledge prevailing in specific Southeast Asian societies.

These linkages can be seen in a number of concrete areas, for example in the emergence of consumer culture throughout the region and especially in its major urban centres, and in the continuous debates in some parts of the region about the definition or creation of "Asian values" seen as somehow emerging from the "collectivist" East with its roots in Hinduism, Buddhism, Confucianism or Islam, as opposed to the values of the allegedly "individualist" West with its roots in Christianity (Seah 1977; Dumont 1986). Revealingly, most, if not all, debates about "Asian values" see the ultimate source of these values in religion, not in some Asianised form of secular humanism. The debate is also interesting in that it demonstrates indigenous social theory (and theorists) at work. An extremely neglected aspect of social change in Southeast Asia has been the role of indigenous social thought or of such thought that has taken and transformed an outside intellectual tradition (e.g. Marxism or psychoanalysis) into something quite localised. The role of such thought, the place and function of the indigenous producers of culture—writers, intellectuals and religious thinkers—and its contribution to the heritage of mankind are widely ignored, especially in "development studies". Such thought has however shaped social change, the reception of innovations, responses to such major shifts as the end of colonialism or the emergence of mass consumption, just as much as it has in the West. Such indigenous social thought has close links with religious thought, with local forms of literary, theatrical or musical expression, with the visual arts and with film and media and to ideas about and experiments with education and alternative forms of social life.

The social forms of Southeast Asia are of great complexity and historical antiquity and cannot be understood through simple formulae, but only through a close examination of their culture, social structures, belief systems and of the articulation of these with political and economic structures and with ecological regimes. The tendency to begin with concepts derived from the West such as "feudalism" should be handled with care. Since the historical expansion of the West mainly through its varieties of colonialism—various in style and with differential emphasis on economic, political, religious or cultural domination—there have been common experiences such as the penetration of capitalism, imposition of Western political models, integration into the world economy and the new international division of labour, technological domination by the West or by Japan, the emergence of new classes and often the widening of social differences and new forms of poverty and of course extensive industrialisation and urbanisation. These common experiences have not been responded to in the same way, precisely because of the interplay between the new historical forces and indigenous cultural patterns. This interplay has in turn created new types of social formation—peripheral capitalist societies, multiethnic states and so forth which then themselves enter into the complex dance of relations both with the old metropolitan countries and with each other which has created in turn such possibilities as Asean. While economics may be dominant in these relationships, it is not determining since actual outcomes emerge from the interplay of economics and culture. Any theory of contemporary or historical Southeast Asian social formations must necessarily be a theory of social transformation.

Any attempt to create such a theory should contain three key elements: an appreciation of indigenous concepts of social organisation, a critical and contextualised applications of concepts derived from Western historiography, political economy and cultural theory and a view of the past which does not impose closure on the paths for the future still open to contemporary Southeast Asian societies. Such a theory would also have to take into account five major structuring processes: state formation and the emergence of modern concepts of the nation (Anderson 1991); patterns of social inequality including such factors as cultures of bureaucracy, the reproduction of power relations at the local level, gender, and what is conventionally called "social structure"; patterns of ideology and culture including religion, value systems, ideologies and what used to be called "world views"; modes of ecological and technological organisation; and the management of contact with other cultures, including questions of on what principles each society defines and perceives itself—race, religion, mode of political or social organisation or geography for instance.

The issues here are thus in a very real sense philosophical and also moral ones. Any model of society contains moral ambiguities. One classical expression of this is orientalism which, while in some ways genuinely desiring to stress the originality and uniqueness of Asian cultures, did so at the expense of radically romanticising and exoticising them. Much contemporary sociology of development has the opposite effect however. While ruthlessly and rationally uncovering the economic patterns of capitalist penetration, it renders its subjects pathetic by creating little sense of the actual vitality, cultural richness, sources of hope, struggle and resistance that are actually present in even the most "underdeveloped" society.

In reality what Jonathan Friedman has called "material logic" and what he calls "cultural logics" are not only related like parts of a Mobius ring, but both are also located within change. But whether we can then use the vocabulary that Friedman proposes: tradition, modernity and post-modernity (Friedman 1989) is very much open to question. If "traditional" as "pre-modern" means the non-adoption of Western preoccupations with rationalisation then perhaps much of Asia has succeeded in escaping Weber's "Iron Cage" and have instead succeeded in creating civilisations very different, which capitalism and colonialism have indeed distorted, but have never fully dominated .

This book is a contribution to the understanding of the role of values in development in contemporary Southeast Asia. As such, it has several objectives. The first of these is to demonstrate through a variety of case studies the ways in which values and development interact and inform each other. The second is to enter into dialogue with some of the most interesting theoretical trends that have emerged in the Western world as attempts to grasp the nature of social transformation. The third is to expand the conventional notion of "development" to include issues of culture, religion, ethnicity, language and the nature and position of the producers of discourse about development (i.e. intellectuals), all currently issues peripheral to most mainstream sociology of development. The fourth is to explore some promising models of social change and to delineate some of the major intellectual issues involved in applying them to the concrete analysis of contemporary Southeast Asian societies.

This book does this in its first part through several theoretical moves. The first of these is to consider the relationship between values and social structure. As I have been arguing in this chapter, values cannot be seen as free-floating entities, but are in reality embedded in and expressions of modes of social organisation. The second is to explore what is actually meant by "values" and to develop a methodology for the analysis of such values in relation to practical issues in human development in Southeast Asia. This leads fairly naturally to a discussion of one of the major models for understanding contemporary social transformations that has so far been very little utilised in the analysis of Southeast Asian societies, notably postmodernism. This section reviews what is meant by this controversial term and how and to what extent it may relate to the understanding of social change. Clearly, in any discussion of development, economic factors loom large. The next two chapters consider the relationships between economics and sociological and cultural factors and attempt to relate the economic changes identified in postmodern theory to the realities of Southeast Asia today, including the fact that much of the region is still rural and contains many social groups and economic practices still well outside the ambit of postmodernity, and even possibly of modernity. The final chapter in the first section deals with one of the major Western classical theorists of social change: Max Weber. Weber in particular dealt centrally with questions of value and of religion and so the issue of the relationship of Weber's ideas to understanding the relationship between values and religion and development in today's Southeast Asia is highly appropriate, especially as Weber himself was not only a theorist of modernity and its rationalising tendencies, but also a critic of those same tendencies.

The second part of the book deals with a range of applications of these theoretical frameworks to a set of central and concrete case studies within the region: the question of urbanisation, the links between religion and capitalism, the position and role of Southeast Asian intellectuals in development discourse, and discourses of race, their connection to ideology and use of allegedly "scientific" models from outside of the region both geographically and in terms of cultural traditions.

Overall then the book both illustrates connections between values and development within Southeast Asia and links development discourses within the region to wider theoretical debates about social transformation and about the role of values in relation to social change, an issue that has been a key question for the social sciences since their emergence in the 19th century. These debates are not only something that occurred in the past. They inform, implicitly or explicitly, almost all contemporary discussions of the nature of the state, the ideal society, the nature of political culture, the sought for balance between tradition and modernity. They also provide the links with emerging trends in social theory reinvigorated by input from several sources. These include renewed interest in religion and the anti-secular tendencies found worldwide and certainly throughout much of Southeast Asia, an anti-materialist reaction that has set in to too much consumption amongst the new middle classes, and widespread interest in ecology and its implications for social change and social futures throughout the region.

Ecological thinking is especially interesting as it articulates clearly with the central place of nature in the thinking and philosophical traditions of many Asian cultures. Whereas in Europe nature is largely seen as something other than and even as set against human beings who dominate it through technology, in much of Asia nature is seen in intimate relations to humans and as part of the constitution of human society (Callicott and Ames 1989). Cosmology in such a context is not just a physical model of the universe, but equally or even principally a set of values. Recent ecological critiques of anthropcentrism in the West actually have a long pedigree in Asia, especially in the parts dominated by Buddhism and Shintoism. The concept of "ecological values" that has emerged as part of this critique and which includes values such as conservation and sustainable uses of nature, reverence for life, mutual responsibility for each other's and the planet's welfare and social justice as "eco-justice" (e.g. Skolimowski 1992) reflects principles that have long been present, even if not articulated in this form, in many Asian religions and philosophical traditions. In this view any kind of sustainable progress is dependent on certain basic or foundational values in which human life is actually rooted. The elimination of natural species and other cultures in the interests of economic development and the spreading of consumer culture is fundamentally unacceptable from this point of view, which from an interestingly fresh angle breathes new life into the old Marxist notions of "species being"—our essential nature as human beings and of alienation—the state of not being in tune with this mode of being. The ecological viewpoint also suggests that enormous wisdom about what kind of development is possible or desirable resides in traditional cultures which have maintained their sense of values intact.

At another level altogether the question of values and development poses new ways of looking at many of the questions currently central to a number of branches of the social sciences. One major example of this is the sociology of the prominent British scholar Anthony Giddens. Giddens has suggested, in formulating his own influential theoretical position known as "structuration theory" that the central issue in the social sciences is answering the question of the relationship between agency and structure—between individual social actors and the large scale organisation of society—or in simpler language between the micro and macro. Giddens develops a sophisticated answer to this question which interestingly does not deal at all with the question of values as mediating between the two levels, nor does he consider the possibility that from certain value or religio-theoretical perspectives, the problem does not exist in this form at all (Giddens 1983). Giddens' whole model implies a view of the self, and thus of agency, which is highly ethnocentric in nature. From this one example alone, the theoretical importance of linking values to wider dimensions of society should be apparent.

A second example emerges from the debates on postmodernism. David Harvey, a major commentator on this theory (Harvey 1989), has suggested that a key to understanding the modern world and the emergence of postmodernism lies in the linking of changes in the world economy and associated cultural changes. With the move from "Fordism" or rationalised production line style manufacturing to "post-Fordist" or flexible accumulation style capitalism a chain of cultural consequences have been triggered showing up not only in such literally concrete forms such as architecture and of course in the forms of consumer culture, but in changes in the organisation and perception of time and space—what he terms "space-time compression". Again the question of values enters here in a subtle way. Harvey, like Giddens, does not directly discuss values, but unlike Giddens they are implicit in his whole model which is actually about the relationship of values and macrosocial change.

A third example, in which the issue of values and culture is even more central, is in contemporary debates about the relationship of modernity and identity, both collective (cultural) identity and individual or self identity. A constellation of major themes in sociology has recently emerged in relation to the attempt to grasp the nature of modernity—its nature, characteristics and the historically specific forms that it has taken, and of identity—both individual and collective and of the relationships between modernity and identity. Out of this have sprung a range of debates about postcolonialism, feminism, race, intellectuals and "development" and about the ability (or even the right) of social sciences based on or rooted in Western philosophical paradigms to represent "The Other". One of the effects of this has been to move debate from an exclusive concern with the problems of the West (as in Giddens' work) to a concern with the rest of the world and in this case Asia (Clammer 1995; Gomes 1994).

Questions of "identity" necessarily involve questions of philosophical anthropology, of how identities are constructed in the contexts of gender, ethnicity, religion and nationality. Especially when the issue of identity is seen in collective rather than purely individual terms, the question of culture takes central place and with it once again the problem of values. The creation of an identity whether individual or collective does not simply (or even) involve the search for some kind of essence. It rather implies the attempt to locate oneself or one's culture in terms of a framework of values—a world view understood not only as a cosmology, but equally as an orientation to that cosmology—to practice in other words. This is why, and quite correctly in my view, the seminal work of Pierre Bourdieu on the foundations of the social sciences deals as its central concern with the nature of practice (Bourdieu 1977). This methodologically helps substantially to overcome the ethnocentricity of much Western scholarship on the question of identity such as that of Giddens (1991) whose discussion of the issue specifically and quite consciously ignores any societies except English-speaking North Atlantic ones.

The world has become a very complex place. Information and production systems have changed their natures, objects (things) have become mobile and subjects (people) have become more mobile than ever before in human history. New classes have been created and new underclasses have appeared, post-industrialisation—so-called in the advanced economies—has led to both the burgeoning of the service sector and to the export of (often polluting) industries offshore to the developing world, demand in the north has severe ecological effects on the south, tourism has become one of the world's biggest industries and globalisation has major impact on national and local cultures (Lash and Urry 1994). From whichever angle one approaches development questions the issue of values remains central. Indeed ultimately "development" is precisely about values, the quality of human life, the enhancement of human potential, relationship to the natural environment and defining and pursuing the proper ends of human existence. As human beings are culture-bearing creatures necessarily the discussion of factors which have remained largely peripheral to mainstream development thinking (see, for example, what is considered to be development thinking in Preston 1985) needs to take a more central place—culture itself, religion, values of a non-religious origin and beliefs about the world, including scientific and quasi-scientific ones.

This can be done both through the delineation of general analysis of values-constructing activities and through the examination of cases and instances where this activity takes place. This book attempts to blend these two approaches and to do so in the context of a specific geographical region. But while the cases presented here are localised in context, it is also true that they have comparative implications. This is partly because many developing countries have passed through similar experiences of colonialism, export-led industrialisation and subsequent environmental pollution for example. Almost all have had to negotiate the relationship between their local cultural and religious traditions and the more universalising forces of urbanisation, industrialisation and globalism. And all have certainly faced the problem of defining the nature of the kind of development that they want and of its relationship to the values that they want to improve or enhance. This is a continuous and historical process and as such a constantly evolving one. Southeast Asia is in conventional terms one of the fastest developing areas in the world today. It is also a region of rich and living cultural traditions, religious diversity, ethnic complexity and ecological variety which has been shaped by centuries of inter- and intraregional cultural contact, trade and political influences. While the question of values is central in any part of the world, it is certainly well illustrated in Southeast Asia, a region which has not only received, modified and reproduced models of culture and belief, but which has also created its own and will continue to do so in the future out of the interaction of globalism and its own local conditions.

References

Alatas, S.H. (1977a), *The Myth of the Lazy Native*, London: Frank Cass.

Alatas, S.H. (1977b), *Intellectuals in Developing Societies*, London: Frank Cass.

Anderson, B. (1991), *Imagined Communities*, London: Verso.

Banerjee, D. (ed.) (1985), *Marxian Theory and the Third World*, New Delhi and Beverly Hills: Sage.

Bourdieu, P. (1977), *Outline of a Theory of Practice*, Cambridge: Cambridge University Press.

Callicott, J.B. and R.T. Ames (eds.) (1989), *Nature in Asian Traditions of Thought*, Honolulu: University of Hawaii Press.

Clammer, J. (1985), *Anthropology and Political Economy: Theoretical and Asian Perspectives*, London: Macmillan.

Clammer, J. (1995), *Difference and Modernity: Social Theory and Contemporary Japanese Society*, London: Kegan Paul International.

Dove, M.R. (ed.) (1988), *The Real and Imagined Role of Culture in Development: Case Studies from Indonesia*, Honolulu: University of Hawaii Press.

Dumont, L. (1986), *Essays on Individualism: Modern Identity in Anthropological Perspective*, Chicago: University of Chicago Press.

Friedman, J. (1988), "Cultural Logics of the Global System: A Sketch," *Theory, Culture and Society* 5: 2-3.

Giddens, A. (1983), *Central Problems in Social Theory: Action, Structure and Contradiction in Social Analysis*, London: Macmillan.

Giddens, A. (1991), *Modernity and Self-Identity: Self and Society in the Late Modern Age*, Stanford: Stanford University Press.

Gomes, A. (ed.) (1994), *Modernity and Identity: Asian Illustrations*, Victoria: LaTrobe University Press.

Harvey, D. (1989), *The Condition of Postmodernity*, Oxford: Blackwells.

Ileto, R.C. (1989), *Pasyon and Revolution: Popular Movements in the Philippines, 1840-1910*, Quezon City: Ateneo de Manila University Press.

Jomo, K.S. (ed.) (1993), *Islamic Economic Alternatives: Critical Perspective and New Directions*, Kuala Lumpur: Ikraq.

Lash, S. and J. Urry (1994), *Economies of Signs and Space*, London: Sage.

Mahathir Mohamed (1970), *The Malay Dilemma*, Singapore: Donald Moore Press.

Preston, P.W. (1985), *New Trends in Development Theory*, London: Routledge.

Said, E. (1985), *Orientalism*, Harmondsworth: Penguin Books.

Seah, C.M. (ed.) (1977), *Asian Values and Modernisation*, Singapore: Singapore University Press.

Skolimowski, H. (1992), *Living Philosophy: Eco-Philosophy as a Tree of Life*, London: Arkana.

Sulak, S. (1992), *Seeds of Peace: A Buddhist Vision for Renewing Society*, Berkeley: Parallax Press.

Chapter 2

SOCIAL STRUCTURES AND VALUE SYSTEMS IN SOUTHEAST ASIA

Sociologically speaking Southeast Asia is an area of both great diversity and of certain profound unities or continuities. Although individual cultures vary considerably in their details, they can also be grouped into broad categories which share many common structural features in terms of such characteristic aspects of society as patterns of marriage, family, descent and inheritance.

In this chapter we will focus on this dialectic of unity and diversity, focusing on two closely related themes: the social structure, meaning the basic patterns of social organisation (marriage, social stratification, power and leadership), and the ways in which these organisational features are reflected in and underpinned by systems of values, such as traditional views of rank, status, authority, law and human relationships. These two levels of social structure—the actual institutions and the values that underlay them always exist, although the relationship between them varies from culture to culture—in some cases being mediated primarily through religion, in others through concepts of descent and inheritance, and in yet others through the relationship of those cultures to land, sea or natural resources. The cosmology (values) of a people always take concrete sociological and cultural forms. In practice in Southeast Asia the focal point of the relationship between the two levels or aspects is most often found to be kinship—an area of intimate interest to everybody and which by its very nature embodies many of a cultures' profoundest (although often unexpressed) views of human relationships and of the links between those relationships and biological, ecological, economic and political processes. A good example of this is the "bilateral principle" very widespread amongst indigenous Southeast Asian peoples, which dictates that descent and the inheritance of property takes place through both male and female lines. This has many implications for male-female relationships before, during and after marriage, for the status of women, for systems of land tenure and for the possibility of accumulation of economic capital, amongst others.

The focus of this chapter will be on the indigenous peoples of Southeast Asia, understood as being those peoples of long historical settlement in the region who have developed their existing social structures *in situ*, and have not, at least primarily introduced them from outside. This largely excludes from our consideration the so-called "immigrant peoples" who form a usually small, but often economically significant, proportion of existing national populations. Chief amongst these peoples are the Chinese who have settled throughout the region in considerable numbers (and who actually form a majority in Singapore) and whose typical social structure—a strong patrilineal pattern of descent, a closely knit organisation of clans and dialect and regional associations, and an underlying religious ideology of ancestor veneration—is very different from that of the typical indigenous cultures. Other important minorities are Indians, mainly Tamils and other south Indian peoples, and Sikhs from north-western India, Arabs and many smaller groups including Jews, Parsis, Ceylonese, Pakistanis and Nepalese, all of whom have contributed to the social, cultural, religious and linguistic mosaic of Southeast Asia.

So while our emphasis here will be on those cultures recognised as traditionally Southeast Asian, we must acknowledge that these cultures themselves have been often deeply influenced by the impact of the immigrant peoples, by their own historical migrations and by the influence of imported religions. Living in close proximity to another culture often leads to the borrowing of some of its most attractive features. This has happened throughout Southeast Asian cultural history, and it continues to happen today. A good example of this would be the Baba or Peranakan Chinese of Malaysia, Singapore and Indonesia who, while remaining ethnically and religiously Chinese, have adopted Malay-style dress and cuisine and a language which, while still containing Chinese elements, is basically a Malay patois. Many of the indigenous peoples themselves have a migratory history, good cases in point being the hill peoples of Thailand, the seafaring Bugis of Indonesia or the shoreline dwelling Orang Laut of the Malaysian and southern Thai coastlines, and indeed many of the majority peoples, including the Thai proper, have only relatively recently settled within their existing political borders. Many of the religious beliefs and institutions of

Southeast Asia have also come from outside—Buddhism, Islam and Roman Catholicism being the most prominent examples with contemporary influence, although historically other now more submerged traditions, such as Hinduism in Thailand, Cambodia and Indonesia (still extant formally only in Bali) and Confucianism in Vietnam, have played a very important role. Today there is continuous interaction between the indigenous traditions and value systems and these imported products, so much so that in many cases what is indigenous and what is not has become impossible to distinguish, so indigenised has the imported system become.

Towards a Classification of Social Types

Before we examine in detail some of the main varieties of regional social structures we should initially sketch a very broad scheme of classification. Here we find that we have three principles at work: one religious, one sociological, one ecological. On the religious dimension a four-fold classification emerges:

1. the largely Therevada Buddhist north, including Burma, Thailand, Cambodia, and to a lesser extent Vietnam, which is mainly Buddhist, but of the Mahayana school;
2. the Muslim south, including Malaysia, southern Thailand, and Indonesia as far east as Bali and the southern Philippines;
3. the Christian east, including most of the Philippines and large communities in eastern Indonesia, including Ambon, Irian Jaya and Kalimantan; and
4. the "tribal" or animistic cultures of northern Thailand, the Vietnamese hill country, Irian Jaya, the northern Philippines and the Orang Asli (aboriginal) peoples of Malaysia.

This is of course a simplified model—many Vietnamese are Catholic, many hill peoples are Christian, and so on, but it does indicate the general pattern. On the sociological dimension we find a broad classification into unilineal and bilateral kinship systems. The former are sub-divided into patrilineal systems, of which the Vietnamese provide a good example, and matrilineal, of which the classic example is that of the Minangkabau of Sumatra. There are many examples of the second, two being the Malaysian

Malays and the Iban peoples of Kalimantan and Sarawak. On the ecological dimension we find the division into those cultures based on lowland wet rice cultivation (such as Thais, Malays and Javanese; those on hill (dry) rice and swidden cultivation (the Thai hill peoples, Iban, Orang Asli); and fishing and trading (Bugis, coastal Malays and Filipinos, Orang Laut).

The immigrant peoples tend to be concentrated in urban trades and services and in plantation agriculture (rubber, oil palm, pineapples, market gardening). The interplay between religion, kinship and ecology is something that should be stressed.

Models of the Social System

Having now set out the general context, we will explore in some detail a number of selected examples drawn from these categories of social organisation.

Unilineal Systems. A society of this type is one in which kinship is organised in the form of a descent group tracing its origins from a common ancestor and in which the inheritance of property, status or name passes either through the male line, in which case the society is patrilineal, or, less commonly, through the female line, i.e. from mother to daughter, in which case the society is matrilineal. Examples of the first type co-exist with a variety of ecological systems, including both upland economies (usually a mixture of dry rice, vegetable gardening, hunting and gathering and sometimes also the cultivation of opium, practiced on a shifting or "slash and burn" basis) and lowland wet rice economies. An example of the former is that of the Lamet people of northwestern Laos, a Mon-Khmer speaking people with an interesting religion that is a mixture of animism, centred on a common hill peoples' belief that rice, alone of all plants, has a soul, and ancestor worship, a common feature of many patrilineal societies. Status is linked to a relationship between economic success and religion, since to undertake the sacrifices to the ancestors requires considerable wealth. Work and marriage (acquiring one or two hardworking wives) are not only for subsistence, but also for prestige competition. Buffaloes in particular are a high value investment, the income from which is ultimately invested physically in bronze drums and socially in buying in wives for a man's sons. The high social status associated with such affluence is marked by the attainment of the noble status of Lem which attract further wealth and admiration, but which is not hereditary or necessarily permanent—a Lem must constantly maintain his position through promoting regular feasts, otherwise the status is lost. The basic units of social organisation are the seven patrilineal clans into which the Lamet are grouped. Each clan has a totemic name and all members of a clan are considered related, the clans are exogamous, and each village consists of two or more clans. Marriage thus takes place between unrelated members of different clans, and bride-price is paid to the girl's parents. A Lem's daughter is costly, which prevents poorer Lamet marrying into high status families and this creates a kind of class system. A Lem himself however may be able to afford more than one wife. Unmarried male children sleep in a community house and not in their parents' residence, unless they sleep with their girlfriends in her parents' house, which is considered quite acceptable. All Lamet are farmers, and there is little ranking except on the basis of wealth and little division of labour between men and women or between men, except for the existence of shamans (who are also farmers) and the village leader or *xumia*, whose position is hereditary in the male line, but whose authority is limited to supervising the community house, to fixing the ceremonial cycle and to sacrificing to the village spirits.

A very contrasting form of patrilineal organisation is that of the Vietnamese, partly because the direct Chinese influence on their culture is so apparent, and much more so than on any other Southeast Asian culture, a fact that still deeply effects relations between Vietnam and China, bound together by cultural ties, but political rivals for long historical periods. The most Sinicised of all Southeast Asian peoples, it may be that the vigor and expansionist energies of the Vietnamese are a combination of their native qualities and the organising and socially disciplining effects of a Chinese type of social organisation. Essentially a lowland, wet rice people, concentrated in the Red River basin of the north and the Mekong delta of the south and shunning the mountains of central Vietnam which are occupied by hill peoples of a very different culture and ecology, traditionally the Vietnamese subscribed to a very hierarchical emperor system, modelled on that of China and undergirded by a Confucian ideology, and supported by a bureaucracy entered through competitive examinations based on a mastery of the Chinese classics. This system lasted until 1915 when it was abolished by the French colonial rulers and when it had in any case been undermined by the phasing out of the writing of Vietnamese in Chinese characters and their replacement by the more accessible system of *quoc ngu* romanised transcription during the nineteenth century. This centralised system co-existed with, and was indeed often very separate from, the largely autonomous villages dominated by the land-lord class, and who were sometimes also members of the scholar class. A thoroughly ranked system from emperor down to landless peasant thus emerged in Vietnam in contrast to Thailand or Burma, with the additional important feature that, unlike in the princely system of Thailand, a commoner could in principle enter the highest social ranks through merit by way of the examinations. This relative "tightness" of the Vietnamese social structure (its highly ranked nature) is to be seen not only in the formal structure, but also in the organisation at the local levels, where villages were closely knit communities, partly because of the labour requirements and degree of co-ordination necessary to carry out successful wet rice cultivation on a large scale. Each village had a ceremonial centre—the *dinh*, the home of the village's patron deity, and a great deal of co-operation took place within villages and often villages specialised in a particular craft such as silk or paper manufacture, or, on the coast, fishing or boat-building.

As any student of Chinese society knows, the lineage is an ideal way of organising this kind of complex ecology, and the Vietnamese recognised this and adopted a patrilineal system with a limited number of surnames and the ideal of the large extended family as the preferred residential unit. Unlike the Chinese, however, surname exogamy does not apply, and women retained the right to own and inherit land separate from their husbands and there is considerable sexual division of labour (shopkeeping being largely a women's occupation, for example.) It is worth that this high status of women and their dominance of certain niches in the economy, is very widespread in Southeast Asia. Each patrilineal clan is headed by the eldest male in the senior branch and deceased members of the clan are memorialised by ancestor tablets kept on the ancestral altar, and while ritual leadership goes to the eldest son, other sons inherit equally, except for the land for supporting ancestral rituals, which is nominally held in trusteeship by the eldest son. A sonless couple, who will have no heir, no support in old age and no one to tend their soul-tablets may adopt a boy, or, if they have a daughter, persuade the son-in-law to reside with them and act as a son. Another noteworthy feature of the Vietnamese situation is that, unlike in Thailand, relatively few men enter the monkhood in a country where the Mahayana school of Buddhism, rather than the Theravada variety, predominates, along with an admixture of Confucianism, Taoism, a rich local pantheon of spirits and more recently a number of indigenous syncretic cults such as the Cao Dai which have drawn on local traditions, the older imported traditions and on Roman Catholicism, which has been a significant influence since as early as the 17th century.

For our final model of a unilineal social organisation we will turn to a third and very significant variation—that of a matrilineal culture, and here our example will be the Minangkabau people of west Sumatra in Indonesia. The Minangkabau are not a small society, having about 5 million members in the Padang highlands, and others scattered in Java, especially in Jakarta, in Malaysia, especially in the states of Malacca and Negri Sembilan, and even further abroad, and this migration, or Merantau is not only a traditional feature of Minangkabau life, but is a product to a great extent of the matrilineal structure. Each Minangkabau is a member of his mother's clan and a man can use, but not sell, the land of his matriclan. Authority, and symbolism, come through the women—and the residential group centred on the mother's house is called the "womb". A man may not always even live with his wife after marriage, but in his mother's house, and he visit the wife who lives in her mother's household. The husband is thus not the primary protector of his wife—that role is taken by her brother, who is of course a member of her lineage, while the husband in turn protects his own sisters. Households that trace their descent from a common matrilineal ancestor are called *kampung*, the head of which is the senior maternal uncle, the *penghulu andiko*. A group of *kampung* form a *suku*, several of which comprise a village. Historically (until 1844)there was a king, whose position was inherited patrilineally, but who had little authority, and even then between the local society and the king stood the "Great Lord" who was responsible for social and political affairs concerning the matrilineages. The sacral position of the king or "Great Lord" was further undermined by the advent of Islam and the existence of an extensive body of largely matrifocal customary law or *adat*, an important topic to which we will return. In traditional Minangkabau society we see a classic example of a matrilineal system at work. But today the system is under siege as ancestral land is sold off for commercial reasons, which vitally undermines the source of female authority, and as more people migrate not as bachelors as was traditionally the case given the ambiguous status and property rights of young men, but as families who live as a nuclear unit in, say, Jakarta, and so can no longer maintain the principle of matrilocal residence, and in which sex roles are entirely redefined in a more "western" way.

Bilateral Systems. Bilateral kinship systems (or "cognatic") ones are systems in which descent is through both the male and female lines. Such kinds of society are very common in Southeast Asia and include in addition to many smaller cultural groups such as the Atjehnese of northern Sumatra, such major populations as the Javanese, the Thais, the Malays and other anthropologically well-documented societies such as the Iban of Kalimantan and Sarawak. Indeed one of the distinctive anthropological characteristics of Southeast Asia is the wide distribution of cognatic forms of social organisation.

Like the Vietnamese, the Thai peoples (who include not only the lowland Siamese, but also related peoples in Laos, Burma and Yunnan) have historically been a vigorous and expansionist race who developed a sophisticated political system based on kingship and a complex culture with its religious base in Therevada Buddhism. Although almost certainly originally mainly a hill people, the modern Thais developed a lowland wet rice agriculture heavily dependent on irrigation. As a result Thai villages, rather than clustering like Vietnamese ones, are often strung out along the banks of rivers and canals. The management of rice production also contrasts with the Vietnamese model—co-operative work is common, but on an informal and labour-sharing basis, and free mixing of the sexes occurs during group activities like transplanting. The typical Thai family is small, husbands have no supreme authority, women have considerable influence in the family and often have economic roles outside of the household and girls as well as boys inherit land and property. The main route through which men can claim any authority is Therevada Buddhism, which gives them a higher ritual status than women, and many men spend at least a brief period at some point in their lives as a monk, an action that confers both merit and status. Although Thais do have family names passed through the fathers, these are not much used (and the neighbouring Burmese, who share many cultural features with the Thais do not even have these) and because of the bilateral descent system large numbers of relatives exist on both the husband's and the wife's sides. Villagers frequently intermarry and so over generations almost everybody in a village may come to be kinsmen, and this eases co-operation, borrowing and general social intercourse. Generosity and sharing are highly regarded social values and are inculcated early in Thai children who are treated with great fondness and indulgence which leads to a great sense of independence in adulthood. The Thai strikes the observer as much more of a free agent than many of his Asian neighbours—self-reliant, poised and able to make individual choices. Choice of spouse, for example, is relatively free, elopement is not uncommon, villages are traditionally autonomous, and while religion, centred in the village Wat or temple, plays a pervading role in Thai culture, Theravada Buddhism does not do so in a heavy-handed or moralistic way. All these features have led many scholars to characterise Thai society as "loosely structured"—a society of considerable personal freedom of choice and behaviour. In fact, this term is not really accurate. In sociological terms Thai society is no more "loose" than the neighbouring Burmese, or the Javanese and only appears so in comparison with the Vietnamese or Chinese patterns. It is true that Buddhism contains less moral prescriptiveness than the Islam of the Malays or even the Catholicism of the Filipinos, and this does create an atmosphere of tolerance. But underlying this is an actually very hierarchical society, rich in status rankings from royalty down through officials, teachers, monks, elders and relatives. Thai society is replete with the symbolism of rank and status and titles and uniforms abound to a greater degree than in any other Southeast Asian society, except perhaps the Javanese. The language itself encapsulates this as forms of address and pronouns vary with the rank of the person addressed and one's own rank relative to his. Some of these hierarchical ideas were certainly borrowed from Hinduism, which has had considerable influence on Thai court ritual. Here then we have a society both bilateral in kinship and strongly ranked.

This tension between social egalitarianism at one level and ranking at another is found in other Southeast Asian cognatic societies, such as the aforementioned Javanese, where another "loose" kinship system of usually nuclear families coexists with an elaborate regal-ritual hierarchy, a system of court cities and sacred places, a language with many levels of formality and politeness and an address system based on rank, whether aristocratic, academic, kinship or occupation. Each of these systems contains its own specific dynamic. The Javanese mother is the centre of the Javanese household, sisters remain close after marriage, post-marital residence is often matrilocal and the inside areas of a house are considered "female". Kinship terms are based on a generational system, so that rank and respect are built into the ways one addresses older or younger relatives. Other notable characteristics of the relative flexibility of Javanese kinship however are the very high divorce rate, and the prevalence of feasting (*Slamaten*) to mark lifecycle events. One important feature of cognatic systems is that while more "democratic" in terms of social relationships, they have economic drawbacks, since it is difficult to accumulate property or capital since goods are dispersed in each generation to an often wide range of descendants. Amongst the Malays of Malaysia and Singapore for example there is a very individualistic system of property ownership and parents may give or leave property to whomever they please, and not necessarily even to their own children. Children in turn feel no strong obligations to support their own parents, especially as they may not live with them, but with an uncle or an aunt. This residential separation is often intensified by again a high divorce rate. Yet another variation is that of the Iban of Borneo who, while practicing cognatic kinship, and having families that are economically and ritually autonomous (known as *bilek*), overcome some of the disadvantages of the Malay system by grouping together into the famous Iban long-houses, varying in size from four to as many as fifty *bilek*, and where duties and obligations are shared and where a cohesive community of a "village within one house"comprising cognatically related kin can be sustained.

Customary Law, Leadership and Cosmology

The coexistence of the introduced "high" religions and the indigenous "folk" tradition has never been altogether easy: in almost every Southeast Asian culture there is a continuing tension between the two. This expresses itself in many ways—in the Philippines with the emergence of "folk Catholicism" and syncretic cults; in Malaysia with the flourishing of traditional spiritist beliefs along side those of orthodox Islam and the expression of these in an indigenous system of folk medicine based on the activities of spiritual healing specialists called *bomoh* and *pawang*; in Indonesia with the tension between those who follow traditional Javanese religion with its strong mystical and Hindu undertones (*abangan*), and the *santri* or followers of reformist Islam; in Burma between Buddhism and the propitiation of a huge range of spiritual beings called nats. Nowhere is this clearer than in Minangkabau society with its matrilineal kinship on the one hand and its male oriented Islam on the other. Here the tension is expressed in terms of *adat* or customary law which recognises matrilineal custom as opposed to Islamic law (historically associated with the patrilineal royal family.) This is a problem that occurs throughout the Malay world, where "outside" authority is seen as being vested in men (and legitimised by the formal religion), while "inside" authority in the home) is vested in women and sanctioned by custom. In Minangkabau society, *adat* is seen as "female", emphasising the community as over against the Muslim law, the *syariah*, which emphasises the male-oriented, individualistic, "outside" world. A continuing social problem in Minangkabau has been the management of the fact that Islam tends to undermine the matrilineal basis of the traditional society, a problem intensified by the emergence of Muslim schools and of the Kaum Muda Islamic reform movement of the early part of this century, that had its roots in Sumatra.

This single example illustrates a region-wide theme: the imported religions both support and undermine the indigenous social structures. They undermine by suggesting an alternative cosmology to that of the traditional belief system, and they often support by providing legitimation fro a system of ranking. One of the initial attractions of Islam to the animistic Malay sultans was that it provided a rationalised and structured world view. The same was true of Hinduism, the effects of which can still be seen in Thai and Cambodian political ideas and rituals, and of course in Bali, the only Southeast Asian culture still to practice a form of Hinduism and with it a modified form of the caste system. Customary law has furthermore been challenged by the growing hegemony of the state based modern legal systems, which do not usually accept the legitimacy of local laws, except in specific cases such as domestic and matrimonial disputes (where Muslim law still applies in Malaysia and Singapore for example). This in turn effects concepts of leadership in Southeast Asia. Again we can identify several main models—patrilineally-based authority (Vietnam), a quasi-Hindu hierarchy (Thailand, Bali, Java), a kingly model (Thailand, traditional Cambodia), a ritual model (the Lamet headman) and a model where authority is imposed by the community but not desired by the recipient (as in the Orang Asli tribal groups of Malaysia.) Traditional leadership came out of three main sources—religious legitimation, position in the kinship system and economic role or wealth. Even as the societies of the region undergo rapid social change, many of these traditional forms continue to persist, at least as ideals, even as they face forces that threaten to transform them. We certainly cannot accept the idea that, in comparison with India or China or even Japan, Southeast Asian societies were or are classless. On the contrary equally prevalent although different or modified systems of stratification have existed for long historical periods, and to these is being added the complications of modern ideas of class and occupational rankings based upon professions and criteria that have no traditional counterparts. The struggle between these competing conceptualisations of human order is likely to be another major theme of the immediate future, as is the question of the sociological and value transformations brought about by large scale economic changes and the erosion of the ecological basis upon which the traditional systems of stratification were based.

Unities and Diversities

Part of the fascination of Southeast Asia as a region to study is its enormous diversity and complexity linguistically, ecologically, ethnically, culturally and sociologically. In practice all these levels interact with one another and with the historical forces that are transforming them. Religion has been a profound influence on social organisation and institutions and ecology both sets limits to social possibilities and provides stimulus to adapt social forms to overcome these ecological limitations. Some of these dimensions we have been able to set out here, but there are potentially many more—the patrilineal Christian Toba Batak of eastern Sumatra, the Therevada Buddhist Burmans, the many hill peoples of Thailand, Burma and Laos, the Negrito peoples of the interior of Malaysia, and others. But as we view this diversity, certain continuities also emerge:the great unities of religion that provide value orientations to their members over large geographical areas, and especially Therevada Buddhism, Islam and Catholicism; the parallels in structure between kinship systems; the similar forms of social hierarchy and the attempts, often by way of customary law, to come to terms with challenges from the outside world. Several other factors also stand out—the significance of economic patterns for social structure, and especially the differences between the settled lowland wet rice farmers and the semi-nomadic shifting cultivators of the hills, to say nothing of the maritime communities such as the Bugis of Indonesia with their economy of trade, boat building, fishing and, traditionally, piracy. Then there is the independence and economic ability of Southeast Asian women, the patterns of childhood socialisation which each society has developed to inculcate its particular social forms, but with the common elements that children are highly prized and cared for and are taught values of generosity and sociability; and the dialectic of egalitarianism at the family and local levels, but of hierarchy at the societal level, with, in many cases avenues of access to rank through the accumulation of wealth (as with the Makassarese of Celebes or the Lamet), through education (as with the Vietnamese) or through religion (as with the Buddhist Thais or with many of the Muslim peoples where status and religious attainment are linked, such as by undertaking the Haj or pilgrimage to Mecca. Another common feature of many Southeast Asian societies is the role of feasting in promoting or maintaining rank or social status, a phenomenon that stretches from the hills of northern Thailand to the outermost islands of eastern Indonesia.

While it is true that the pressures of modernisation, political changes and urbanisation have modified or even swept away some of these features, for the most part they have been adapted to meet the new conditions without sacrificing the underlying values, especially in the rural areas. For this reason the emergence of class as a basis for social stratification, while changing the old forms has also often been assimilated by them the new elites turn out to be the old elites in a new guise. Southeast Asia has a long history of indigenous urbanisation and it is interesting to note that in Singapore, the most urbanised society in the region, it is often the Malays who have adapted best, not the Chinese, because of their cultural values, strong religious base and flexible social structure. Indeed underlying and basic to the social organisation are values, and, to hazard a generalisation, Southeast Asian values largely are and will continue to be based on a deep religiosity, a perception of the happy individual as one integrated into a co-operative group, but with the possibility of reasonable social mobility in an ordered cosmos. Meaningful human relationships are seen as essentially social relationships, standing in a symbiotic relationship with nature, the provider of the rice which is the stuff of life throughout the region.

To conclude, a Malay example (representative of a wide cultural area from southern Thailand to the Philippines) helps us to sum up the whole. In Malay society, there are three fundamental principles of social organisation: *darah*, or blood ties involving obligations and duties; *muafakat* or agreement and settlement of disputes through discussion and consensus; and *kesayangan*, or love or sentiment that should characterise all close relationships. The social, the moral and the religious are seen as a whole, and the voluntary and active submission to this order of things creates harmony. This idea succinctly summarises and expresses the varied yet shared social genius of the traditional and indigenous cultures of Southeast Asia.

References

Burling, Robbins (1975), *Hill Farms and Paddy Fields*, Englewood Cliffs: Prentice Hall.

Keyes, Charles (1976), *The Golden Peninsula*, London: Macmillan.

Murdock, George (1960), *Social Structure in Southeast Asia*, New York: Wenner Gren Foundation.

Peacock, James L. (1973), *Indonesia: An Anthropological Perspective*, Goodyear, Pacific Palisades.

Chapter 3
VALUES AND HUMAN DEVELOPMENT

Without doubt what is now considered the acceptable paradigm of development has shifted from a purely technical one to one that emphasises sustainability, ecological responsibility, distributive justice and culture. Critiques of past patterns of development and of the models which were dominant in the recent past and still continue in some of the international aid agencies have often concentrated precisely on the lack of human and cultural content in the prescriptions and policies hitherto applied to the solution of poverty and other major development issues. The emergence of non-governmental organisations (NGOs) as a major force in international development has been largely a response to the failure of the established models to provide creative and successful answers. The diagnosis of what has gone wrong of course has many elements, but one of the recurring themes has been the neglect of values embodied in culture and expressed in behaviour—which determine people's view of the good life (and therefore of the meaning of development for them) and their response to policies. The failure of many development policies is traceable precisely to the absence of any attempt to incorporate such values into the formation or execution of plans. When attempts are however made to explore the role of values in the process, they are soon discovered to be absolutely central to people's response and motivation (Dove 1988).

This is not only true of "development" situations. An emergent theme in sociology generally has been the rediscovery of culture, a category formerly left mainly to anthropologists who in any case tended to treat it in a fairly conventional way. The re-emergence of cultural studies in sociology has revealed the extent to which culture is implicated in all human social activity (including the economic), and the extent to which previously repressed or ignored dimensions of culture, such as popular culture, are actually central to the understanding of everyday life and life-worlds. Culture itself is multidimensional, of course, and in this context attention will be paid to only one, but one very central dimension which has itself tended to be neglected, that of values. The first step then will be to decide the meaning of values and to set out the way in which a consideration of values illuminates some of the most significant aspects of the meaning of development and the application of development ideas to concrete situations.

Values in this context will be taken to mean the belief systems, world views and ideologies espoused by people and expressed through culture. Some values are very explicit, for example those enshrined in religious doctrines. Others are less explicit, for example those embodied in religious *practice* which may or may not have a clear relationship to formal beliefs or theologies. Some values derive from religion, some from politics and often from everyday practices such as agricultural cycles and orientation to nature, kinship relationships or the various ways in which emotional life is culturally patterned and modified, for example through literature or the media. Some values are of the kind that structure basic experiences (cosmological attitudes and ideas underlying the nature of social structure), others are instrumental (moral values, treatment of the natural environment.) Values will be embodied in and expressed through religion, cultural practices, social organisation, political ideologies, psychological structures, conceptions of human needs, quality of life and human rights. The analysis of values very fruitfully brings together two usually separated levels: philosophical anthropology or the ontological conceptions held by a people on the one hand, and fundamental questions of development, such as the very *meaning* of development and the nature of the desired good life being pursued through development on the other. Here we will explore the nature of values not as a philosophical problem, but in relationship to a range of basic questions in human development. The choice of the specific issues discussed here indeed illustrate the question of values very well, since the choice of problems itself reflects a value orientation, and one that will be argued here: that certain questions are indeed fundamental to the development debate.

The Nature of Development

The key question in development studies is the nature of development itself—whether it is conceived of primarily as economic growth, better distribution of existing resources, sustainable and ecologically responsible expansion of the economy, poverty alleviation, pursuit of greater levels of political participation and democratisation, greater attention to the rights of women and children, liberationist or "wholistic" images of development stressing the rounded encouragement of human potential including its psychological, spiritual and cultural dimensions, or the "conscientization" approach.

Values clearly enter deeply into all of these possibilities, since development is itself primarily about values. For example the question of whether development should promote equity (Dube 1984: 25-27) is not only a question of technical economics, but very much involves political and moral decisions. If it is decided that development *should* promote equity, then policy and strategy follow but do not lead. Issues which are usually considered to be outside of the scope of technical development planning consequently become very relevant at both the theoretical and practical levels. Religion is clearly one of these—as a source of world views, ethical prescriptions and even as a model of the factors which ultimately govern relationships. The latter can be seen most classically in the "Weber Thesis"—the argument that the origins of capitalism lie not only in the material conditions of pre-industrial England, but most importantly in the religious value orientation of the post-Reformation Calvinist Protestantism which, when put together with the material conditions, created the conditions for the emergence of modern industrial capitalism (Weber 1987). Variations of this thesis have been enormously important for explaining the *lack* of development in societies not sharing this Protestant tradition, or for explaining the parallels to a Protestant ethic like ideological complex especially in Confucianism, seen by not a few scholars as being the basic factor in the rise to industrial-capitalist prominence first of Japan (Davis 1992) and subsequently of the "four little dragons"—Taiwan, South Korea, Hong Kong and Singapore—of East and Southeast Asia.

This interaction of "technical" and "world view" factors can be seen very clearly in debates about basic needs and the quality of life. Basic needs can be seen only as survival needs—food, water, shelter and reproduction; or they can be seen as encompassing a much broader range of attributes of humans, including cultural, psychological and spiritual needs. Galtung, for example, has divided needs into the four major categories of security needs, welfare needs, identity needs and freedom needs and sees, beyond absolute survival needs, all needs as basic: there is no hierarchy as in Abraham Maslow's well-known "hierarchy of needs". Security needs include the need for protection against violence; welfare needs include nutrition, shelter, medicine and schooling; identity needs include self-expression, work, recreation, affection, religion, political activity and esteem; and freedom needs include choice of residence, occupation, social contacts, way of life and free association. Building on this, Dube expands the categories to six: survival needs (nutrition, security, etc.), societal needs (creation of viable communities), cultural and psychic needs (including privacy and creativity), welfare needs (protection of the vulnerable), adaptive needs (flexible relationship to the social, cultural, psychological and physical environments and ability to respond to and to modify them), and progress needs (problem-solving capacities) (Dube 1984: 78-84).

Closely related to the question of basic needs is that of the quality of life: "an inclusive concept which covers all aspects of living including material satisfaction of vital needs as well as more transcendental aspects of life such as personal development, self-realisation and a healthy eco-system" (UNESCO: 1977). This conception of the quality of life, like those of basic needs, contains both objective factors such as food and subjective components essentially involving cultural, aesthetic and religious elements. The significance of "alternative" approaches to development is very apparent here since almost always they are characterised precisely by their attempts to redefine the bearing of the subjective elements or values on the objective ones. Concern with sustainability and the curbing of high consumption lifestyles, with appropriate technology or with alternative energy sources for example all reflect this central concern.

An unavoidable consequence of these demands for alternative voices to be heard is that they politicise the debate. Demands for alternatives requires that those who wish to implement them have access to political structures, to planning agencies and to institutions. Even more radically, alternatives may require the dismantling of existing agencies and structures and the creation of new institutions for human resource development. The rise of these demands can be seen in populist movements in some developing countries, including the emergence of new forms of social movements which place values at the core of their activities—for example, the Sarvodaya movement in Sri Lanka (Zachariah 1986), the emergence nationally and internationally of NGOs as powerful and very visible alternative voices and in the "conscientization" movement beginning largely with the work of Paulo Freire (Freire 1972) and his work with politicising Latin American peasants as an integral part of teaching them literacy, but spreading since then to Southeast Asia as part of a broader liberationary stream often, as in the Philippines, with links to liberation theology (Nagliliyab 1988). Conscientization has also become an idea that has spread into the Asian feminist movement and this has had important implications for revaluation of the place of women in development in Asia (Katoppo 1981) and of other groups previously marginal to official or technical development thinking, such as youth (Itty 1984). The original link between conscientization and education has also refuelled debates about the relationship between development and education, the role of non-formal education and educational alternatives such as those proposed by Ivan Illich (Illich 1976).

In summary then, the setting of development goals requires attention to values. The selection of long term over immediate goals for example is a value-decision that may have immense implications (sustainable development as opposed to fast short-term gains or ecological considerations taking priority over rapid profits being examples). In other words the way in which time itself enters into considerations of development is itself a values question. Human needs, perhaps the central concept together with ecology in any responsible theory of development, requires a value perspective. As Dube points out (Dube 1988: 53-58) even the most biological of needs (for food or sex, for instance) are expressed through cultural channels—dietary rules, theories of nutrition, rules of kinship and so on. Becoming human itself requires the process of socialisation and education; to be human requires the expression of aesthetic capacities and creativity. Conscientization "may be understood as a process of cognitive and evaluative transformation, especially in the poor of the world. It enables the individual to contemplate the environment and the human condition and gain an understanding of the forces that are shaping the contemporary world" (Dube 1988: 88) and as such is essentially the process of recognising and expressing values in action. To deepen this perspective it is now necessary to turn to some cases in which value analysis contributes to the actual formation of development goals and policies.

The Social Analysis of Values

Methodologically there are a number of different ways in which the nexus of values and development can be approached. The Weberian possibility has already been mentioned. Others include the "modernisation" approach which contrasted the values and sociocultural features of "traditional" and "modern" societies to the detriment of the former which were seen as inhibiting economic and technological innovation (e.g. Rostow 1952) and the related view that achievement motivation must be inculcated in the entrepreneurs who are seen as leading economic growth (McClelland and Winter 1969). More recent approaches are those of Hofstede who has concentrated on work values as the key to understanding differential levels of development (Hofstede 1980), and of an increasing number of psychologists who have attempted to trace the connections between values and belief systems and development (e.g. Sinha and Kao 1988). Each of these approaches has its characteristic problems, but they all share the danger of essentialism—ascribing to an entire culture a single set of psychological characteristics. When this problem is added to that of assuming a simple-minded notion of development such that certain values are "functional" and others are "impediments" to that development (e.g. Sinha and Kao 1988: 14), the psychological approach, while adding some insights, is fraught with methodological pitfalls. One of these is that the concept of values is itself extremely broad in these studies, encompassing "attitudes" (themselves very difficult to measure empirically), work orientation, family organisation, religious beliefs, concepts of power and hierarchy, attitudes to authority, social interdependence, pleasure, levels of individualism/collectivism, and general psychic structures (such as ego-orientation). The psychologist's tendency, as seen throughout the Sinha and Kao volume, is towards an ahistorical approach that pays no attention at all to the social construction of values.

The result is an approach devoid of a critical dimension, since "values" are just seen to exist in some free-floating form separated from actual social and political processes. The inadequacy of this approach is apparent when it is contrasted with the whole thrust of contemporary cultural theory with its emphasis on the ways in which identities are fluid and constructed—in gender studies for example, in relation to concepts of femininity and masculinity, in ethnicity, or in studies of colonialism and postcolonialism

(Bhabha 1994). The idea of "values and development" itself needs handling carefully since to conceive of "values" on one side and (economic) development on the other is to create a false dualism. Economics itself is deeply value-laden and is perhaps the most value-saturated of all the social sciences (McClosky 1985), so even at this level the causality postulated by the psychologists of the relationship between values and development does not hold. If development is seen in a more wholistic way, then it is also the values themselves, or the selection of unsuitable values (for example, purely materialistic ones) that provide the basis for development. Part of the problem indeed is that of the values associated with the term "development" itself. If other terms are substituted—for example "civilisation" or "the civilising process"—the whole nature of the debate changes.

This all suggests several perspectives on the analysis of values:

1. Values are not simply "natural" or essentialist, but are socially constructed and as such have a history, are part of a field of power relations and have origins. The analysis of the genesis of values and the context of their first appearing is as important as their relationship in the present to other social forces.
2. Values are dynamic and strategic. That is to say they change, the "same" values may mean very different things in different social settings or in different historical periods. They are also used by people in pursuing individual or collective goals, and as such are highly politicised. New ways of looking at the world constantly emerge which, while they may and usually do have strong continuities with the past, also succeed in rearranging the elements in such ways that very fresh world-views emerge (e.g. postmodernism, the New Age movement, Marxism, psychoanalysis, new religious movements.) As such it is often more fruitful to approach values not in themselves (in which case they often appear as very abstract, generalised and free-floating), but through the social vehicles which embody, express or attempt to advance them—for example, social movements.
3. Values are not "neutral" in at least two senses. Firstly, they may embody hidden ideological agendas. Education is a very good example of this, where claims about the expanding of the mind and

the promotion of growth may and often do conceal class, gender- or race-based programming which actually leads to quite contrary results (as demonstrated most effectively in Willis 1981). Secondly, values can have unintended consequences. The individualistic theology of Weber's Protestants, designed to open a direct channel to the Divine without intermediaries, has had the long-term effect of making it extremely difficult for such Protestants to develop any serious social theory or social analysis.

4. Failures in development need not be the result of failures to take into account values and beliefs: there can be purely technical reasons, or ones of a political nature.
5. Attitudes and values (constantly conflated by the psychologists) are extremely difficult to measure precisely, largely because they are not precise and people may not be clear what their attitudes are (or feel they "should be") until forced to clarify them. The same is true of many beliefs. To use unclarified values as a basis for development policy and planning is bound to produce unintended consequences and may be almost as bad as not taking such values into account at all.
6. Values must be described ethnographically, i.e. identified in their social setting—for example, the empirical nature of relationships, religious practices, use of languages, expression of emotions, attitude to time; and must also be critically evaluated in terms of the patterns of power, dependency or domination that they reproduce.
7. The nature of the supposed causal relationship between values and other factors, in this case development, must be carefully spelt out. This is especially important because values are not separate from development nor can they be, since any concept of development once deconstructed proves to be itself loaded with values. "Values" are not over against "development" but are integrated with it. A problem arises, however, when attempts are made to design technical "value-free" development programmes. In practice and philosophically, however, this cannot be done.
8. A "values" approach methodologically is in great danger of drastically oversimplifying the actual complexity, uncertainty and gen-

eral messiness of actual cultural practices and belief "systems" (actually usually very unsystematic). Attempting to structure the value-systems of societies as diverse as Indonesia, Thailand, Japan, the Netherlands and the United States on the basis of the four dimensions of individualism, power distance, uncertainty avoidance and masculinity (even if any real operationalisation of these term were possible) is frankly absurd, although this is exactly what Hofstede attempts to do (Hofstede 1988). A basic problem with this approach, apart from its mania for creating categories into which the richness of actual and highly complex and often contradictory cultural practices can be forced, is that it reproduces all of the problems of the older national character studies and the weaknesses of the culture and personality school of anthropology without adding any understanding of the processes of the social construction of values or their dynamic qualities. The result is a form of sophisticated academic stereotyping which is fundamentally a form of racism.

Themes in Values and Development

Given these methodological caveats, it is possible to identify a number of areas in which the analysis of values and the study of development can usefully be put together. While the psychological approach yields little fruit, it is suggested here that a more sociological perspective on values as socially constructed means of understanding the world, orientating oneself to its demands and interacting with it in ways that convey meaning is a valuable way of approaching the whole question of development. This can be illustrated by briefly reviewing a number of themes, which while not exhaustive, do provide an indication of the possible range of relationships between values and development.

1. If human development in its broadest sense is intended, the beginning point has to be a philosophical anthropology concerned both with the nature of human beings as they are, and also with what they might become. Most existing philosophical anthropology is very much western in its presuppositions however. To begin to discuss the nature of humanity from the point of view of say

Thai, Javanese, or Japanese perspectives, would involve rephrasing the issue in fresh terms that would inevitably incorporate elements of ecology (different physical and climatic conditions), history, language and of course religion, with Buddhist, Islamic, Shintoism and syncretic mystical tradition coming to very different conclusions. This suggests two principles: that values can only be understood on a comparative basis and that the abstract discussion of values is pointless as in practice they are rooted in a complex dialectical relationship with religion, nature, age, sexuality and other basic components of being human. And if broad human development is really intended, questions of economic development may have to be subordinated to or incorporated within priorities that have to do with non-material development-expanding creativity, spirituality, psychological as much as political liberation and so on (Daly 1973). A problem with much current "values and development" thinking is not only its limited sense of development, but also its assumption that it knows what the values are. In fact they can only be discovered (often with some difficulty) by empirical analysis, often of such apparently unlikely areas as popular culture (Sirvent 1986), recognised as shifting and strategic orientations rather than as fixed essences and treated with a critical view as to their links to possible mechanisms of power in the society.

2. An example of this in action would be the current debates on culture and development. Such approaches rightly recognise the way in which culture deeply affects the ways in which development is perceived, the way in which policies are reacted to or implemented, the ways in which they fail and the significance of deep-rooted patterns of cultural response to change. Whereas in the past such factors were seen largely as impediments to development, it is now recognised that they are also reflections of wisdom and accumulated experience. Ethnoscience, for instance, has uncovered the ways in which traditional agricultural practices and the beliefs on which they are based are often highly adaptive, efficient and ecologically responsible, far more so in fact than some of the modern energy, pesticide and fertiliser,intensive techniques

suggested to "improve" agriculture. Indigenous knowledge—of farming, medicine, irrigation, forestry, animal husbandry, fishing or whatever—is recognised as the outcome of long experience, not as a reflection of "primitiveness".

This is a very positive development, although this particular debate about culture needs deepening and linking to current debates in cultural studies which themselves are remaking approaches to social reality, being much more critical about the forces that produce, and sustain cultural practices, are concerned with the mechanisms that culture uses to reproduce itself and are very much aware of the politics of culture (Rosaldo 1993). Tradition, for example, can now be seen not as immutable patterns extending from the past, but as something constantly created, remade, reinterpreted, invented and very much used for strategic purposes, often of a highly political nature.

3. A second example would be the question of human rights. Here we have a perfect instance of values at work, again at two levels. The first is the question of the role of human rights in relation to development. Is the goal of development the advancement and establishment of human rights? Or can certain forms of development (say, economic growth) take priority over human rights? Is it legitimate to suppress human rights in the interests of political stability, and to argue that democracy and a free press slow down development (as has been done by Singapore's Lee Kuan Yew, for example)? The second is the question of the definition of human rights. Are they universal or are they culture bound? And to what extent do those who argue for the latter actually do so out of political motives rather than on the basis of anthropological analysis? The question of human rights in relation to cultural relativism (Vincent 1986: 37-57) is especially interesting, since it is also a question of "culture and development" and also illustrates the way in which anthropological knowledge can be used ideologically. Interestingly the typical list of basic rights—to life, liberty, property, and economic and social rights (Cranston 1973)—makes no direct reference to cultural rights. But here the connections between rights, culture and development are especially

strong, since most practical development questions have a rights dimension—land reform, the status of women, environment and energy or access to legal protection, for example (ICJ/CAP 1982). The right to legal representation, the passage of laws in the interests of workers and minorities as well as owners and majorities, for example, demonstrates not only a debate about values at the obvious level (people should have access to legal protection), but also at the deeper level of concepts of jurisprudence and the way in which courts operate according to cultural as well as legal principles. Or rather legal principles are cultural principles expressed in a particular coded form. Not surprisingly debates about human rights often take the form of demands for legal access (Scoble and Wiseberg 1985).

4. Values, being at least in part socially constructed, are liable to manipulation, especially for political ends. Two examples that illustrate this are the debate about the genetic basis of intelligence and its relationship to meritocracy in Malaysia and Singapore. The first case—in which attempts were made to utilise scientific or quasiscientific material to support the idea that intelligence is basically genetic (nature) rather than a product of social environment and education (nurture) in order to justify a policy on meritocracy based, especially in the Singapore case, on race. In both countries the arguments were closely tried to specific political agendas—in the Malaysian case the maintaining of Malay dominance and in Singapore the protection of Chinese dominance. The values questions here are multiple: the justification of meritocracy, the contentious use of race and the distortion or selective use of scientific data (Chee and Chan 1984), the suppression of cultural and social factors in favour of purely biological ones.

   The second example is even more appropriate. In 1988 the Singapore government suggested the idea of creating a national ideology based on what they termed "shared values". After some debate within the government five such values were identified: nation before community and society above self; family as the basic unit of society; regard and community support for the individual; consensus instead of contention and racial and religious harmony. These "values" are interesting for many reasons—their vagueness, their culturalist assumptions, their implicit recognition of the lack of any founding myth or charter in a political culture that is symbolically impoverished, their premise that all of the different religions and cultures that make up Singapore do in fact have common values, their exclusion of any discussion of human rights, equality or gender. The White Paper which set out the government's proposal reveals an ideology which as I have argued elsewhere is actually statist, patriarchal, Confucian, and highly conservative and which attempts not to create change but to preempt it, partly by giving the government a monopoly over moral discourse and partly by recasting the image of Singapore society as being a "consensus" society rather than a pluralist one (Clammer 1993).

Both these cases and other examples of attempts to create such values can be used by the state in its attempt to define the nature and direction of development and to actually prevent people's participation by deciding for them the nature of the values which they are supposed (at least publicly) to hold.

5. What characterises both of the above examples is that they suppress the role of religion, allegedly in the interests of communal harmony. But in fact religion continues to play a major role in all Southeast Asian societies, both in terms of political significance and in terms of private practice and belief. It is not surprising then that indigenous development thinkers have turned to religion as the source of values that provide the basis for meaningful living and alternative forms of development. In its different ways this same theme can be seen in Islamic fundamentalism in Malaysia, Catholic liberation theology in the Philippines, the Charismatic Movement in Singapore, politicised forms of Buddhism in Thailand and for that matter the spread of the "new religions" in Japan.

What all these have in common is the attempt to define and practice humane and satisfactory lifestyles. And the themes are often much the same—ecological responsibility, anti-consumerist, the promoting of satisfactory human relationships, usually non-violent methods of struggling for social change, self-sufficiency, and generally "development as if people mattered" (Sivaraksa 1992). Empirically religion is central to the network of values that constitute Southeast Asian cultures and as such, regardless of the personal religious views of development practitioners, it needs to be placed equally centrally in debates about development. Again, of course, a critical perspective is necessary as it always is. Religion can be used to oppress as well as to liberate, to create alienation instead of to overcome it, to become politicised instead of liberatory and thus, when it betrays its own true nature, a source of false values rather than true ones.

6. A final example is that of ecology. Amongst the debates currently raging in the development field now, this is probably the most conspicuous. The developed world has finally woken up to the fact that its style of growth (especially industrialisation) has profoundly damaged the natural fabric of the earth through pollution, resource depletion, over urbanisation and the destruction of bio-diversity. The ecological movement has been a timely response to these problems, now of a global scale. But this movement is opposed by at least two powerful groups: industrialists on the one hand and the governments of some developing countries on the other. The special interests of the former is in a sense understandable; the position of the latter is interesting because it either denies the ecological threat or argues (as has happened say in Malaysia) that developed countries have no right in the name of ecology to dampen the growth of developing countries. And since growth means some measure of environmental destruction, the developing world has the right to do what it likes with its environment, even as the "first world" did before it.

    This argument is interesting for several reasons. It overlooks the question of ethical responsibility to the environment and to other species who also inhabit it and it fails to recognise that whatever the history of the developed world may have been, the world has since changed. The condition called by some "postmodernity" is now upon us—the world is one eco-system, interlinked at all levels and the political and economic logics of the past no longer work. The problem here, in other words, is not just political expediency and lack of economic imagination, it is also a question of "old mind" attempting to address new problems, when in fact "new mind" is urgently needed. There is a time-lag in values, in other words, with old paradigms still being used to address very new problems that do not have precedents. Within the ecological movement itself similar values-struggles are taking place, for example, the debates between reformists or conservationists on the one hand, and "deep ecologists" who proffer much more radical solutions on the other (Fox 1990).

Values and Structures and Institutions

Anthony Giddens has argued (Giddens 1983) that the basic theoretical issue is to link action and structure in a coherent way to relate the activities of individual social actors to the broader processes that make up society (classes, for instance). Of equal importance, and parallel to Giddens' problematic, is the linking of values and development, of attempting to understand the relationship between individual beliefs and social structures. This is a question that has been approached in many ways, especially by scholars concerned with the sociology of religion in which certain basic questions have to be asked: where do beliefs come from? how are they modified by their social context? how do religious beliefs and religious institutions relate to one another? how do religious beliefs affect non-religious activities such as economic practices? At least since Weber sociologists have been attempting to answer these questions. While no one abstract answer can be given, certain principles can be set out and have hopefully been defined in this chapter.

It has been necessary to see values as socially constructed, as dynamic, as manipulable and as having a complex and often internal causal relationship to other factors. It has been necessary to adapt a critical approach to values and not to regard them as simply neutral. Negative values occur as well as positive ones, but which is which cannot always be decided *a priori* but through the practical working out of their consequences for human life and the societies in which they occur. The psychological approach to values, while of some utility, needs to be approached with great care and the methodological problems of dealing with values have necessarily taken up a good deal of our discussion here.

Three further points need to be added. The first is that the way in which values are handled in relationship to development cannot be defined in an abstract and universalist manner. Different national traditions of sociology, drawing themselves on the underlying world views of their respective cultures, approach the question in different ways. The nature of the colonial experience (or lack of), educational methods, gender roles, dominant religions, political system and economic structures will all influence the ways in which the value-development issue is expressed. There is a question in the sociology of knowledge here—the conditions under which knowledge is provided, reproduced and consumed affects the understanding of the linkages between values and development (Clammer 1982).

The second is that the best way to analyse values is through the exploration of culture. This means, as has been suggested earlier, that the values debate needs to be linked closely to developments in the rapidly expanding area of cultural theory, and also to enter into very close dialogue with cultural anthropology, the discipline that has most consistently placed culture at the centre of its concerns and which is comparative and has historically been closely involved with the study of developing countries (Turton 1988).

The third is that values are not free-floating. They are largely created by and expressed through institutions, and so the analysis of institutions—schools, churches, temples, families, corporations, lineages, and so forth—and the analysis of values goes hand in hand. Here we have stressed the analysis of values, but it must be said again that values and institutions while analytically distinct are in practice totally intermeshed. As Foucault has shown, basic values relating to criminality, madness, sexuality, health and the body are all totally interwoven with the evolution of institutions—the prison, the clinic, the asylum, the medical profession, the school. Foucault has also demonstrated the relationship between values and power, a point also stressed here. A similar analysis could be extended to other areas—to selfhood, ideas of hierarchy and social inequality, of individualism (Dumont 1986), of religious belief.

Development then is about values, and values are ultimately about the development of the human person. Finally the two should not be seen dualistically, but as aspects of each other: human development is a term which encapsulates this—the expansion of the capacities and freedoms of the person, in the context of supportive not oppressive institutions with achievement of a rounded humanity dwelling responsibly in nature and as far as is possible free from want—as the final goal.

References

Bhabha, H. (1994), *The Location of Culture*, London: Routledge.

Chee, H.L. and C.K. Chan (eds.) (1984), *Designer Genes: I.Q. Identity and Biology*, Petaling Jaya: INSAN.

Clammer, J. (1982), *Sociology and Development: Problems and Prospects from the Perspective of South and Southeast Asia*, Singapore: RIHED.

Clammer, J. (1993), "Deconstructing values: the establishment of a national ideology and its implications for Singapore's political future," in G. Rodan (ed.) *Singapore Changes Guard: Social, Political and Economic Directions in the 1990s*, Melbourne: Longman Cheshire and New York: St. Martin's Press, 34-51.

Cranston, M. (1973), *What Are Human Rights?*, London: The Bodley Head.

Daly, H.E. (ed.) (1973), *Toward a Steady State Economy*, San Francisco: W.H. Freeman Company.

Davis, W. (1992), *Japanese Religion and Society*, Albany: State University of New York Press.

Dove, M. (ed.) (1988), *The Real and Imagined Role of Culture in Development Case Studies from Indonesia*, Honolulu: University of Hawaii Press.

Dube, S.C. (1984), *Development Perspectives for the 1980s*, Petaling Jaya: Pelanduk Publications for the United Nations Asian and Pacific Development Centre.

Dube, S.C. (1988), *Modernization and Development: The Search for Alternative Paradigms*, New Delhi: Vistaar Publications and Tokyo: United Nations University.

Dumont, L. (1986), *Essays on Individualism: Modern Ideology in Anthropological Perspective*, Chicago: University of Chicago Press.

Fox, W. (1990), *Towards a Transpersonal Ecology: Developing New Foundations for Environmentalism*, Boston and London: Shambhala.

Freire, P. (1972), *Cultural Action for Freedom*, Harmondsworth: Penguin.

Giddens, A. (1983), *Central Problems in Social Theory: Action, Structure and Contradiction in Social Analysis*, London: Macmillan.

International Commission of Jurists and Consumers' Association of Penang (1982), *Rural Development and Human Rights in Southeast Asia*, Penang: CAP.

Illich, I. (1976), *Deschooling Society*, Harmondsworth: Penguin Books.

Itty, C. I. (ed.) (1984), *Searching for Asian Paradigms*, Bangkok: Asian Cultural Forum on Development.

Hofstede, G. (1980), *Culture's Consequences: International Differences in Work-Related Values*, Beverly Hills: Sage.

Hofstede, G. (1988), "McGregor in Southeast Asia," in D. Sinha and H.S.R. Kao (eds.) *Social Values and Development: Asian Perspectives*, New Delhi: Sage.

Katoppo, M. (1981), *Compassionate and Free*, Maryknoll: Orbis.

McClelland, D.C. and D.G. Winters (1969), *Motivating Economic Development*, New York: Free Press.

McClelland, D.N. (1989), *The Rhetoric of Economics*, Madison: University of Wisconsin Press.

Nagliliyab (1988), *Organizing People for Power*, Quezon City: Claretian.

Rosaldo, R. (1993), *Culture and Truth: The Remaking of Social Analysis*, London: Routledge.

Rostow, W.W. (1952), *The Process of Economic Growth*, New York: Norton.

Scoble, H.M. and L.S. Wiseberg (eds.) (1988), *Access to Justice: The Struggle for Human Rights in Southeast Asia*, London: Zed Books.

Sinha, D. and H.S.R. Kao (eds.) (1988), *Social Values and Development: Asian Perspectives*, New Delhi: Sage.

Sirvent, M.T. (1986), "Human development and popular culture in Latin America," in C.A. Mallmann and O. Nudler (eds.) *Human Development in its Social Context*, London: Hodder and Stoughton, 190-212.

Sivaraksa, S. (1992), *Seeds of Peace: A Buddhist Vision for Renewing Society*, Berkley: Parallax Press.

Turton, D. (1988), "Anthropology and Development," in P.F. Leeson and M.M. Minogue (eds.) *Perspectives on Development: Cross-Cultural Themes in Development*, Manchester: Manchester University Press.

UNESCO (1977), *UNESCO's Policy-Relevant Quality of Life Research Programme*, Paris: UNESCO.

Vincent, R.J. (1986), *Human Rights and International Relations*, Cambridge: Cambridge University Press.

Weber, M. (1987), *The Protestant Ethic and the Spirit of Capitalism*, London: Unwin.

Willis, P. (1981), *Learning to Labor*, New York: Columbia University Press.

Zachariah, M. (1986), *Revolution Through Reform: A Comparison of Sarvodaya and Conscientization*, New Delhi: Vistaar.

Chapter 4
POSTMODERNITY AND MACRO-SOCIAL CHANGE

This is a theoretical topic, and deliberately so, as I believe that it is necessary to address in a fundamental way some of the key issues underlying empirical debate about contemporary social transformation, whether it refers to relations between states, between social groups or classes within states or between society and emerging but non-state social forces such as transnational corporations and information technology. To address all the issues that these questions raise within the ambit of a single chapter is obviously impossible, but I will attempt here to at least sketch out an approach that makes it a little easier to theorise the relationship between the complex and macroscopic forces currently leading or creating social change.

A basic problem for sociology has long been that of understanding the relationship between values, structures and institutions. Indeed there are some who see the explanation of the links between action or behaviour on the one hand and collectivities, structures and institutions on the other as being *the* central problem of social theory (Giddens 1979, 1981). At one level this is a problem of understanding how individual behaviour issues in, reproduces and in turn is affected by large scale sociological structures, and "structuration theory" has arisen to address this (Cohen 1987). But at another level, and at one frequently mentioned but not fully explored, this is a variety of the problem that anthropologists used to call "cultural lag". That is to say the phenomenon of values changing at a rate faster than, or different from, the structures and institutions that may have originally given birth to those very values, or at least nurtured them in the past. Or of course the order can be reversed: the difficulty of institutional innovation is often that the values do not exist that would supply the soil for the institutions to take root. An important component of the study of social change necessarily becomes the analysis of the relations between values and institutions (or structures), regardless of whether this relationship is expressed at the micro or macro levels.

While there are a number of paradigms available for the analysis of these relationships, I will argue here that the potentially most fruitful is that known by the generic name of "postmodernism". Postmodernism actually represents a congeries of theories, not all of them in agreement with each other, but that address the common theme of the nature of contemporary ("post-industrial" or "late capitalist") society with specific reference to the *cultural* transformations that have occurred in the transition to this type of social formation. Three important dimensions of this are:

1. the identification of emergent social forces and institutions characteristic of the contemporary era;
2. the significant role given to the role of culture (and therefore values) in understanding social transformation; and
3. a totalising perspective that dissolves disciplinary distinctions between sociology, economics, political science and cultural studies in full awareness of the multi-causal nature of social change.

The central role of culture here is important, since a general characteristic of writers who consider themselves to be or are widely considered as "postmodernists" is the possession of a theory of culture that argues that foundationalism—a view of society based upon the "grand narratives" of religion, Marxism, structuralism, feminism, etc., is now obsolete and has been replaced by a culture of consumption—hedonistic, democratic, eclectic, in which any number of language games can simultaneously compete, with none having any special authority or legitimacy (Lyotard 1984).

My role here is not to set out a history and analysis of postmodernism: that has already been done and continues to be done in a large and growing literature (e.g. Lash 1990; Harvey 1989). Rather it is to draw on elements in the debate about the nature of contemporary society that I believe are fundamental to an understanding of current social change. Many of these ideas have been generated precisely by the arguments pertaining to the issue of whether we now live in a "postmodern" world and if we do, what are its characteristics. To talk about these issues it is not actually necessary to use the word "postmodern" at all if one feels that the term has already become too loaded, confused or too associated with a particular anti-foundational epistemology. To avoid this some have suggested alternative terms such as "late modernity" (Giddens 1991), "late capitalist" (Mandel 1975) or "post-industrial" (Bell 1976). While there are equally problems with these notions too, common to all of them is the idea that the contemporary world is different in some fundamental ways from even the recent past, and that these changes are reflected in culture, social organisation (or disorganisation), class, micro- and macro-economic patterns, technology and psychology. My objective here will be to attempt to identify these changes and in doing so demonstrate both an appreciation for and a critique of the broad "postmodernist" position. The objective then will be to explore the usefulness of certain strands of contemporary cultural theory to explaining macro-trends in the world as we now see it changing around us.

There are of course many potential starting points for such an objective. An obvious one would be to take one or more empirical areas where the question of change is being addressed. These might include changing class structures and in particular the emergence of new classes (technological professionals, the "new rich" in some developing countries, etc.); institutional innovation (new kinds of educational networks, NGOs, the organisational restructuring of firms to take account of economic, technological and consumption shifts); the analysis of social movements and their impact; shifts in culture and values (Bellah 1985) or of course the activities which typically take place under the rubric of the "sociology of development" which is by its very nature to do with social change. All these things can be done, and are being done, but such empirical analysis takes place in the context of broader epistemological shifts. Postmodernism itself, for example, could not exist were it not for the emergence of an intellectual climate (or an anti-intellectual climate) that has displaced the concern with traditional social problems to a great extent with a preoccupation with aesthetics, literary criticism and selfhood. This is not necessarily a bad thing: it may reflect the emergence of genuine problems that have been suppressed in the past by positivist, structuralist and generally non-reflexive sociologies, although of course it might also reflect a flight from the critical problems of modern history. Broadly I would argue that postmodernism is not trivial: although it may not express itself as such, and indeed often adopt a posture exactly antithetical to those non-conservative sociologies that have most directly engaged the highly problematic and ambiguous nature of the world (Marxism, world-systems theory and critical theory typically), it potentially is an absolutely necessary source for the description, critique and changing of the contemporary world. Postmodernism is, or implies (despite its claims that it is an anti-theory) a theory of social change, in many ways a very radical one. It also articulates with (although this does not yet seem to have been systematically analysed) other emerging ideas about social change—"New Age" theories, new forms of religiosity, ideas about social organisation buried away in communes and other "intentional communities", theories of "future shock" and the argument that we are now (to use Capra's term) at a "turning point" (Capra 1982) in which older positivist epistemologies and the authoritarianism and uniformity that they implied, and the forms of social organisation that supported them, are now redundant.

Dimensions of Change

The onset of postmodernity is evident, according to its theorists, in the shift to a post-industrial society in which reproduction rather than production becomes the norm, in which knowledge is technologised and where the computer becomes the central artefact of society (Lyotard), where the distinction between the real and appearance becomes dissolved as we inhabit a world of "simulations" (TV images, Disneylands, "real plastic") which come to be the world that we inhabit (Baudrillard 1983) in which tradition and history evaporate and time becomes discontinuous to be replaced with the ephemerality of the present, and which culturally sees the ascendancy of eclecticism, the collapse of the distinction between high and mass culture and the reproducibility of cultural objects (e.g. paintings) which makes their originality or even their authorship irrelevant. There are a number of problems with this account of the world: it assumes that "the masses" (to use Baudrillard's term) are taken in by the simulatory nature of media and information technology, that alternative meaning systems (e.g. religion) have collapsed and that a totally commoditised culture has arisen within (or indeed is) late capitalism. Indeed in Baudrillard's account this leads to the "end of the social" in which norms, grand narratives and classes all disappear, indeed there are no "masses" even, but a black hole into which all meaning, reference and representation collapses (Baudrillard

1983): all have imploded in the system of simulations. Leaving aside the nihilistic implications of this view of things, there are several positive and several negative conclusions that can be drawn, which together constitute a valuable checklist of contemporary social forces.

These include the following:

1. We see here a revival in a fresh form of the traditional discipline of the sociology of knowledge. The basic plank in the postmodernist platform is that changes in knowledge are a fundamental factor in triggering the transition to a post-industrial society and that these forms of knowledge (reflected in art, literature, film and "world view" and therefore in values) are closely tied up with technological and production organisation ("post-Fordist") developments within rather than beyond late capitalism. The media, something usually on the margins of mainstream sociology, thus becomes central. In postmodernist theory, however, it becomes central in its role *within* advanced capitalist societies. A serious gap in the analysis however is the role of media in relations *between* societies and in the representation or misrepresentation of not so much the individual other as the collective other. Debates about the new world information order encapsulate this very well, as it is widely recognised that the flow of the information and its control and content is a factor in perpetuating inequality between societies. It is in other words, a very real form of power. The postmodernist recognition of the central role of knowledge is important and has methodological implications too, as it suggests that evidence of major social shifts can be found as much in (again for many sociologists such marginal areas as) art, literature or popular culture and architecture, as in such "classical" areas as social stratification. It is significant that a great deal of the best writing on postmodernism is that which has dealt with architectural evolution as emblematic of the accompanying social changes (Jameson 1984; Harvey 1989).
2. The urbanisation of the world is itself a major social trend. However, in conventional urban sociology the topics often taken for analysis—gentrification, suburbanisation, ethnic zoning, migra-

tion, are often under-theorised. But at the same time urban planners, geographers and political economists, to say nothing of architects themselves, were engaged in the study of urban form. Where the insights of the various fields, mixed with the challenges of postmodernism, came together with the older style interests, an explosion of interest in urban issues resulted. Amongst the issues emerging from this have been the linking of urban changes to the globalisation of capital (Massey 1984), changing power relationships within and between cities, changing conceptualisations of space and the links between these and images of society, and the appearance of urban spaces designed to provide "spectacle" and entertainment while promoting consumption (atrium-hotels, shopping malls, theme parks) which ignore local traditions and contribute to the "fragmentation of geographical loyalties" (Zukin 1988) typical of the postmodern world. The challenge here is to move beyond the tendency of postmodernism, to concentrate on the "sensual" form of cities, to a more critical vocabulary that can encompass the aesthetics of cities with their perpetual rebuilding and restructuring, the constant capitalist innovation that changes them (e.g. fast food chains). The class use of space, consequent changes in the lived experience of built-space, the impact of modes of transport (the private car, the subway), the role of tourism and the abandoning, in many major cities, of "modernist" attempts at urban reform (e.g. the build-up of inner city or satellite towns of high-rise apartment blocks). We recognise then that urbanisation is not just the physical concentration of people: it is a lifestyle, consumption, a creation of both opportunities and problems (such as the "new poverty" of the inhabitants of Japan's big cities faced with huge housing bills, high transport costs, inadequate suburban facilities and the stress of spending hours daily on grossly overcrowded public transport simply to reach the place of work), all of which are symptoms of underlying economic (capitalist) forces.

3. A central problem of contemporary society is that described by Habermas as a "legitimation crisis" (Habermas 1976). Often this is seen (although not exactly in this way by Habermas himself) as

the perennial difficulty for the state, for elites or indeed for any power bloc, to maintain its ascendancy and hegemony. Stability of control (the issue again being one of power) cannot be guaranteed through the means of violence: it is necessary to *legitimate* dominance. Since Foucault, however, we recognise that there has been a major shift in the way that the maintenance of power is to be understood. As Bauman puts it, "Seduction and repression between them, make "legitimation" redundant. The structure of domination can now be reproduced, ever more effectively, without recourse to legitimation; and thus without recourse to such intellectuals as make the legitimation discourse their speciality. Habermas's "legitimation crisis" makes sense, in the final account, as the intellectual perception of "crisis" caused by the ever more evident irrelevance of legitimation" (Bauman 1988).

Seeing the situation in this light revolutionises the old idea of "social conflict". Competition is no longer simply or crudely class struggle or ethnic conflict or the circulation of elites. It becomes indeed a question of assault on hierarchies, but the important thing to note is that these hierarchies are largely *symbolic*. Bourdieu's notion of "symbolic capital" (Bourdieu 1979) comes to centre field here. The object of (much) struggle is not material but epistemological: it is to obtain the right to name, classify and define, for those whose name create reality. There are two upshots to this: the theoretical one is that we need to reexamine what we mean by "power", and the empirical one is that all around us we see examples of the destabilisation of previously secure hierarchies (in art, in patriarchy, in religion, in academic disciplines, in international relations, in economic status groups.) The postmodernist attack on metanarratives ("There is no reason, only reasons": Lyotard) while itself an intellectual attack on foundationalism, is also symptomatic of a broader (although by no means total) loss of faith in those metanarratives. This implies widespread scepticism, relativism and interest in the non- or ir-rational which, together with the spread of the "narcissistic personality" identified by Lasch (1980) and the increasingly mobile (geographically, occupationally and psychologically) society with its throwaway mentality (the rapid obsolescence of everything, including human relationships) and too rapid (for most people) rate of technological and social change identified by Toffler (1970) rapidly undermines the "sanctity" of established institutions and hierarchies.

When combined with the actual historical decline of western global domination (the collapse of colonialism), the emergence of unexpected new power blocs (OPEC), the sudden demise of old adversaries (the Cold War), and its replacement with regional conflicts (the Gulf War), the weakening of states before the globalised power of multinational firms, rapidly accelerating ecological crises, medical ones (AIDS), ethnic ones (e.g. in Yugoslavia and the former USSR), economic ones (evidence of global recession) and religious ones (the rise of "fundamentalism" in surprisingly diverse contexts), there would indeed seem to be a legitimation crisis. But while many are convinced that there is indeed a crisis—of economy, ecology and consciousness—disagreement soon breaks out as to whether the crisis is cyclical or terminal. If the former, it will presumably soon adjust itself with relatively little inconvenience to most of us. But if the latter, then what we see is a fundamental break: modernity is over and a new epoch is upon us. And this is the position of the postmodernists, although it is very debatable whether the features they identify as being "postmodern" actually are, or whether they represent the last gasps of high modernism, the point of transition, to some thing which as Marx sensibly noted, it is wise to keep quiet about as we can never know the exact form of the future. What is significant about the present juncture is not only the severity of the global crisis and the apparent lack of any systematic model of how to deal with it (not only no grand narrative, but as the postmodernists would argue, there can *no longer be* a model), but also the unprecedented number of social movements (e.g. feminism) that are both contributors to our current state of being, and also uncertain, beyond local goals, of how to fundamentally solve anything. Indeed if Lasch is right (Lasch 1986) nobody is trying any longer to solve anything beyond the protection (physically and psychologically) of one's self and immediate environment. The issue that in the last resort the postmodernists have identified is a crisis of history: the past no longer has or is a source of legitimacy, the present is fluid, without structures, and the future can no longer be anticipated as liberatory. Science, philosophy and the grand narratives (e.g. Marxism) have failed (except the latter, significantly, for Jameson). The crisis then is fundamentally an epistemological one, and it is a real crisis for the postmodernist because the theory of postmodernism itself, beyond identifying the transition, can do nothing to help, since progress and meaning have been rejected. Essentially then there is no place for values in a postmodernist reading of our present situation.

4. The centrality of *culture*—something that until recently has been pushed to the margins of mainstream sociology—is an essential part of this new model. This is not to say that the concept of postmodernism is only restricted to culture: indeed the argument of this essay is exactly that it needs to be retrieved from this limited usage and seen as applicable to the social, economic and political realms as well. I will not here develop a detailed argument of why culture is central to the understanding of social processes: hopefully by now this can be taken for granted. Rather I would like to point out some important implications of this. A key element in the postmodernist understanding of our present condition is that politics has changed because culture has changed. A decentred, deconstructionist, "post-structuralist" view of culture—its intertextuality, lack of authority, unconcern with issues of authorship, genius or leadership—is radically democratic, but in a way that calls into question the traditional understanding of individualism and collectivism, since a whole new image of the self and therefore of the interrelationship of selves (i.e. "society") emerges. The result is only a new "political culture" (or even, if we were to follow Baudrillard here, the end of politics as we have previously known it) as a radically new *cultural politics*. This has two levels: one of the struggle to establish new regimes of signification within cultural practices (the arts, literature, film, psychology, the social sciences, etc.), and the other is the impact of these new repre-

sentational strategies, or what Jameson calls "cognitive mapping" (Jameson 1988), on social practice (political life, class relationships, everyday life, economic behaviour and even international—including intercultural and interethnic relations.) Aesthetics and politics are thus deeply intertwined and are in a very fundamental sense dimensions of each other—something incidentally true not just in late-capitalist societies, but in relatively more "traditional" ones too—such as China, where the link between art and politics has always been quite explicit (Kraus 1991). The impact of the media (Baudrillard's "simulation" again) in promoting this is visible in the whole process of the creating of images and "personalities" on TV: not to appear well on television is the most fatal flaw that a US presidential candidate can have. The result is "simulated politics" to use Kellner's term, which raises a key empirical question: "It remains to be seen whether the oppressive realities of contemporary capitalist societies are producing a new proletarianisation of the underlying population, or whether the glitzy joys of its culture and consumerism will continue to entrap the majority. . . in its massified and commodified pleasures, and its simulated politics" (Kellner 1988: 262).

Whatever empirical decision is made here, this quotation points (apparently unconsciously) to one of the key mediators between the two levels of cultural politics: consumption. It can certainly be argued that there are two main features of late capitalism: its transnational character and its promotion of consumerism on a mass scale. Consumerism deeply affects values, aesthetic sensibilities, meaning systems and patterns of interpersonal relationships. Self-identity, status, the worth of individuals, leisure-time habits, body-images, sexuality, etc. are all transformed by the reproducibility, interchangeability and discardability of contemporary objects of consumption. The boundaries between high and low culture are dissolved, and the eclecticism, ephemerality and pastiche nature of products so celebrated by one wing of postmodernism appear. Spectacle replaces involvement, "relationships" displace love and a completely ahistorical view of time takes over. While the criticism can be made that a good deal of postmodernism's description of contemporary culture, while valid, only applies to a tiny proportion of the urban population of the "First World", the perception of consumerism (or what Erich Fromm calls the "having" mode displacing the "being" mode of existence: Fromm 1982) as lying at the heart of contemporary society in the so-called advanced societies, is, I believe, essentially correct. And because of the transnational reach and international penetration of capitalism, consumerism is becoming an almost universal way of life. This takes us to a yet deeper level, one where we can invoke Critical Theory's view of mass culture as essentially corrupting in its glorification of consumption over other modes of existence, engineered by what are basically cynical, greedy and self-serving capitalist forces—TV companies, the mass press and of course advertising. Interestingly we see here again both the strengths and the limitations of postmodern theory: the ability to perceive and describe very real cultural trends, while failing to develop a deep enough critique of their full meaning (with some conspicuous exceptions, Jameson and Harvey being amongst the main ones.)

The expansion of media and information systems has paradoxical functions: it unifies (or rather homogenises) by the very act of creating a mass culture, but yet promotes pluralism by the nature of its programming. A travel programme creates awareness of alternative ways of life: a nature programme can promote ecological and/or anti-industrialism sentiments. The potentially propagandist nature of the media thus cuts both ways precisely because of the "postmodern" context in which the media itself operates: it is powerful but yet not authoritative.

Underlying this is something that I will later return to: the need for a fresh look at theories of power. But this is not all, for this selfsame context creates new fault lines in the distribution of traditional political categories. Much of what used to be on the "right" is now on the "old left"; the "New Right" that has arisen in a major way in Europe in the same environment that has seen the rise of "green" politics is in many ways the reflection of neo-conservative principles in the values of a mass public rather than simply the recycling of old Tory politics; the "New Left" is beginning to look a little tired in the face of a fragmenting political culture that has not only thrown up "postmodernism", but also what is being called "postmaterialism"—which finds its friends on both the "right" and the "left" (Gibbins 1989). "Lifestyle", far from being any longer just a Sunday colour supplement buzz word, has become a serious political and moral issue, reflected interestingly primarily and some commentators are suggesting that class be reconceptualised in terms of consumption categories rather than in terms of its traditional indicators. The postmodernist shift from content to style can be seen operating at many levels. We clearly need a new term here too: perhaps "technoculture" to reflect the connection not simply of economics and culture, but of technology and culture.

Before moving on from this topic, there is one more issue that needs to be discussed. Traditional politics has been characterised by the domination of large organisations (parties, trades unions, machines), the tendency to centralisation and the rapid transition from, in Weberian terms, the charismatic to bureaucratic modes. This view of political organisation has been seriously undermined from three related, but separate directions: from postmodernism (e.g. Lyotard 1970) which attacks the rationalism of traditional political discourse and its tendency to reproduce the very repression that it often claims to be directed against; from poststructuralist, and especially Foucaultian analyses of power; and from the new social movements of the post 1970s with their focus on micro politics and the organisation of everyday social practice. Restraint (the conservative version of political order) is replaced by libidinality and the expression of feelings, the desire not to have "power over" anything, and the rejection of external laws. Efficiency, domination, power, patriarchy, bureaucracy, and the State itself are, according to this analysis, becoming increasingly undermined by postmodernist cultural tendencies. Localism replaces universalism. Stable discourse or stable power can no longer be assumed. Once again we find a link between non-representationality in culture and anti-authoritarianism in politics. And we find in postmodernist theory a very powerful model for unmasking the links and causal claims that bind together contemporary society, something that is being done in interesting ways not only by postmodernists themselves, but by the theorists of the new social movements also (e.g. Guattari and Negri 1988).

On the Global Scale

Amongst the possible criticisms of the postmodernist interpretation of the shift to a post-industrial social and cultural order is the objection that this position is an elite one which, despite its claims to an interest in popular culture, really only reflects the lifestyle of the first-world urban elite, and ignores not only the great class and ethnic variations in everyday life in the industrialised countries, but especially the position of the "third world" and especially its non-elites. The counter-argument to this would be that postmodernism is essentially the theory of the cultural logic of late capitalism, and as that capitalism expands it penetrates all levels of society in the first world and eventually most levels of society in the third world, and has similar effects wherever it reaches. The actual response to the penetration not of primary but of late capitalism is a fascinating empirical question, and there is a lot of evidence that with the spread of television, the mass print media, etc. there is a great deal of uniformity in effects.

In fact, postmodernism itself cannot be understood in terms of a static model of capitalism, but of the expansion of capitalism on a global scale. But as soon as we state this we see an interesting tension developing, leading to a resolution. Seen from a critical (typically but not necessarily Marxist) perspective the expansion of capitalism, while it produces more things, also produces more subtle but unmistakable servitude, regulation, disciplinary procedures, necessities. But at the same time modernity, the historical partner of capitalism, has as a central part of its project the objective of liberation (from nature, tradition, the uncontrolled). When put together, the resulting tensions create contradictions which can only be resolved by the transition to postmodernism, where a late post-Fordist capitalism based on new flexible modes of accumulation and committed to the creation of a universal culture of consumption, necessarily coexists with a mind-set concerned with the transcending of the restraints of modernist civilisation (see, for example, the argument of Bell 1976).

Under these circumstances new identities begin to emerge throughout the global system. These identities (sense of self, relationship to space and time, relationship to the body, to nature, to the unconscious, to belief) vary substantially with context, but they are *all substantially changed* by their necessary position within a world system which is now hegemonic. This argument of course is not that of neo-conservative commentators such as Francis Fukuyama who see liberal values everywhere replacing authoritarian and traditional values. The postmodernist argument is actually neutral as to the actual *content* of emerging values, which could well turn out, in a world facing what seems to be an endless succession of crises, to be very authoritarian ones. The moral vacuum at the heart of Lyotard's system with its failure to develop any theory of justice or in Baudrillard's elitist cynicism regarding "the masses" clearly shows that while as a description of late capitalist culture postmodernism may be all too accurate, as a prescription for action or solution, it is weak indeed.

But significantly many commentators see "traditionalism"—reflected in the persistence of nationalism and the rise of religious fundamentalism—as responses to (even if not called by this name) postmodernity. There is a certain theoretical failure of nerve here, a kind of reflex naive functionalism which tends to appear whenever the genuinely new emerges (it has to be explained away in terms of pre-existing categories). In fact the thrust of the postmodernist argument is that something new is emerging comparable to the emergence of capitalism itself from feudalism. Of course there are continuities, there always are, but these should not blind us to what is new in our present situation. The tendency to retreat into atavism at times of crisis is all too apparent, but partly because adequate theories of the present and of the nature of social transformation, have not been worked out in convincing ways.

A significant element of such a theory would be the understanding of the world system itself: patterns of trade and accumulation; of the increasing peripheralisation and underdevelopment of some areas (e.g. much of Africa) on the one hand with the expansion of new modes of intensive capitalist activity (e.g. parts of Southeast Asia, Korea; the international division of labour; labour flows; the role of MNCs; shifts in local economies with respect to one another; patterns of employment and unemployment. From this essentially economic analysis ("the material logic") emerges the "cultural logics" with which the economic crisis is expressed: concern with ethnicity, religious fundamentalism, racism (as in France, Germany and increasingly Austria), return to "roots" and the seeking for quasi-traditional value systems, e.g. neo-Confucianism in East and parts of Southeast Asia (Friedman 1988). What is commonly understood as the linkages between the micro and macro levels reappear here, but cast into a new form: the relationship between the material and cultural logics operating simultaneously within the global "economy", a good word since it implies a total ecological system. In a very real and indeed radical sense *all* social groups (including the remaining vestigial tribal ones) are integrated into the world system, if not in terms of identity, then economically; if not economically then politically; if not politically then ecologically: "the acid rain falleth alike on the just and the unjust."

The applications of the model sketched out here—broadly termed "postmodernist"—need next to be applied to a range of empirical examples. Classical postmodernism (if we may be allowed such a term) has concentrated (even in its Jamesonian Marxist/utopian variety) on the analysis of culture: its qualities and mechanisms of production and reproduction. The next step is to apply the ideas to larger scale social, economic and political processes and institutions. Examples of this would be precisely to those so often labelled "traditionalist"—religion, ethnicity and nationalism. Others might include social movements (feminism, ecology, peace, educational, health and communitarian ones especially), seemingly more abstract processes such as power, flexible accumulation, localism and the burgeoning interest in chaos theory. And at a very macro level, an analysis of the state itself would be a priority, together with the question of the emergence of new classes.

It should not then take too much imagination to see that issues such as the new nationalisms, growing local and regional as opposed to global conflicts, the relationships of firms (especially TNCs) to states, are all linked to the fundamental shifts in the total system. Although it is difficult to think simultaneously in both global and micro terms, in material as well as in cultural terms, this is what is necessarily involved here, as Bourdieu has shown with his concept of "habitus". The theoretical necessity is for a conceptual revolution, the elements of which lie all around us (in Bourdieu, in the postmodernists, in the new social movements, in contemporary literary theory), which requires new ways of analysing the relationships of space and time to economic processes, of technology to structures of feeling, of art to politics, of the body to cosmology. If Harvey is correct in his perception that "There has been a sea-change in cultural as well as in political-economic practices since around 1972" (Harvey 1989) then correspondingly new forms of social theory are necessary to deal with this.

World-systems analysis (as enshrined particularly in the world of Immanuel Wallerstein), while quite rightly stressing the interrelationships of the economic, the political and the social, have tended to explain the global system using categories (e.g. the State) which themselves need to come under close critical scrutiny. Understanding that an increasingly integrated world economy has for the most part made national boundaries superfluous, especially in an era of satellite TV and the facsimile machine, is an important advance. But it may not go far enough, as not only is the legitimacy of the state being called increasingly into question, but so is the viability of the firms that constitute the major institutional expression of the world economy. Similarly in political science there has been a resurgence of l950s' style modernisation theory to explain late 1980s' political developments—and with it the refurbishing of exactly the kinds of ideas that Baudrillard for example attacks as now hopelessly outmoded—such as the idea of "civil society" and its almost inevitable expansion—although interestingly enough even civil society theory argues that this essentially means the growth of institutions independent of, and so a challenge to, the State. (cf. Almond 1987; Pye 1990). Indeed there seems to be almost an inevitability at work here: that even as analysis led to the understanding of the emergence of authoritarian regimes in newly capitalist states (e.g. in Southeast Asia), so now it is carrying it beyond that point to a viewpoint stressing the strong pressures working against authoritarianism from a variety of traditional, neo-traditional and postmodernist sources.

Conclusion

A revolution in the traditional sense seems to be an unlikely scenario in much of the newly or late capitalist world. But then it may not be necessary, as a very different kind of revolution may be taking place before our very noses. Indeed classical revolution—the replacing of one kind of authority of domination with another—may have been rendered obsolete.

This is not to say that much of history for the next decade or two will not be made up of fierce rear-guard actions on the part of states, transnational corporations and authoritarian bureaucracies, educational organisations, trades unions and the like, to stave off the unfolding future. There are also consequences for policy: while the state may have had a vital role in economic development in the past in NICs such as Singapore and Taiwan, it has become evident that what was once a positive (at least in a capitalist sense) force has now become a dead-hand. Labour and information have become extensively internationalised, as has finance. The management of domestic economies has become in fact a problem of managing the world economy, but in practice this cannot be done: the old assumptions about management no longer apply; possession of an MBA is becoming more of a liability than an asset.

We thus end up with a situation in which, like it or not, globalisation has occurred and with it the transformation of relationships between the global and the local, of everyday life, of sense of identity (especially as a result of the reflexivity characteristic of post, late or high modernity), and the collapse of expertise (no one is really an "authority" on how to manage the world any more, and many of the worst mistakes, e.g. in development planning, are made precisely by the "experts". These transformations can collectively be termed "postmodernity" (without necessarily having to commit oneself to the complete collapse of metanarratives, the total relativity of language-games, etc. characteristic of much of the "literary " or artistic postmodernism.) Seen in this light the theory of postmodernity carries within it powerful, indeed indispensable, tools for the analysis and critique of our present situation and at the same time, by stressing creativity and imagination rather than structures, roles and the whole vocabulary of the over-socialised conception of man, permits alternatives: an open future modified but not dominated by the past, with which the present is in many ways discontinuous. New religious, social, ethnic or national movements are not then just the resurgence of "tradition", they are often (as in Japan for example) the *invention* of tradition, modes of managing the uncertain present and mechanisms for creating those alternative futures, gestures at least towards how things might be. And if the world is now different, the social sciences, and in this case specifically sociology, will have to be different too, especially in its need to bring together its hermeneutical and critical functions (Smart 1991). The plasticity rather than the rigidity of the present is surely its key characteristic, and while we can argue over the exact extent to which the contemporary world is a break with the past rather than the reflection or transformation of continuities, the subtle perhaps but nevertheless fundamental distinctiveness of our present era needs recognition and the development of theoretical tools for its analysis. And this is not just a passive or academic matter: it requires equally the development of social, educational and political responses to the open future. The failure to do this will result in the seemingly easy (and certainly familiar) but ultimately disastrous course of simply resurrecting the past models (racism, fundamentalisms, authoritarianisms) because of our fear of the future. Decay of the present great systems (Vacca 1971; Eco 1986) need not usher in a new "middle Ages", since both our reflexivity (and hence our ability to be aware of the problems) and ability to inject transformative energy by way of alternatives, is potentially greater than the forces of entropy. The question of values in other words lies at the root of the understanding of institutional and social transformation.

References

Almond, G.A. (1987), "The Development of Political Development," in M. Weiner and S.P. Huntington (eds.) *Understanding Political Development*, Boston: Little, Brown.

Baudrillard, J. (1983), *Simulations*, New York: Semiotext(e).

Baudrillard, J. (1983), *In the Shadow of the Silent Majorities or, the End of the Social*, New York: Semiotext(e).

Bauman, Z. (1988), "Is There a Postmodern Sociology?" *Theory, Culture and Society* 5, 2-3, p. 222.

Bell, D. (1976a), *The Cultural Contradictions of Capitalism* London: Heinemann.

Bell, D. (1976b), *The Coming of Post-Industrial Society*, Boston: Basic Books.

Bellah, R.N. et al. (1985), *Habits of the Heart*, Berkeley: University of California Press.

Bourdieu, P. (1979), *Outline of a Theory of Practice*, Cambridge: Cambridge University Press.

Capra, F. (1982), *The Turning Point*, New York: Simon and Schuster; London: Wildwood House.

Cohen, Ira J. (1987), "Structuration Theory and Social Praxis," in A. Giddens and J. Turner (eds.) *Social Theory Today*, Stanford: Stanford University Press.

Eco, U. (1986), "Towards a New Middle Ages," in M. Blonsky (ed.) *On Signs*, Oxford: Basil Blackwell.

Friedman, J. (1988), "Cultural Logics of the Global System: A Sketch," *Theory, Culture and Society*, 5, 2-3.

Fromm, E. (1982), *To Have or To Be?* New York: Bantam.

Gibbins, J.R. (ed.) (1989), *Contemporary Political Culture: Politics in a Postmodern Age*, London: Sage.

Giddens, A. (1979), *Central Problems in Social Theory: Action, Structure and Contradiction in Social Analysis*, London: Macmillan; Berkeley: University of California Press.

Giddens, A. (1981), "Agency, Institution and Time-Space Analysis" in K. Knorr-Cetina and A.V. Cicourel (eds.) *Advances in Social Theory and Methodology: Towards an Integration of Micro- and Macro-Sociologies*, London: Routledge and Kegan Paul.

Giddens, A. (1991), *Modernity and Self Identity: Self and Society in the Late Modern Age*, Stanford: Stanford University Press.

Guattari, F. and A. Negri (1988), *Anti-Power*, New York: Semiotext(e).

Habermas, J. (1976), *Legitimation Crisis*, London: Heinemann.

Harvey, D. (1989), *The Postmodern Condition*, Oxford: Basil Blackwell.

Jameson, F. (1984), "Postmodernism or the Cultural Logic of Late Capitalism," *New Left Review* 146.

Jameson, F. (1984), "Cognitive Mapping," in C. Nelson and L. Grossberg (eds.) *Marxism and the Interpretation of Culture*, Urbana and Chicago: University of Illinois Press.

Kellner, D. (1988), "Postmodernism as Social Theory: Some Challenges and Problems," *Theory, Culture and Society* 5, 2-3.

Kraus, R.C. (1991), *Brushes With Power: Modern Politics and the Chinese Art of Calligraphy*, Berkeley and Los Angeles: University of California Press.

Lasch, C. (1980), *The Culture of Narcissism*, London: Abacus.

Lasch, C. (1985), *The Minimal Self*, London: Picador.

Lash, S. (1990), *Sociology of Postmodernism*, London: Routledge.
Lyotard, J.F. (1982), *Driftworks*, New York: Semiotext(e).
Lyotard, J.F. (1984), *The Postmodern Condition*, Manchester: Manchester University Press.
Mandel, E. (1975), *Late Capitalism*, London: New Left Books.
Massey, D. (1984), *Spatial Divisions of Labour*, New York: Methuen.
Pye, L. (1990), "Political Science and the Crisis of Authoritarianism," *American Political Science Review*, 84, 1.
Smart, B. (1991), "Sociology, Ethics and the Present," *Thesis Eleven*, 30.
Toffler, A. (1970), *Future Shock*, London: The Bodley Head.
Vacca, R. (1971), *Il Medioevo Prossimo Venturo*, Milan: Arnoldo Modadori Editore.
Zukin, S. (1988), "The Postmodern Debate over Urban Form," *Theory, Culture and Society* 5, 2-3. p. 433.

Chapter 5
SOCIOLOGICAL CONSIDERATIONS IN ECONOMIC DEVELOPMENT

Economic reform does not take place in a vacuum, but always in a context of social, cultural, political and ecological circumstances. And it does not only have economic consequences but, whether successful or not, has profound effects on all dimensions of the societies in which it occurs, even influencing things as apparently remote from economics as patterns of religious belief and practice. This chapter will address three issues: the question of what sociological factors can be identified in Japan's experience of modernisation and the possibility of their replication elsewhere; the identification on the basis of this and with reference to comparative examples of the sociological conditions that seem to promote or retard certain kinds of economic reform; and the question, vital to any balanced understanding of development processes, of the sociological consequences of economic reforms, which contains within itself the question of whether in all or even in most cases, reforms at the level of the economy are even desirable from a sociological point of view. The overall objective is to relate the economic and the sociological in such a way that a coherent and more wholistic picture of the nature of development emerges in which the necessity of economic changes is balanced by an understanding of social costs.

The necessity for such an approach can be argued on a number of grounds. One of these is, of course, the theoretical need to be able to relate the economic and the sociological in a systematic way. Another is the requirement of being able to see the actual impact of what may appear to be "rational" economic policies on the everyday lives of those they affect and to understand what actually happens "on the ground" when new forms of economy begin to penetrate pre-existing forms. A third involves the attempt to explain why, despite the prescriptions of economists, many underdeveloped societies remain that way, and not a few find their situation actually getting worse. It is, or should be, obvious, in other words, that development is not a matter of economics alone, and indeed, if the end point and purpose of economics is to produce the good society, then a cogent argument can even be made for the subordination of economics to social goals. Our objective may be to overturn Marx with Weber: to create the conditions in which values come to determine our relationship to the material rather than allow our material conditions to determine our values.

Lessons from the Japanese Experience

Recent tendencies to look upon Japan as, if not an exact model, then at least as an inspiration for other countries embarking on the path of technology-based development, are in many ways well founded. Emerging from a long period of almost medieval stability and social order at the end of the Tokugawa era (1603-1867), Japan underwent a process of intense and rapid modernisation following, at least in externals, western patterns. A bureaucracy was organised, staffed mainly by former *samurai*, the foundations were laid for a modern educational system, industrialisation was initiated, a national army and navy were created, shipbuilding, medicine and other aspects of technology were transformed. And within a short time Japan moved from almost complete isolationism to becoming a colonial power. As is well known, this path led rapidly, despite the widespread dissemination of Marxist and other internationalist views, to the militarism which culminated in Japan's involvement in World War II. And it should also be remembered that the period from the Meiji reforms through to 1945 was also one of bad working conditions for labour, the destruction of much of the traditional rural economy and the incorporation of large numbers of young women into the industrial workforce for the first time, the suppression of organised labour and a withering in the bud of embryonic attempts at democracy. All these conditions—a highly centralised and authoritarian government, the rise of capital at the expense of labour, the decline of the rural sector and the major role of the military and of oligarchies in political and economic life—can all be seen in the recent or contemporary history of many of the industrialising societies of Southeast Asia. This fact should encourage us not to think of the Japanese economic "miracle" in totally positive terms, but to recognise the problems and massive social dislocations that accompanied primary industrialisation in Japan.

But of course the Japanese experience does not stop with the war, but continues on into the postwar reconstruction of both the economy and the society and its successive transformations into the economic superpower that it is today. But even then we should keep in mind the social costs that have very obviously accompanied this process and the social sacrifices that have made it possible. The often-heard slogan "Rich Country, Poor People" has more than a grain of truth in it. Japan may then provide a model of an unexpected, but especially valuable type, in which the disadvantages, problems and costs of following the route of capitalist style, industrially-based development can very clearly be seen, as well as the advantages of a high consumption, energy intensive and resource poor but democratic political economy.

There is tremendous and continuing debate amongst historians about the exact conditions that facilitated Japan's achievement of modernity (e.g. Smith 1989, McCormack and Sugimoto 1988, Jansen 1985). Here I will attempt to summarise those sociological factors which in my estimation have played the most significant roles. It is important to approach these not simply as a list of elements which, if replicated elsewhere, will bring about the same results elsewhere, but synergistically. That is to say it is not only the presence of the individual elements, but also the ways in which they combine and influence each other that is crucial to their effective working. With this in mind we can now attempt to summarise these factors, not in any special order of priority, but with constant attention to their interlinked nature.

1. *Population.* The Japanese population has expanded rapidly in the postwar era and now exceeds 120 million, and has only recently reached the point of demographic transition. This figure, which puts Japan in the top ten most populous countries in the world, is interpreted within Japan as leading to excessive crowding. This, however, is a myth. Although Japanese like to think of Japan as a small country, it is not. The apparent overcrowding comes not from ratio of population to land area, but to over concentration in a small number of large cities. In any country sustainable population depends essentially on the ratio of population to resources and efficient agriculture and then intensive industrialisation

which together with Japan's position as a world trading economy has permitted a large population with long life expectancy. A large population with reasonable income levels of course creates a large internal market, and in the Japanese case high expectations of quality together with the systematic creation by capital of a consumer society have produced high levels of internal economic energy driven by escalating demand. At the same time the *belief* in the crowded and vulnerable nature of the Japanese economy has fuelled overseas expansion, initially through colonisation and later through trade, investment and the shifting offshore of labour-intensive and lower-technology industries both to offset the high yen and labour costs in Japan and to penetrate other markets, for example in Southeast Asia (Clammer 1993). A large population with a perception of scarcity and insecurity (although one could argue with an objectively sound economic basis except for some energy resources such as oil) would seem to be a key factor in releasing economic energies.

2. *Education.* Ronald Dore (1965) and others have argued that the early stages of economic take-off in Japan were made possible by a literate population. With the postwar expansion of universal education and the rapid growth of higher education, both state-funded and private, the creation of a highly educated population has reached unprecedented levels. Japan now has almost total literacy, one of the world's highest proportions of high school leavers enrolled in tertiary education, an enormous network of supplementary, vocational and special interest (e.g. foreign languages) schools and colleges and a society in which both the value system (often attributed to Confucianism) and the mechanisms of social mobility (Ishida 1992) are closely linked to educational achievement and the respect for learning. Certain features of Japanese education stand out as especially important in my estimation. Firstly, education has extended to women who are highly represented in all levels of education including the tertiary level. This has meant not only a highly trained workforce across gender lines, but also ensures that young children are brought up by literate and well-educated parents, especially the mother with whom they

spend the most time. Secondly, the educational process does not only involve the inculcation of facts, but is very much also a total method of socialisation which stresses co-operation, achievement of goals in a group and basic ethical values and quasi-ethical values such as honesty and tidiness (White 1990). Thirdly, a large amount of time and attention is given to the study of mathematics and science subjects, which when combined with high levels of literacy, is clearly functional for economic success. Japanese students spend more hours in school and spend more time on mathematics and science that those of any other industrialised country. And fourthly, education does not finish at the point of graduation from high school or college. Quite apart from the network of opportunities for continuing education especially in skills-based subjects such as languages, Japanese companies provide very extensive facilities for training and further education on an in-house basis. The lack of graduate business schools in Japan is not a result of lack of interest in management training, but a reflection of the fact that such training is provided by the companies themselves.

3. *The role of the State.* A factor which clearly crosses the boundary of the sociological, the political and the economic is that of the role of the state. Throughout early modern, modern and contemporary Japanese history, the state has played a major role in structuring social and economic activity, manipulating markets, managing the infrastructure such as roads, controlling taxation, promoting land reclamation, and so forth. And it has done so in modern times in large part through the creation of an efficient bureaucracy, entry to which is based on education, which is not corrupt and which, while subject to the inevitable structural ills of all bureaucracies, is largely respected by society at large and which provides a very desirable career for some of the very brightest graduates despite relatively low wages and often very long working hours. (For a now classic case-study which includes the sociological dimension see Johnson 1982.) The bureaucracy has promoted certain patterns of industrialisation, promoted offshore investment and carefully protected Japanese industry and agriculture as well as the retail sector from too much foreign competition.

4. *Amongst the more specifically sociological factors should be included the relatively homogeneous nature of the Japanese population, which has both promoted easier identification with the national entity and has almost eliminated conflicts and divisions based on ethnic pluralism, tribalism and linguistic variation.* This sharing of identity, even though it can take the negative forms of discrimination against minorities and exclusion of outsiders, does help to promote common values, which themselves prove to be very functional when applied to economic growth. These would include the high evaluation of education, high levels of saving, patterns of co-operation and mutual assistance, the largely non-confrontational characteristics of the culture, the nature of managerial styles, and attitudes to labour and to service. Social organisation, and especially the presence of stable families as the norm, with gender roles which while backward by the standards of some western commentators, do provide a situation in which working men are given a supportive environment and are basically released from domestic duties, children receive socialisation that converges with that provided in the schools, and in which many of the social functions of the state such as care of the elderly are at least in theory, undertaken by the family. Positive attitudes to technology and a religious system which certainly does not in any way retard economic activities and in some cases such as the Nichiren form of Buddhism actively encourages it, strengthen those values which, in conjunction with education and the family system, provide what has proved to be an excellent economic environment.
5. *Additional background factors with sociological implications would include the nature of the Japanese ecology which has required co-operative labour relations, especially in the rice growing areas, but to some extent in all agricultural sectors and in the Shinden or land reclamation and new village schemes begun during the Tokugawa period.* Ecological and geographical conditions have also from quite an early date predisposed the Japanese towards urbanisation and urban centres, again from quite early dates, became centres of commerce, culture and artisanal and craft activity long before the advent of industrialisation.

If then we start from the idea of Japan as a "model" for economic transformation it is apparent that a specific group of factors—social, cultural and ecological have contributed to the country's rise to economic power. But the specific nature of this combination of factors requires some further comment. The first is that, as other countries have found when they have attempted to transplant aspects of Japanese technique to their own situation, simply adopting one factor by itself rarely works. An obvious example of this would be attempts to adopt "Japanese-style management" in a number of Southeast Asian countries such as Singapore. While some detailed elements such as quality control circles have been successfully adapted, in other respects the transplanting of Japanese styles has failed because of cultural factors. In the Singapore case higher levels of individualism, lack of commitment by either workers or managers to the company leading to frequent "job hopping", very bureaucratic control mechanisms within organisations and top-down decision-making styles together with differing attitudes to work on the part of Singaporeans has rendered a Japanese model in any strict sense quite unworkable. Similar experiences have been reported from Taiwan, the Philippines and elsewhere in the region.

The second is that the Japanese success story is to a great extent a success in terms of abstract national income and for the large industrialists. Very high costs of living, unaffordable housing, rising pollution and environmental degradation, long working and commuting hours, short holidays and severe social pressure to compete and perform are the lot of the average worker and salaried employee. It is also often forgotten that only a minority of Japanese work for large corporations, and an even smaller minority enjoy so-called "lifetime employment". In fact the Japanese economy is heavily based on small business, family-owned shops and eateries and sub-contractors for the major corporations. All of these are vulnerable to fluctuations in demand, have low capitalisation and high costs and do not enjoy economies of scale. Employees in these sectors do not have lifetime employment, and even those workers who do are finding that with the current (1993-4) recession bonuses—which form a large part of salaries—are being cut, part-time workers are being laid off, new hiring has stopped or declined and that women in particular are finding it hard to find salaried work and in some cases those with theoretically permanent status are being pressured into taking early retirement or are being relocated to unattractive subsidiaries or remote locations. A concept gaining popularity in Japan is that of *shin bimbo* or the "new poverty", or as it is sometimes phrased "rich country, poor people".

Thirdly, Japan's postwar economic success was in large part due to the availability of markets and markets that furthermore were not overly defended by protectionist sentiments. Whether or not the old saying is true that the best route to economic success is to loose a war against the Americans (in any case hardly a recipe for future development!) it is the case that Japan, on becoming a postwar US ally, enjoyed access to the world while receiving US military protection and was also a major beneficiary economically of US involvement in Korea and then subsequently in Japan. This has created international market access while keeping Japanese military spending down to around 1 per cent of GNP and historically allowed Japan access to advanced technology upon which indigenous industrialisation could be based without high R&D costs. But for a newly industrialising economy now entering the world trading economy for the first time (other than as a simple supplier of commodities) the trading system is already largely rigged in favour of the early entrants, much of the market is already saturated and lack of scientific infrastructure makes competition in high-technology innovation very difficult. The only alternatives are to become recipients of foreign capital much of which comes because of lower costs and brings with it at least some degree, often a high degree of foreign control, and to only have access to relatively low and often more polluting and energy-inefficient technology. A good case in point would be the Malaysian car industry. For nationalistic reasons of unclear economic rationality (but probably to do with ideas of employment creation and transfer of technology) the Malaysian government decided that it needed a car industry. The result was what while technically a joint venture with Mitsubishi Heavy Industries is actually largely controlled by the Japanese and has involved the transfer of what is now low technology for building a poorly made and underpowered car based on a design now a decade old (the Mitsubishi "Lancer" model). Most components are imported from Japan and simply assembled locally. The resulting car—there was initially only one model, the "Proton Saga"—was indeed bought by innocent Malaysians of middle income in the belief that it was indeed a Malaysian car. Subsequent problems with the project have involved the small size of the domestic market, difficulty of access to overseas markets already dominated by "real" Japanese and European cars, the fact that early models of the car did not meet North American technical and emission standards and managerial problems due to the unwillingness of the Japanese parent company to transfer responsibility to Malaysians who were mostly employed in subordinate managerial capacities. Numerous other examples could be given from elsewhere in Asia of similar patterns of economic reform whose ultimate value is very questionable. The point here is not to criticise the Japanese experience, but to warn against hasty adoption of that (necessarily unique) experience as a model and to remind its fans that there have been costs, in particular social ones, and that the export of that model or of one like it is likely to bring with it similar costs.

Economic Reforms in Southeast Asia

The Japanese case then provides a kind of theoretical paradigm. Other countries in the region have had varying degrees of success with other patterns of economic reform, and it is also important to review some of these. Here I will concentrate on Southeast Asian examples, since this region contains both some of the most successful economies and some with major problems.

Singapore is seen as one of the most successful capitalist economies in Southeast Asia. Until 1963 the country was a British colony with an economy based largely on the British military bases and on entrepot trade, both regionally and as the import-export point for commodities bound from or to Malaysia, Indonesia and even Burma. It was composed of a mix of Chinese and Indian immigrants, indigenous Malays and mixed-race Eurasians. The social infrastructure was weak (education, housing, etc.) and few inhabitants had any particular loyalty to Singapore as such. Between 1963 and 1965 Singapore was a constituent state of the Malayan federation, but in 1965, mainly for political reasons, left to become an independent nation-state. At the same time the British announced the withdrawal of their troops and naval and airforce divisions. The military bases were a major source of employment and of income for the local community, so this was a potentially devastating decision. The first independent government then found itself with a tiny country, politically at odds with its immediate neighbours (Malaysia and Indonesia), with an uncertain economy, a volatile ethnic mix of people with no particular commitment to the country and with no common language, with a weak infrastructure and with the major threat of the communist movement in Malaysia and militant left-wing labour unions and students at home.

The initial solution to this group of pressing and potentially overwhelming problems involved three interlinked policies: the creation of an indigenous economy based on export-led industrialisation; the creation of a social infrastructure and especially of a massive public housing project designed both to provide employment and stimulate the local economy and to tie people to Singapore on the assumption that ownership of a home would encourage people to put down roots; and the creation of a national identity through an explicit attempt at what was locally called "nation-building" through the establishment of a strong state apparatus, the promotion of national symbols—flag, national anthem, sports teams, etc.—and by way of the mechanism of compulsory military service for all men as a condition of citizenship (proposals to extend this to women too have never taken off, although women are encouraged to voluntarily join the armed forces and many do). Benefiting from an influx of foreign capital—labour costs were then low and educational levels and knowledge of English, legacies of the colonial period, were quite high—liberal trade regimes in the region and internationally, close defence links with Australia and New Zealand which guaranteed military protection under the SEATO treaty, a population of immigrants inclined, as immigrants so often are, to hard work, long hours and the pursuit of wealth and an ideal geographical position in the centre of Southeast Asia and on air and sea links between Europe and the Middle East on the one hand and Australasia and the Far East on the other, the "first industrial revolution" was launched.

The success of the first stage of industrialisation soon had the effect of attracting further capital, banking services, a widening range of airlines and shipping services and visitors who, while finding little of real cultural interest, did find low-cost shopping and a safe environment. But at the same time costs and the cost of labour also began to climb. Government policy itself at one time was to push up wages and to increase employers costs through compulsory contributions to the Central Provident Fund in lieu of any provision for pensions. The huge sums of money accumulating in the CPF were in turn used by the government as investment capital. Later, CPF funds could be used by individual contributors for purchasing a house and for certain approved investments, for example in the recently privatised Singapore Telecoms, since otherwise the high rates of saving were having the natural effect of depressing consumption in an already small local economy (a population of 3 million in 1993). As costs began to rise it was evident that Singapore could not survive as a manufacturer of low value-added goods such as textiles, since international capital would simply relocate to cheaper locations and local capital would be rendered non-competitive. Policy then shifted (and the high wage policy was part of this) to driving out inefficient industries and moving towards financial services, automated high technology industries, tourism and the manufacture of high value-added products while maintaining some of the economy's traditional strengths such as oil refining, ship repair and port services. The result was the so-called "second industrial revolution" with the economy changing structurally. The general expansion of the economy absorbed easily those displaced from the out-going labour intensive industries, and indeed at the moment Singapore, like Japan, is a labour-short economy which relies on contract labour from Malaysia, Thailand and India for workers in construction, from Korea for workers in assembly, from the Philippines for domestic labour which releases educated Singaporean women into the workforce and to professional workers from Hong Kong, Europe and the rest of the world for high skilled functions.

In sociological terms several points can be made here. The first is that policies directed at bringing about high levels of economic growth were not from the outset divorced from social policies. In fact, the two are so closely intertwined that it is hard to tell them apart. The housing policy that was mentioned before was noted as an exemplar of this. By creating a massive public housing project several aims were accomplished at once: stimulation of the local construction and related industries, creation of demand for labour, creation of a sense of belonging in those who bought homes, integration of ethnic communities through proximity of living, working and shopping in the same residential or commercial estates, social control of a divided population through the close supervision of the estates by the administering authority, the Housing Development Board, and the creation of close links between the state and private enterprise. Other examples would be the creation of what in Singapore are known as "statutory boards" which include the above-mentioned HDB, the Urban Redevelopment Authority (URA), the Port of Singapore Authority (PSA), the Economic Development Board (EDB) and the Development Bank of Singapore (DBS). The latter is of some interest as from its initial role as a bank to manage government investments it has extended into retail banking and was the first bank to extend its retail hours beyond traditional banking hours for the convenience of workers, and to begin Saturday afternoon opening which has forced private and foreign banks to extend their hours and facilities in order to compete. Massive investment in education including government-sponsored kindergartens, two universities, three polytechnics, two art and design colleges and numerous vocational and technical schools has produced a skilled and upwardly mobile population. Similar investments in roads, hospitals and community centres creates the sense of an efficient and well-ordered society with the best infrastructure socially and physically in Southeast Asia.

Again, of course, there are costs: high levels of social control and political surveillance, a controlled press, a rather sterile local cultural scene, a very bureaucratic approach to management and a high level of political authoritarianism. Nevertheless Singapore does demonstrate what seems to me to be a very important principle: that sustained growth and a sustainable social order (one not riven by huge income inequalities for instance) is best achieved not by postponing attention to the social infrastructure and the development of human capital, but to linking it from the outset to economic reform in such a way that they form a unity. It is true in Singapore of course that many of the imperatives for this were and continue to be political: they are not done for the love of people, but to ensure their political loyalty. Even so the fact is that Singapore has grown from a minor ex-colony in 1965 to a fully developed industrial country by the mid-1990s which is in many ways the envy of its neighbours. This has been done with some changes of policy that have indeed made it possible for Singapore to anticipate and keep up with the rest of the world and to hold down the inflation and overheating that often accompany high growth policies. The country as a result has become rich, but increasingly expensive. But these fluctuations in economic policy have often been paralleled by unnecessary and confusing fluctuations in social policy (total reversal of family planning policies, closing the second university and then reopening it, creating a state medical system and then privatising it, etc.) This is primarily a result of the over politicisation of life in Singapore and of the continuing attempt of the ruling party to maintain a monopoly on power even when economic rationality very clearly suggests the need for less control, more political pluralism and the encouragement of more genuine entrepreneurship which has suffered from overly bureaucratic control. Singapore in fact represents a curious form of advanced peripheral capitalism which is in fact far from being a free market economy, but is actually closely managed by the state at all levels. Given for example some of the disastrous overseas investment forays by the government itself, this raises the significant question of how to detect the point at which strong state intervention, which may be functional in the early stages of growth begins to become counter-productive (Rodan 1993).

Thailand, currently the highest growth economy in Southeast Asia, however represents a very different set of problems and solutions. Here we have a case of a society originally very much agrarian in its economy, that has never been formally a colony and which embarked on high growth policies relatively late, having moved through an intermediate phase of labour intensive industry (textiles, toys, agricultural equipment) and tourism. High growth has included the development of petrochemicals, liquid gas, manufacturing and assembling of electronic goods and agribusiness. It has also brought with it pollution, deforestation, rampant urbanisation especially in the primate city of Bangkok, massive rural-urban migration leading to the decline in the traditional agricultural sector and major changes in labour patterns such as the movement of large numbers of young rural women into factory work, the expansion of child labour and widespread prostitution. Working conditions in factories are often bad, labour legislation is weak, the rate of unionisation low and abuses are common. Living conditions are often bad for urban workers as the infrastructure transport, schools, medical facilities, water, sanitation and electric power—quite apart from housing itself—is not designed for the sheer number of people now crowded into areas designed for far less inhabitants. Thailand is of course very much bigger than Singapore, is still largely rural, has had serious insurgency problems until quite recently and started its growth pattern with high levels of population and low levels of education.

But Thailand does have the advantages of a relatively homogeneous population ethnically and linguistically, and fairly common value systems based on Buddhism.

Essentially Thailand represents the case of a rural society undertaking industrialisation at too fast a pace with little attention to the parallel development of the social infrastructure. This is instructive for it is a wonderful case of exactly what happens in reality when market forces, so beloved of major funding agencies, are actually allowed to flourish unchecked. Labour legislation has lagged far behind the development of capital, and environmental legislation is even less developed. Growth first has brought inflation, labour practices that are unacceptable by international standards, corruption and pollution. If the state is too strong for its own good in Singapore, it is too weak in Thailand. As capitalist-based companies are not charged for the social cost of their own growth they naturally ignore the provision of the necessary infrastructure. In other words, large scale exploitation of both social and ecological varieties takes place on a large scale. The result of economic reforms without parallel social policies (or at least of adequate ones) and without a parallel development of the legal framework has been freedom for capital but often bondage for workers. And although the economy in GNP terms has been expanding rapidly, this has not been balanced by equal distribution or by a taxation structure that forces those who benefit to contribute to the social infrastructure. The result is likely to be that rates of growth will begin to fall off as foreign investors are alienated by poor physical facilities and confusing legal provisions and as local ones, especially Thai-Chinese capital is moved overseas as is already happening. Thai investors are already heavily involved in the high growth areas of southwest China and in Vietnam, which they see as being the next as yet unexploited frontier.

This may be instructive as it is likely that Vietnam will be a kind of speeded up re-run of the Thai experience: very high rates of capital infusion, rapid development of polluting labour intensive industries, emergence of systematic abuses of workers, a confused and inadequate framework for legal regulation of industries, displacement of rural dwellers and massive rural-urban migration with no coherent compensating policy for the development of sound agriculture. The presence of both the IMF and the World Bank more or less guarantees that this will happen. Vietnam is also actively entering the aid trap-accepting large sums of money that needs one day to be repaid at interest and which will ensure massive foreign presence and control. One compensating advantage that Thailand does have is the presence of active NGOs which attempt to monitor and influence the so-called development process, something that Vietnam with its Stalinist legacy does not have.

Examples can of course be multiplied. The Philippines provides yet another variation. In this case we have an ex-colony (of both the Spanish and the Americans), largely rural in character, but with the characteristic problems of concentrated urbanisation in the Manila-Quezon City conurbation, rural-urban migration and problems caused by the withdrawal of the US armed forces which was a major employer. Despite decades of aid and market-led "development", poverty levels are actually increasing and with poverty another form of environmental degradation is occurring. Here again there are many issues including the effects of a long period of authoritarian government and its associated "crony capitalism" (i.e. large scale structural corruption), the distorting effect (as in Thailand and Indonesia and increasingly in China) of the role of the military, not only in the political process, but in the economy as well, a very badly paid public bureaucracy, years of internal insurgency, regionalism, high rates of population growth and the crucial need for fundamental land reform, which no government has yet had the political will to carry out. In the Philippines we see a mixture of ineffectual internal attempts to effect reform, deep structural problems originating in the "feudal" nature of much of the society, especially the rural sector, and attempts from the outside, especially from the big funding agencies, to push the economy towards an increasingly pure market model. The result has been disastrous. But from these examples and others that can be referred to in passing, a general picture of the role of sociological factors begins to emerge and can now perhaps be clarified.

Sociological Dimensions of Economic Reform

To talk in terms of "sociological considerations in economic reforms" is to imply that economic reform is primary, and the sociological factors are either obstacles or functional to the achievement of such reforms. This view needs a little careful unpacking however. What we have implied so far is that certain patterns of social structure and culture may indeed form the context in which successful reform has in fact taken place. But we have also implied that:

1. Social goals themselves may be and need to be the goal of economic reforms and that economic changes should rarely be an end in themselves;
2. The most successful modernised economies in Asia are precisely those that from the outset have linked economic and social policy into a single package;
3. There is no single recipe, but different combinations of sociological factors and institutions may all equally well provide realistic bases for alternative patterns of economic reform; and
4. To separate economic from social considerations (and from related environmental ones) is to court disaster.

It also needs to be pointed out that it is not only that sociological factors provide the "obstacles" or "advantages" that make economic reforms possible or make them"stick" when implemented on the ground, but that it is also economic development that makes it possible for many aspects of the social infrastructure to develop too. Without poverty alleviation programmes, for example, attempts to raise educational standards, promote many types of rural reform and to expand the political community will fail. There is in other words in any given instance, a complex dialectic between economy and society: changes in the composition of capital very deeply effect patterns of work, employment and the spatial organisation of society (Harvey 1989).

To develop these issues several kinds of questions need to be posed. There are obviously many different varieties of economic reform which tend to appear in different political environments, for example, heavily managed capitalism as in Singapore, bureaucratically administered capitalism as in Japan, an attempt to mix markets and socialism as in China or an attempt to retain the socialist framework while allowing limited access to capitalism as in Laos. The assumption sometimes made that "economic reform" = monetarist, free market and deregulated policies is not sustainable on either empirical or theoretical grounds. It is entirely justifiable for instance to ask *who* exactly benefits from a certain pattern of economic reform and whether such reforms promote higher levels of equable income *distribution* as well as raising the per capita GNP. Certain forms of "structural adjustment" policies for instance, which while removing subsidies in the interests of "efficiency" cause heavy burdens to fall on lower income groups; fiscal policies such as taxation reform can if not very carefully planned and implemented increase the tax burden of those on fixed but low salaries, while entrepreneurs of much higher income avoid appropriate taxation (Gans 1973).

Furthermore, the obstacles to the effective implementation of economic reforms, even assuming that those reforms themselves are appropriate and well thought out, are often a mixture of sociological and political factors. Amongst these would be the role of the state and the effectiveness of its bureaucratic apparatus, the common problem of good policies but lack of trained personnel, administrators and entrepreneurs to actually carry them out, distortions introduced by corruption and inefficiencies stemming from over regulation such as excessively complex licencing procedures, suppression of organised labour or indiscipline and greed on the part of organised labour, and the kinds of ideological barriers that can be constructed by governments. Yet other problems may arise from the intersection of economic and political factors such as compulsory over-high rates of saving or the effects of privatisation which may reduce the size of the state but only to increase costs to consumers or where, as in Singapore, basic social facilities such as hospitals and telecommunications have been privatised and minor devolution of responsibilities to "town councils" in public housing estates has occurred, while in fact the government continues to regulate these sectors.

A third group of issues arises from the behaviour of the economic elites themselves in any given country. The very appearance of such elites and the unequal spatial distribution of wealth (e.g. between provinces) in China has produced quite radical social changes. In a market economy it is natural that the behaviour of such elites will tend towards maximising their own benefits. Thus we see overseas Chinese capital in Southeast Asia flowing into China initially and now Vietnam and not being used to generate economic growth at home in the local environment. Such elites are important social actors and are frequently (e.g. in Indonesia) the mediators between government generated economic policy and the rest of the society. Any study of the interplay between economy and society needs to pay attention both to classical sociological issues such as the nature and role of the bureaucracy, and also to the broader social structure understood not only as family and religion, but in terms of new class formation, the social organisation of elites, the sociological nature of entrepreneurship, patterns of communication and influence between elites and government and elites and masses (including political institutions), the social organisation of work practices and patterns of social inequality and social mobility.

We can thus begin to classify sociological factors in economic reforms into categories, all of which however interact with each other in practice:

1. Values, or what is commonly referred to in the management literature as "culture". These include values in the sense of, say, desire for social equity (socio-political) and also ones that, for example, promote a desire for Islamic banking (socio-religious) as well as culture in its more everyday sense of life patterns, diet, dress, language and so forth. Clearly these values are of central significance in economic reforms and have major practical consequences, as in the just mentioned example of Islamic banking.
2. Structures which refers both to institutions and to the ways that these are organised into social hierarchies. If the family is an example of an institution, caste is an example of the ordering of families into macroscopic patterns. In the analysis of economic change, the study of institutions is frequently not given sufficient prominence. But the building of institutions and the effective utilisation of existing ones, including such elements as leadership has proved to be vital at both macro (building of administrative, legal, fiscal and educational institutions) and micro (the provision of small scale credit to local industries or to networks of women engaged in marketing) levels as well as in the creation of social forces which mediate all of these such as literacy (Clammer 1976).
3. Processes such as the impact of schooling or the transformation of work. Work indeed is one of the most significant of these, since the effect of economic reform is often seen first and most visibly at this point. Economic changes create shifts in the spatial, temporal and physical conditions of labour, in the psychology of work and

in the values, practices and rituals that accompany it. Migration within and between societies, which has itself become a major socio-economic phenomenon in the contemporary world, is both symptomatic of these shifts and in turn creates new patterns of labour and lifestyles.

Amongst the points that need to be made as we move towards a conclusion are the following:

1. *Economic policy has rather different meanings in different socio-political contexts.* In very underdeveloped countries it is most likely to mean primary poverty alleviation measures, and the sociological issues involved are likely to be the confrontation of reform and tradition, the attempt to modernise the social structure so as to improve the delivery of development measures, to maximise the efficiency of policy implementation and to minimise the severe social disruptions that can occur when rapid forms of change begin to take place. In socialist countries (e.g. Laos) or in those that still have a strong and distinctive non-secular value system as their ideological basis (for example, Brunei, with its cultural foundations in Islam), reforms will be more likely directed at raising of living standards while preserving both the value or ideological system and the distinctive features of the social structure, such as commune organisation or the family. In the NICs, policy is more likely to be directed towards a mixture of industrialisation, infrastructure development (such as roads and energy), and modernisation of the agricultural sector (as in Malaysia or Thailand). In countries which have achieved developed country status (Japan, Singapore, Hong Kong, probably now Taiwan and very soon South Korea) emphasis is likely to be on a move towards services, managing the social problems created by rapid growth and coming to terms with the social conditions that emerge with a mature economy, such as the political and leisure demands of a growing middle class.
2. *The location of any given society within the global economy.* Whether national governments like it or not, they are being very rapidly

drawn into a post-nationalist age. Media, the international flow of information and the interdependencies of the world economy have created a situation in which no economic policy makes sense unless it is contextualised in global terms. The impact of aid, the nature of world trading patterns, the role of international agencies such as GATT, patterns of protectionism and the emergence of new blocs like NAFTA and EC, are all now part of the environment for any economic planner. Attention, in other words, needs to be paid to the organisation of international society and the way in which this articulates with the local society, in the conceptualisation and implementation of economic reform.

3. *Economic reforms have consequences which are often socially undesirable: inflation, overheating, rural unrest, growing income inequalities.* At the very best they bring with them ambiguities: for instance inviting in foreign MNCs while it introduces some investment and employment generation, also tends to introduce a now very well documented set of problems. The emergence of religious fundamentalism and ethnic unrest can also in part be traced to the problems arising from too rapid economic and social change. The point here is not to recommend the abandoning of economic reform (which would cause equally severe problems), but to indicate that sufficient experience, comparative case studies and economic and sociological expertise now exists to anticipate such problems and so far as is rationally possible, to incorporate their effects in planning.
4. *To recognise that economic reforms are not just a question of planning (i.e. bureaucratically imposed models from above), but very much a question of the involvement of those who will be effected, of intermediate social agencies such as NGOs, and of the mobilisation of existing social resources.* Examples of this might include local-level decision-makers, the utilisation of social networks to provide feedback and monitoring mechanisms for assessing policy on the ground, the promotion of self-reliance (Dube 1984: 33-35) and democratic decision-making procedures, and the identification of real human needs not in theoretical terms, but as defined by members of a society themselves.

5. *Some major theoretical questions are inevitably raised here too including the central issue of whether we are collectively entering a "postmodern" world in which the older "Fordist" methods of industrial production (production line, labour intensive) are being rapidly replaced by robotics, just-in-time flexible inventories and new patterns of capitalist accumulation and modes of operation.* In so far as we are, these fundamental changes in technology, economic structures, management and employment are bound to affect everybody. A new form of the "late development effect" begins to appear: not that developing countries can leapfrog into development through by-passing intermediate stages (through technology transfer, for example), but that any newly industrialising country suddenly finds itself inheriting all of the problems of a world economy actually making the transition at this historical moment to *postindustrialism.* Alternative views however suggest that, while it is true that the developed or over developed societies (or rather economies—all societies are "developed" even if not modernised) are now passing into their postmodern-postindustrial stage, what is happening on a global scale is the deepening of the international division of labour. This is achieved by the rich countries moving into the services and financial/information-based stage, while exporting the less desirable, polluting and labour-intensive productive operations to developing countries. The First World thus becomes post-Fordist while the developing world only gets to become Fordist. Behind this specific debate is a major question. The analysis of complex change is itself an underdeveloped field, but the *management of change* is itself effectively impossible unless methods for the understanding and description of change can be evolved, and to a great extent it is of course the contribution and responsibility of sociology precisely to undertake this analysis of social change.
6. *We have already suggested that institutions play a central role and that one of the major sociological aspects of economic reform is the effective utilisation of existing institutions or the creation of new ones.* This point relates back to the question of values. In some cases values need to be preserved, in others they need to be created or en-

> hanced (for example, positive attitudes to nature, or towards the value of agriculture). In any case such values are not free floating: they need to be encapsulated in institutions. The creation of workable institutions then becomes a central aspect of the sociological dimension of development.

Since the mid-1980s, for the first time in postwar history, people in the developed economies of the west and in Japan when polled about their attitudes to the immediate future, anticipate a worse one based on grave doubts about the viability of their existing form of industrial civilisation. This is very significant and indicates not only a need to understand this pessimism, but also the urgent need for alternative scenarios of the future. This is not said to encourage utopianism (although the construction of imaginary futures can be a healthy and helpful exercise), but to encourage informed debate on sustainable and livable possibilities and the means of reaching them and as an antidote to the paralysing effects of pessimism. Development is very much about, in the best as well as the worst senses of that word, political. And politics is the science of the desirable society.

A single empirical instance with which to conclude illustrates most of these points very well. This is the issue of land reform. In many of the rural societies of Southeast Asia, the problem of poverty in the countryside is intimately linked to the nature of land ownership, and of the relations of power which stem from command of this primary resource. Many of the rural poor do not own land, or if they do it is marginal. As a result they are forced either into the cities (Thailand, Indonesia), onto agribusiness style plantations (Malaysia) or to work on the virtually feudally run estates of large, and often absentee, land owners (Philippines). Those who do own land have problems with marketing produce and with raising yields. They too often join the exodus to the cities leaving their land unworked. In some cases (Thailand, for example) this land is then bought up very cheaply by speculators or even by middle-class city dwellers who would like a place in the country. Agriculture becomes not only less a paying proposition for the small farmer, but becomes socially less and less attractive. Big commercial farmers who do still farm raise yields, with government approval, by the use of chemical fertilisers and pesticides. The result is a crisis in the countryside: pollution, displacement of labour, dependency on the part of estate workers, declining fertility, switching of crop choice from subsistence food crops to export ones for First World markets and often major social inequalities, rural violence, insurgency and a downward spiral that makes farming even less attractive.

In many cases the fundamental answer is land reform—the breaking up of big estates, redistribution of land to owner-occupiers, improvement in marketing, access and social infrastructure, promotion at a national level of awareness of the value of agriculture and security arrangements. In the example of land reform the intersection of economics, politics, culture, ecology and sociological factors can be clearly seen. Any policy which set about to address the question of land reform would necessarily need to take account of all these factors and of their complex interaction. Which illustrates very well that one of the biggest challenges for development specialists of whatever ideological colour is the bringing together of the economic and the sociological both at the theoretical level and at the level of practical application. The resources exist intellectually to do this, not least through the recovery of the wholism of the old sense of the term "political economy " (Clammer 1985).

References

Clammer, J. (1976), *Literacy and Social Change*, Leiden: E.J. Brill.

Clammer, J. (1985), *Anthropology and Political Economy: Theoretical and Asian Perspectives*, London: Macmillan.

Clammer, J. (1993), "Nihon to Tonan Azia, " *Sophia*, Winter.

Dore, R. (1965), *Education in Tokugawa Japan*, Berkeley: University of California Press.

Dube, S.C. (1984), *Development Perspectives for the 1980s*, Petaling Jaya: Pelanduk Publications for the UN Asian and Pacific Development Centre.

Gans, H. (1973), *More Equality*, New York: Vintage Books.

Harvey, D. (1989), *The Condition of Postmodernity*, Oxford: Basil Blackwell.

Ishida, H. (1992), *Social Mobility in Contemporary Japan*, Stanford: Stanford University Press.

Jansen, M.B. (ed.) (1985), *Changing Japanese Attitudes Toward Modernization*, Tokyo: Charles E. Tuttle.

Johnson, C. (1982), *MITI and the Japanese Miracle: The Growth of Industrial Policy, 1925-1975*, Tokyo: Charles E.Tuttle.

McCormack, G. and Y. Sugimoto (eds.) (1988), *Modernization and Beyond: The Japanese Trajectory*, Cambridge: Cambridge University Press.

Rodan, G. (ed.) (1993), *Singapore Changes Guard: Social, Political and Direction in the 1990s*, Melbourne: Longman Cheshire and New York: St. Martin's Press.

Smith, T.C. (1989), *Native Sources of Japanese Industrialization 1750-1920*, Berkeley: University of California Press.

White, M. (1990), *The Japanese Educational Challenge*, Tokyo: Kodansha.

Chapter 6

THE SOCIAL CONTEXT OF ECONOMIC BEHAVIOUR: ECONOMIC ANTHROPOLOGY AND DEVELOPMENT ISSUES

Economic anthropology is the study of the material dimension of life in its social and cultural context. It studies the way in which the production, distribution and consumption of things enters into the whole fabric of social life, and comprises a vital part of the seamless totality that constitutes a living society. For anthropologists economic concepts are also social ones that reveal in a profound way the basic values, worldview and moral orientations of a society. The fundamental economic ideas of credit, saving, capital, exchange or entrepreneurship, although capable of abstract, general definitions applicable across a range of human societies are at bottom socio-cultural notions. This is true even in modern capitalist societies, or in the context of neo-classical economics which has given many of these concepts their standard textbook definitions. Exchange, for example, at least since the classic work of Mauss (1954), is widely known to be deeply embedded in social relationships, and is often an expression of them. The practise of gift-giving beautifully illustrates these social dimensions, but culture enters into almost any exchange, even the seemingly most "economic".

In a world in which everything seems to have its price, anthropologists draw attention to systems where not everything can be swapped, bartered or exchanged for anything else: some things may not be exchangeable at all (e.g. an heirloom or a piece of ancestral land) or can only be exchanged for certain other things, bark-cloth for a canoe or cattle for a bride for instance, but never batik-cloth (however much and however valuable) for a bride—a notion known as *spheres of exchange* (Barth 1970). Even in a fully monetised economy social relationships and cultural factors enter into exchange. This is evident in Japan where gift giving remains a very important custom and is, in fact, a complex social institution (Befu 1974).

Economic anthropology is thus about the role of things in animating and structuring social and ecological relationships. There is no richer field for exploring this interaction of the material and socio-cultural than Asia: peasants and fishermen, swidden-agriculturalists and forest gatherers, pastoralists and factory workers, traders and plantation labourers interact with one another in all sorts of complex ways and all are caught up in varying degrees with the process of "development", including urbanisation and the spread of a money economy.

Despite this vast geographical and sociological range some preliminary attempt at classification of social types is necessary (for purposes of comparison if for no other reason) provided that we recognise that such general classifications are heuristic—they serve a theoretical purpose, but are not absolute. So perhaps initially a four-fold classification is helpful.

First, we can classify economic systems on a *social* basis: for example, peasants, entrepreneurs, family-owned and run business, or where a particular social group, usually ethnic and/or religious, dominates a particular economic activity.

A second principle of classification is *ecological*: fishermen, hunter-gatherers, rice farmers, for instance.

A third is the Marxist-derived concept of *modes of production*: economic formations defined by the relationship of their participants to the process of production—peasants and landlords, rural plantation or agribusiness labourers and the owners of the establishments or urban factory workers and capitalist proprietors.

The fourth is what we might call *cultural-thematic*, i.e. a classification of socio-economic types based primarily on the presence of certain conspicuous activities of an economic or quasi-economic nature, which might include extensive gift-giving, competitive feasting or conspicuous consumption, which empirically might include Japan, many Indonesian societies and the "big man" phenomenon, usually identified with New Guinea, but actually very extensive throughout Asia. In the light of these categories, what are the main socio-economic types that we need to deal with, and what is their relationship to the theoretical questions that economic anthropology has raised about the interpretation of economic practices in their socio-cultural settings?

Systems of Economic Organisation

Despite variations in detail from place to place, we can make a working list of cases which includes the following:

1. *"Forest eaters"*, to use the phrase of French anthropologist Condominas (1957), or what are more conventionally known as hunter-gatherers. These societies do not plant on a systematic basis and do not breed domestic animals, but live by collecting forest produce, fish and game. They are usually nomadic, building simple shelters from the materials to hand and characteristically are found in the deep jungles of Southeast Asia. Well-documented examples include the Semai of West Malaysia (Dentan 1986), the Penan of East Malaysia and the Muong Gar of Vietnam (Condominas 1957). Gathers are small scale societies entirely, or almost entirely self-sufficient and with a close and often benevolent relationship to their ecological setting. The small size of the social group is itself necessitated by ecological conditions. It is impossible to support large populations with a gathering economy dependent on the relatively sparse and not always easily obtainable resources of the tropical forest.

   Today such groups are coming under increasing pressure to abandon their lifestyle as a result of government policies (governments generally dislike peoples of no fixed abode who cannot be counted, controlled or taxed), logging of the tropical hardwood forests of Southeast Asia and "development", such as the proposed flooding of huge areas of the virgin forest home of the Penan and Dayak peoples in Sarawak for a hydroelectric scheme (Clammer 1987). Although the technology of "forest eaters" is simple, their non-material culture can be correspondingly rich. It is expressed through kinship, religion (Endicott 1979) and "inner" means, such as the "dream culture" of the Temiar and other Malaysian *Orang Asli* groups who have attracted the attention of psychologists, anthropologists and novelists. Even apparently simple economies contain their own social complexities, illustrating very well our earlier assertion about the linking of society and economy, and a very good example of this is the body of rules determining the sharing of game amongst the group. An animal is never eaten individually or secretly, but becomes a resource for the whole community.

2. *Swidden* or *shifting agriculturalists*, are also nomadic or semi-nomadic, but in addition to gathering and hunting they cultivate crops (usually dry or hill rice, vegetables and in some cases opium) and often keep domestic animals (typically pigs and chickens), and inhabit substantial villages or longhouses. Examples of this group are the "hill-tribes" of northern Southeast Asia and Southwestern China such as the Hmong (Geddes 1976; Cooper 1984), the Akha and the Karen, and the Iban of East Malaysia (Freeman 1980). Many of these groups supplement their subsistence activities by trading with lowland peasants, with each other, or with Chinese merchants, with whom they exchange opium for cloth, medicine, guns and luxury goods (watches and radios are not uncommon) in the case of the Thai hill-tribes, or in the case of the Malaysian groups forest products (rattan, game, animal skins). In both instances and to a lesser extent in Southwestern China, those groups on the periphery of the mountains or jungle, or who are accessible by road or river have begun to exploit, or be exploited by, tourism, producing handicrafts for sale to visitors or for "export" to the regional market towns and even abroad. Thus swidden farmers are rarely isolated from outside influence and technology (firearms, axes), fashion, disease and religion have all been introduced in varying degrees from the surrounding world. Shifting agriculturalists typically have complex social structures of lineages and clans, ancestor cults, elaborate ritual systems, pottery working abilities and domestic architecture. Ecologically the swidden agriculturalists are concentrated in the mountainous areas of northern Southeast Asia, and the relatively untouched jungle zones elsewhere, since large tracts of land are needed to support this mobile lifestyle.

The mode of life of these groups has sparked off an intense ecological debate. One school of thought argues that shifting agriculturalists are ecologically responsible. They say that farmers allow adequate time for regeneration of the land used, usually by cutting the large trees and burning off the undergrowth and planting among the stumps and, given their small numbers, do not overexploit animal and plant resources. The other school argues that, on the contrary, shifting agriculture is ecologically disastrous. It destroys primary forest, uses agricultural methods which are inefficient and exhaust the land which is then abandoned to erosion and secondary growth when these people move on and repeat the process in the next place of settlement. Whichever view we take, it is certainly the case that land is not unlimited, and different groups find themselves in competition with one another or with lowland peasants who move up into the hills as they too face land scarcity and overpopulation in the valleys, a process happening in Thailand, China, India, Nepal and Bhutan. The differences in ethnicity and culture between the upland and lowland peoples exacerbates the problems of economic-ecological competition. In an attempt to solve this kind of problem many governments have attempted, usually with limited success, to get shifting agriculturalists to settle down and grow alternative crops such as irrigated rice, fruit and cash crops (Cooper 1984; Tapp 1989 for northern Thai examples).

3. *Peasants*, empirically a large and heterogeneous group, raise some important and difficult theoretical and definitional problems. The common-sense definition of a peasant as a small independent farmer producing mainly for subsistence, but with some surplus for market is all right so far as it goes. But initially, given our common-sense definition, it is possible to see represented in Asia several major types of peasants, beginning with relatively self-sufficient ones who market only a small proportion of their produce and need little in the way of inputs from the outside, either in terms of consumer goods or of agricultural technology, including items like chemical fertilisers. Examples of self-sufficiency still exist, in India, Laos, Burma and many remote parts of Indonesia. Then, as the level of technology rises, accompanied by the necessary inputs of fuel, parts, tools and so on, efficiency and productivity tend to rise, but self-sufficiency decreases. Technological dependency not only creates more direct needs, but also indirect

ones—consumer goods and desire for information, for example—and increased productivity generates a need for markets, which require transportation to reach and which, unless they are purely barter arrangements, promotes monetisation. Examples of this type abound, ranging from the relatively mechanised peasants of the northern rice-bowl area of Malaysia to highly mechanised Japanese rice farmers with their access to large urban markets and a sophisticated "information society". Yet a third, and statistically very significant category, is that of peasants in socialist regimes—throughout Indochina for instance, and most conspicuously in China. The relationship between peasants and their political context is an important one that must be dealt with further.

4. *Fishermen* have long attracted anthropological attention because of their widespread geographical distribution. Much of Southeast Asia is a maritime region, along with Japan, and is oriented towards the sea. And China and India both have long coastlines. The socio-economic organisation of fishermen, like peasants, varies with their ecological location, technology and their relationship to the wider economy. Some fishing, especially inshore fishing, is supplementary to on-shore agriculture, while for others it constitutes an autonomous economy with an associated culture and social structure of its own. Levels of mechanisation range from almost none at all to the sophisticated technology used by Thai, Korean, Taiwanese and Japanese fishermen. Some fishing peoples, like the Bugis of Indonesia, combine fishing with maritime trade or boat-building. Others are essentially shore dwellers who launch their boats from coastal beaches, as with most Malay fishermen (Firth 1946). Some live on or over the sea in villages of stilt houses, as with the formerly nomadic Bajau Laut of Sabah (Sather 1985) while others are still boat dwellers who maintain a mobile lifestyle (Sopher 1977). Not all fishermen use the sea as their primary resource—river and lake fishing also takes place in inland areas, for example on the huge Tonle Sap Lake in Cambodia, and fish farming is on the increase not only in natural waters, but in artificial ponds. Not far from Bangkok large areas of

swampy land have been converted into prawn farms, producing a product of high value both for local and overseas markets.

5. *Hydraulic societies.* The term "hydraulic societies" was coined by the German scholar Karl Wittfogel in a controversial book *Oriental Despotism* (1973) where he argued that typical Asiatic States, and China in particular, were based on the construction and management of large scale irrigation systems that necessitated strong central control. Although much of Wittfogel's thesis is hotly contested, he did draw attention to the profound significance of irrigation in the economic and social organisation of many Asian societies. Therefore I would like to rehabilitate his term to refer to those settings where the creation and management of complex water systems is a crucial element of local culture and ecology. Many societies in Asia have historically developed elaborate irrigation systems—China, India, Sri Lanka, Thailand and Java being examples of societies where water management for agricultural purposes, fishing and inland transportation is, or was, widely developed. An outstanding contemporary example of this however is Bali, where over centuries a complex water management system evolved, linking networks of farmers who shared the same watershed and tying them into ritual relationships centered on "water temples" that both managed the water flow and provided a symbolic framework that unite "economics" and "religion" into a single holistic entity (Lansing 1991). In rice economies the flow of water continues to be a vital ecological, economic and social factor.
6. *Pastoralists* are people whose livelihood is based on the management of domesticated herds or flocks of animals. Traditional pastoralists are usually nomadic, and given the grazing demands of their animals require large open spaces. Examples of such land are surprisingly difficult to find in Asia, where much of it is either under forested, subject to intensive crop cultivation, or is mountainous. So while the keeping of domestic animals as an adjunct to peasant farming is common, and while controlled commercial pastoralism does occur (in the form of dairy) in a few places, large scale traditional pastoralism is almost uniquely confined to Mon-

golia and other lowland parts of central Asia. Only here is space abundant, population densities low and the grazing suitable for horses, sheep and goats available. There is an important cultural dimension to be considered as well. Many central Asian peoples, from Chinese Turkestan right across to Persia, are Muslims and so do not raise pigs, the traditional Chinese domestic animal, but are mutton eaters. The Mongolians, however, are Buddhists.

Pastoralism is not just an economy, but really is "a way of life", often emphasising mobility, independence, a martial spirit and contempt for settled peasants and townsmen. Pastoralists have an almost mystic identification with the animals they herd, who are the source of almost all nutrients and physical possessions (skin tents, for example), except those obtained through barter or trade. Restricted under Mongolian socialism (Jaghid and Hyer 1979) and even more so in Tibet and China, large scale nomadic pastoralism is probably a thing of the past, that will be replaced by commercial farming.

7. *Plantations.* An extremely important part of the economy of Asia since the introduction of colonialism has been plantation agriculture. This is a feature that Asia shares with much of the rest of the former colonised world—the West Indies for example. The particular forms that plantation agriculture took were rooted in the different colonial experiences of the region, and expressed themselves subsequently in different sociological ways that often had profound long-term effects on the whole social structure of the national economy. Thus in the Philippines under Spanish colonialism large scale semi-feudal estates were created. Today much of the rural social structure of the Philippines still revolves around these estates, which are now in the hands of big Filipino landowners and run as "agribusiness". In Indonesia the Dutch created the "Culture System". In Indochina the French established rubber plantations to feed the needs of their own empire. And the British Raj created a massive plantation sector in India and Sri Lanka (tea) and in Malaya (rubber). Under this British umbrella, local (usually Chinese), entrepreneurs established their own plantations for sugar, rubber and later oil palm.

The Malayan case is especially interesting for what it reveals about the relationships of economy, society and politics. First of all, extensive plantation agriculture had a profound ecological impact. Huge tracts of forest land were cleared, to be replaced by uniform rows of rubber trees. While much of this land was unsettled or underutilised jungle, in many cases the natural economy was destroyed and the local Malays moved. The processes also had major sociological effects. The Malays for the most part did not want to work in these aptly named "rural factories", keeping strict hours, filling quotas, and under the watchful supervision of European planters. To solve the labour problem, therefore large numbers of south Indian Tamils were brought in, and while some returned to India at the end of their contracts, many remained. The long-term result was the introduction of a whole new ethnic group into Malayan society which, when coupled with the parallel introduction of huge numbers of southern Chinese, completely and irrevocably altered the social landscape of Malaya and created all of the problems and issues of ethnic pluralism that plague that country.

Many Chinese also worked on plantations, but most soon moved out into independent vegetable farming (a Chinese speciality throughout Southeast Asia and southern China), tin-mining, trade and urban occupations. Most Tamils, however, remain to this day in virtually mono-ethnic rural ghettoes with substandard schools and social facilities, far from the towns, badly paid and with little opportunity for social mobility.

The plantation sector also had long-term economic consequences. Mono-crop primary commodities destined for export are especially vulnerable to fluctuations in world demand, low prices and the challenge of alternative products (e.g. artificial rubber). Many plantations have, of necessity, up-dated themselves into modern agribusinesses, but they all still have one major side-effect. They create or require a labour force of landless workers (either ex-peasants or descendants of the original contract workers) and so create a rural proletariat, which is often badly paid and paternalistically managed, a fact exploited by insurgent movements such as the Communist Party of the Philippines.

8. *Petty commodity production.* Any rural economy requires more than landlords and labourers: it also requires artisans who can produce the technology and goods required by the local economy. In a rural setting small producers are to be found running, or employed in, small-scale workshops, factories or cottage industries, engaged perhaps in weaving, pottery or metal working as their primary activity, although they may well supplement this with gardening, farming or fishing to help make ends meet. A good example of this category are blacksmiths, shoeing horses, fishing cart-wheels and producing tools and agricultural implements. A well-documented example of this kind of economic activity explored the nature and place of petty commodity production amongst the Minangkabau people of Sumatra. It shows not only how the economy of these producers is structured, and how they relate to the agricultural society of which they are a part, but how they are under threat from the bigger capitalist commodity producers in the cities who have economies of scale and threaten the small producers by flooding markets with mass produced and often cheaper products (Kahn 1980).
9. *Traders.* While most people in rural economies engage in occasional trade, some are full-time traders. Trade may take the modern and familiar form of shops and stores with their associated paraphernalia of banks, taxation and bureaucratic licensing and regulation. But there are some equally important forms that fall outside this framework and are widespread in Asia. Two of the most significant are barter and hawking. Barter involves the direct exchange of one commodity for another without the use of money. From time immemorial this has been a normal way of conducting exchange all over the world and it continues all over Asia, such as in the informal barter between Thai hill peoples and lowlanders. Sometimes it is very organised. In the waters south of Singapore it is a daily sight to see inbound Indonesian sailing *prahus* laden with forest products on their way to the official barter dock in Singapore's Pasir Panjang district. They leave again loaded with cassette recorders, textiles and any number of manufactured commodities. Hawking is a more familiar form of petty trade, as

it is very visible in almost every Asian town. Street vendors selling fruit, clothing, trinkets, in marketplaces crowded with tiny stalls or with their produce simply set out on the ground. Little booths or carts are strung out along sidewalks or clustered around bus or train stations selling every variety of local cooked foods and drinks. Sometimes these activities are the sole livelihood of the individuals or families that run these stalls; sometimes they are a supplement to other economic activities, including wage labour. Sometimes they are highly organised and regulated, as in the custom-built "hawker centres" of Singapore; or they are part of the "informal sector", the "underground" and unregulated part of the economy which flourishes in almost every major Asian city.

An interesting feature of trading communities is that they are often ethnically homogeneous. Much of the spice trade in Southeast Asia is in Indian Muslim hands, the coffee shops are monopolised by Mainland Chinese, while the diamond trade throughout Asia is largely Jewish-controlled, and so on. Indeed some ethnic groups—the Chinese in Malaysia or Indonesia, the Arabs throughout the region, the Parsis in India, are automatically associated with trade, even though in practice many of their members may be in other professions or activities. Archaeologists are aware that for centuries there has been trade both within the sub-regions of Asia and across the region as a whole. These linkages are attested to not only by material artefacts—Ming jars in upriver Borneo communities for example—but by continuing networks of trade which are often organised on very traditional lines, such as the now declining plywood timber trade between Indonesia and Singapore, or the enormous networks created by prominent overseas Chinese such as Oei Tiong Ham, with relatives and representative offices in practically every important trading centre in East and Southeast Asia.

10. *Services, Artisanal and Industrial.* With the "modernisation" of Asia, or at least with the industrialisation that has engulfed so much of the world, large numbers of people have been drawn out of traditional rural activities into urban life and factory labour. These are of course not synonymous: urban centres create em-

ployment of a whole range of types, including of course hawking, but especially services, artisanal and industrial employment. Any large city requires a host of services to make it work—transportation, sanitation, banking, bureaucracy, vending of everything needed for the urban lifestyle of that particular place. It also requires people who make and fix things. And if it is at all industrial it requires a proletariat to man its factories. With the increasing urbanisation of modern Asia (see Chapter 8) employment in industry is becoming normal. It has however a range of sociological effects, including disruption of traditional crafts, displacement of rural labour, slums and squatting. We also see a wide incidence of child labour (Weiner 1991) and the extensive employment of women in industries involving repetitive and often low-paid work such as electronic appliance assembling (see Chapter 8) and prostitution. Also, country-specific ones which differ with cultural responses to industrialisation (UNCRD 1991), for example.

Of course we must recognise that in practice many of these types are mixed. Tribal people in India or Thailand often have complex economic and socio-cultural interactions with other groups in society. Pastoralists engage in trade, craftsmen keep a market garden. Indeed traditional craftsmen such as Balinese painters, northern Thai jewellery makers, or Japanese flower arrangement teachers are good examples of a socio-economic group still active in Asia, but who are hard to categorise neatly. This is also true for logging which partakes of some of the features of plantation agriculture, some of swiddening, and some of modern agribusiness. Many small Japanese and Taiwanese farmers spend more time in off-farm economic activities than they spend on them. This overlapping of economic action begins to make more sense when we put it in a yet wider context.

Economy and Society in Asian Context

There are four major elements that we have used to contextualise the empirical economies we have identified: ecological, political, developmental and theoretical.

We have already stressed that every economic system is also an *ecological* one. Each derives from a particular ecological base (forest, sea, climate, mountain, etc.) and in turn modifies that base, often profoundly. The spectacular rice terraces of Luzon that are the product of generations of labour by an upland people are an example of a natural environment being enhanced by this interaction rather than destroyed, with unproductive mountain sides being transformed into a granary. Another is the landscape of Java which today looks like a continuous garden, densely populated and with red-tiled roofed hamlets scattered everywhere amongst the plots, each of which is utilised to its maximum extent. It is hard to imagine that within living memory much of Java was forest and that the primal landscape has been transformed by burgeoning population and intensive land use. Ecology and social structures are likewise closely tied together: forest gathering, while doing little to disturb the environment, does not permit high population densities which in turn tends to keep the size of domestic and social units small and simple in structure. Settled peasant agriculture, however, especially on productive land, creates the conditions for elaborated kinship groups of the kind associated with the southern provinces of China, with their extensive lineages. The links between ecology, economy, social structure and culture are many, varied and complex, and beyond our scope to detail here. But it is important at the very least to stress that economic activity is always contextualised in an ecological setting, and is ultimately dependent on that setting for its viability.

The *political* dimension of the economy is so important and varied that some anthropologists have suggested reviving the concept of "political economy" to help understand the relationships between the economic and the political (Clammer 1985). Economic decisions are often also political ones and vice versa. Individuals or groups often ask themselves: with whom should I enter into an economic alliance? whose daughter will bring the biggest dowry? should I enhance my political status by sponsoring a feast? and so on. Social power in other words is multi-dimensional and it is often necessary to conduct politics by way of economics. But in a more formal sense the political context modifies the possibilities of economic activity. The slowing down, if not the total cessation of shifting cultivation amongst the northern Thai hill peoples, is not because they have suddenly lost their wanderlust, but because the Thai government, for reasons to do with ecology, security, the opium business and the dangers of ethnic conflict with other hill groups or lowland Thais, is trying to stop their perpetual motion both by direct policy means and by the indirect means of linking them ever more closely with the lowland economy, something that is happening progressively to, for example, the Lahu peoples (Hoare 1985). This government intervention is even more apparent in the socialist countries of China and Indochina (Evans 1990) where the role of the state in influencing economic and social possibilities is very pronounced.

The *development* dimension is closely linked to the political, and is often an expression of it. Development activities—road building, well-digging, agricultural extension work and so forth, whether directly intended to promote social well-being, or for other motives (security)—can profoundly affect the natural economy by introducing factors such as access to the outside world, its markets and its tastes, by changing the ecology, by bringing in outsiders (tourists, loggers, missionaries), and by creating new economic opportunities which the more entrepreneurial will be eager to seize. Development, for all its rhetoric, has until recently paid little attention to culture, and as a result has more often than not undermined local value systems, promoted industrialisation and monetisation at the expense of the natural economy, created subsequent distortions in kinship and social relationships, damaged the ecology and has even created the impoverishment it was supposed to eradicate (see Chapter 5). Fortunately, there has been a recent movement back towards assessing the role of culture in development, and this in turn affects the way indigenous economic systems are understood and perhaps incorporated into a more sensitive and balanced understanding of what development means (e.g. Dove 1988).

The *theoretical* dimension. Theory does not (or should not) mean abstraction and systems building; rather it means how to think accurately about the data in the real world that confronts us—in this case real people trying to make a living in various ways, and investing what they are doing with symbolic significance, and tying their relationships with material things into a meaningful bond with their social networks and values. In general terms then, anthropological theories are about how to think about our subject matter, and since economic anthropologists have taken rather different points of view on the interpretation of their subject matter, we need to address this problem as it bears directly on the issue of understanding the economic systems of contemporary, or even historical, Asian societies. This raises a further interesting question: most anthropological theories are the product of the West not of Asia, of the colonisers rather than the colonised, of intellectuals rather than the practitioners of the economic arts that the anthropologists describe. So how relevant is all of this to the illumination of our empirical subject matter?

Modern economic anthropology has up till now been dominated by two main theoretical controversies, between the "formalists", who argue that the basic theoretical apparatus of neo-classical economics is applicable to all human societies, and the "substantivists" who argue that, on the contrary, every society operates according to different systems of economic rationality which arise from each one's specific cultural logic. Alongside this debate is that between Marxist and non-Marxist anthropologists. A more recent development has been the analysis of economic systems through the use of concepts drawn from developments in contemporary cultural theory, including ideas about the consumer society and commoditisation, in which the objects of exchange are analysed as being part of a semiotic system, i.e. systems of signs, rather than just material "things". And some have focused on the emergence of a "global system" which allegedly is progressively incorporating more and more of the world's cultures (e.g. Featherstone 1991).

Most economic anthropologists would agree that economic activity is about social relationships—about the creation, preservation and enhancing of them, and they are also, when necessary, about their termination. Material things, whatever their practical utility, mediate these relationships, even with the supernatural (sacrifice, for instance, nearly always involves a physical or material medium). The distinction, beloved of an earlier generation of anthropologists, between "modern" and "primitive" societies is totally irrelevant here: they all share this fundamental characteristic, and as we have seen in our survey, the range of economies present in contemporary Asia transcends all such patronising divisions of humanity.

Thus economics, properly understood, is a social science rooted in social behaviour, belief, valuation and ideology, but this rooting does not destroy, as Marx for example recognised, the relatively autonomous logic of economic activities. Otherwise, it would not be possible to conceive of the "economic" as a distinct category at all. So although economists often talk as if their subject is purely abstract, even mathematical, the reality is that economics is as embedded in socio-cultural and historical contexts as any other social science or branch of the humanities for that matter (McCloskey 1985). If we see the problem in this way we can recognise that both "formalism" and "substantivism", formulated as mutually exclusive and antagonistic positions, are both false. Each grasps an aspect of the truth and represents it as the totality. Where each has been most useful in fact has been in generating concepts that help to isolate concrete and discussable elements of real economies—such as "markets" and "entrepreneurs", to name but two of the most useful. Whether the term "market" is meant to apply to a physical location for exchange and trade (as in familiar "marketplace" or "market town") or to the abstract and impersonal "market forces" of capitalism, the presence of entrepreneurs (individuals who seize or create economic and technological opportunities to enhance their own material and social standing) is implied.

And here the interesting empirical questions for students of anthropology begin: where are these marketplaces? who are the merchants and entrepreneurs? are they women? of one ethnic group? of one caste? what are the sources of capital? how does the activity of exchange in the marketplace relate back to the social structure and productive capacities of the villages? is the system monetised or are non-monetary media being used in the exchanges? can everything be exchanged for everything else, or are there "spheres of exchange" in which only certain items can be traded for certain others? how do entrepreneurs innovate? and how do they manage what they innovate? what is their social role? how are localised markets related to the wider political and economic structures of the society? And as anthropologists begin to answer these questions they see some interesting social patterns emerge. Entrepreneurs and operators (indeed even manipulators) of market forces are often women. Hawkers in the cities of China and the Chinese-dominated cities of Southeast Asia are often women, and in the Muslim areas of Southeast Asia, for example Indonesia and the east coast states of Peninsular Malaysia, small traders, market stall keepers and shopkeepers are often women, although in the Muslim areas of South Asia this is less likely to be so. Entrepreneurs and traders are also rarely socially isolated individuals, but are actually much more likely to be backed by strong ethnic and/or kin networks: as members of a distinct religious community such as the Southeast Asian Arab communities, famous for their business acumen, or the Indian spice traders of urban Southeast Asia, who are all Muslim (although of different sects), or they belong to a strong kinship group, as with Chinese merchants all over Asia, or to belong to a specific caste, as in the case of the south Indian *Chettiars*, famous as money-lenders.

The important concept of "division of labour" is only a small step from this, and raises some interesting theoretical questions further. We have mentioned examples of economic divisions along the lines of race, religion, caste and sex. But are these a real system of hierarchy, or simply convenient and arbitrary ways of dividing up tasks? In the case of the caste system we see a fairly clear instance of a real hierarchy: a system where occupations are ranked in status by caste (the four divisions of *Brahmins* or priests, *Kshatrias* or farmers, *Vaishas* or traders, *Shudras* or servants and labourers and the untouchables) and by *jati* or sub-caste—potters, leather workers, weavers, sweepers, and so on. The basis of caste is religious, and particularly related to Hindu notions of purity, but it also entails a complex linking of economic and religious status. In the case of ethnic stratification there is different linkage. It may be that in general terms the Chinese in Malaysia dominate urban trades, the Malays the peasant sector and Indians the plantations, but in reality there are Chinese peasants and plantation workers, Malay entrepreneurs, and Indians are statistically over-represented in some high status primarily urban occupations like medicine and law. In certain respects the middle-class Malay doctor has more in common with his Indian and Chinese colleagues than with his ethnic cousins and co-religionists in the *kampong* (village), yet ethnicity (including its important religious component) still divides, or seems to. Which raises a critical question: is this kind of division *class*? And if it is, can a Marxist model be applied to it?

This question is even more important when we realise that, in opening up the issue of the linkage between social stratification and economic inequality, fundamental questions about social justice, the distribution of resources and the need for socio-economic reform, or even revolution, are posed. Economic anthropology then turns out not to be a purely "academic" discipline, but one with practical implications (see Chapter 5). Marxism is characterised by the central place that it gives to the role of classes in society and of the conflict between them. In societies in which industrial capitalism exists on a large scale and where urbanism is extensive (Hong Kong, Singapore, Japan, parts of urban India and Southeast Asia) we can recognise what look like classes—groups defined by occupation, income, education and housing, by their patterns of consumption and by their differential access to both material and symbolic capital (Bourdieu 1984). But what about non-capitalist societies—either socialist ones (China, Indochina) or "pre-capitalist" traditional ones? This whole area was opened up by a Marxist-inspired anthropology, mainly in France (Clammer 1975). Two key notions emerged out of this literature: one, a refurbished notion of *modes of production*, and two, the universality of relations of *exploitation*. Although the notion of mode of production was originally intended by Marx to apply to the broad forms of economic formations succeeding each other in history—primitive communism, feudalism, capitalism and ultimately post-capitalist communism—the idea has become extended to include almost any relationship between a set of economic activities and their associated social structure (a relationship that Marx defined in part as the "social relations of production", although Marx did not seem to have much idea of the significance of culture in this relationship). This has given rise to such concepts as the "domestic mode of production" and the "lineage mode of production", in which a relationship of exploitation exists between those thought to possess social power or symbolic capital, e.g. the elders in a lineage system like that of the Chinese, and those who do not. The elders exercise control not so much through physical forces as through a combination of ideological control (e.g. running the ancestor cult) and matrimonial control, i.e. determining who gets married to whom. This very dubious argument (discussed in detail in Clammer 1978, Chapter One) does raise the important question, however, of the relationship between exploitation and economics. Are most or all of the economies that we have been discussing really ways for one group to exercise social and material power over another?

The Peasant Paradigm

Perhaps the single best context in which all these factors can be seen working together is that of the peasantry. Although the term is often used, it is not always defined, or is defined in a very loose way. But attempts to define a "peasant" raises fundamental questions: is there just one such category that embraces all of Asia? do they necessarily till the soil, or can groups engaged in other activities, such as fishing or in mixed economies also be considered peasant? (a problem that occurs in Firth's classic work *Malay Fishermen* (1946)) are peasants to be considered an autonomous social group, or are they always defined by their place in a set of "feudal" relationships in which they are always the subordinate and dependent partner? do peasants cease to be peasants when they move to cities, as they have done all over Asia (see Chapter 8) or is there such a thing as "peasanthood"—a mind-set as well as some economic characteristics, which continues to define peasants outside of their normal rural setting?

Normally we think of peasants as small farmers operating family-owned or landlord-owned smallholdings, utilising only family labour or a minimum of outside paid labour at peak seasons, and able to maintain a subsistence economy or one with a relatively small surplus which is sold or exchanged in the marketplace. We also often think of peasants as being exploited by landowners, middlemen, providers of credit, seed, fertiliser and consumer goods, as being landless and as the providers of obligatory labour to feudal overlords. Many of these images are indeed, in some places and at some times, correct. But the reality is complex and as James Scott, for example, has brilliantly shown (Scott 1985) peasant societies are both internally stratified (into rich and poor, landed and landless) and maintain very complex links with the world beyond the farm and the hamlet through marketing networks, knowledge about the differential access to credit, agricultural extension services, the media, kin-networks, personal travel, political patronage, education, religion, and other means. In the terms used by Marxist anthropologists, this represents both the "penetration" of a formerly non-monetised economy by the capitalist sector and the "co-existence of modes of production"—the living side by side of a non- or semi-capitalist mode of production and a capitalist one. Both the sheer size of the Asian peasantries (the bulk of the population in many countries) and this pivotal role helps explain their political significance in modern Asian history. Like all our other categories, the peasantry are not a fixed entity, but a historical one, evolving through time as the technological and political context changes and as the world economy as a whole alters its structural qualities. So it is important to remember that peasants are not only a form of economy—small family farmers—but are also underdogs in the total agrarian social structure, despite their large numbers, and possess their own traditional cultures very different from those of both urbanites and other country-dwellers such as hunters and gatherers (Shanin 1971:11). The notion of the peasantry can also be a highly ideological and emotive one—some regarding it as the repository of all virtues once "correctly" politicised, as with Mao, while others see peasants as the epitome of under-development, ignorance and brutishness. Whichever view, or hopefully a more balanced one, we take it is important to remember that the isolated peasant living in an autonomous albeit "feudal" context is largely a thing of the past in contemporary Asia. The reality is a dynamic one: a peasantry increasingly "incorporated" into the national economies of Asia, through marketing networks, political mechanisms, media, the integration of the national economies into the world economy and the spread of a consumer economy. It is useful here to distinguish between peasants in basically capitalist societies and those in centrally-planned socialist ones where sometimes radical forms of collectivisation have been attempted and where peasants have worked out complex accommodations between their traditional cultures and the demands of the new order.

But what happens to peasants when their traditional social structure breaks up? Most become landless labourers providing seasonal help for richer peasants, or work as agricultural labourers on commercial farms and market gardens or on plantations; yet others abandon the countryside and move to cities where they swell the urban population (cities like Jakarta and Bangkok) and many end up in the "informal sector", the often huge unregulated or "underground" economy typical of Asian cities we spoke about earlier. From the point of view of the economic anthropologist these are fascinating forms of economic activity with their own sociological and cultural life-forms, but to policy-makers they are a major problem, not only because from the bureaucrats point of view they represent a big sector of the total economy uncontrolled, untaxed and full of health hazards and strains the infrastructure (roads, sewage, education, health facilities) to breaking point—a fact that will not be lost on anyone who has visited, say, Manila or Calcutta, or almost any other major city in the tropical zone.

Amongst the attempts to solve these problems at source, rather than within the cities themselves and to offset this cityward migration, have been schemes to provide satisfactory employment in or near the countryside. Some of these schemes involve creating industrial centres in small towns and cities, away from the metropolis in an attempt to promote decentralisation and the modest growth of regional cities (Malaysia has followed this pattern with "free-trade zones" in smaller cities like Penang and Malacca). Others promote rural-rural migration rather than rural-urban migration, the best known being the massive Indonesian "transmigration" scheme, involving the resettlement of thousands of Javanese peasants in the outer and underpopulated islands of Kalimantan (Borneo), Sumatra and Irian Jaya. A third category are those schemes which attempt to improve productivity and the rural infrastructure and make life on the land more attractive. Such schemes exist in northeastern Thailand (an impoverished area which is the main source of migration into Bangkok) with road building, village development schemes, irrigation improvements and the like, and in northwestern Malaysia where the best known one is the famous FELDA scheme, a massive government-funded plan to promote the rice-bowl area of the country to maximum productivity (Hashim 1979). Elsewhere land reform has been attempted, especially through the redistribution of the estate land to poor or landless peasants. This is being tried, although not yet very successfully, in the Philippines.

Markets

Markets, the nexus of exchange, are an important subject in themselves which have attracted a great deal of historical and contemporary attention from economic anthropologists (Firth 1970, Belshaw 1965, Polanyi 1957, Geertz 1963, Alexander and others 1957). Most attention in Asian anthropology has focused on physical markets—marketplaces, small market towns and the social organisation of these markets—who sells to whom? what ritual or religious activities are associated? how is the market related to the social structure of the town (e.g. the Chinese middlemen in small Malaysian market towns) or of the countryside? A classic case study is by Geertz (1963) where he explores a small Javanese market town with its social make-up of peddlers and storekeepers, of unskilled workers, and of civil servants and white-collar workers (the local elite). The central economic divide in the town way between the "firm centred", i.e. commercial) trading enterprises and the "bazaar" or flexible and individualised hawking sector. He examined the flows of perishable and imperishable commodities, large and small objects, bulk goods and trickles of small items, and the service, techniques of bargaining, credit and business relationships. While marketing flows obviously differ from culture to culture (the business culture of Chinese shopkeepers being very different in many respects from that of an Indonesian bazaar trader for instance) and depend very much on the scale of the market (the small-town, or rural crossroads market being different from big scale marketing in the large cities, and both differ from the markets that spring up around temples or pilgrimage sites), the central significance of marketplaces of the kind that Geertz describes as the focal point of exchange, credit, entrepreneurship and of social and cultural contact, is very great. To revert for a moment to the language of the old formalist/substantivist and Marxist/non-Marxist paradigms, markets are a major location of *exchange*, although not the location of *production*, the two phases of the economic cycle that precede *consumption*. And in the bigger sense of the term "market" that we earlier identified, local markets often provide the point of contact between a traditional economy and a monetised one. They are where nomads and peasants discover the logic of money and a taste for goods, such as watches, radios or bicycles that their own technology cannot produce.

The Comparative Perspective: Rationality and Ecology

One of the themes implicit in all that has been said up to this point is the necessity of a comparative perspective. Anthropology has long prided itself on being a comparative social science, and in a discussion of Asian economic systems we can see that many of the most interesting points not only illuminate classic themes in economic anthropology, but shed new light on them. One example of this is the old theme of the gift, with which we began. Well documented as it is in many so-called "simple" societies, few anthropologists have thought to extend the idea to "complex" societies. But in Japan we find a gift economy on a huge scale, where not only are gifts given at mid-year and end of year to bosses, school-teachers and those who have done one favours (or who might do them!), but on many other occasions throughout the year, when visiting someone's house and for countless other reasons. A large industry exists to provide, wrap and deliver these gifts, the basic purpose of which, as with many other exchanges, is to create, constitute, or deepen social relationships (Befu 1974). Likewise feasting, a widespread institution with many forms exists in many contexts in Asia: the Chinese wedding feast and the Indonesian *bersanding* to mark a birth, marriage or other life-cycle event, to name but two. But we do not always think to relate feasting to markets, to the ways in which commodities are circulated or to the gradual penetration of capitalism into "tribal" societies, but in practice the Asian economic material points to significant links here (Voss 1987). The mystique of rice as something that has a "soul" is widespread throughout both the Malay-Indonesian and Thai-speaking areas of Southeast Asia, but who would at first sight think to link it with Japanese resistance to opening their rice market to foreign imports? But there is a close connection, for not only do the Japanese eat a different variety of rice from that grown in South and Southeast Asia, but rice for them is deeply tied up with ideas of cultural identity, purity and even their biological make-up.

Two key factors actually tie all these diverse themes together. The first is a theme that has been a central element in a lot of recent discussion in economic anthropology, that of rationality (e.g. Godelier 1972). What our material suggests is that rationality, while no doubt universal in some of its aspects, is deeply cultural and that different economic activities are embodiments and expressions of these rationalities. Second, we must stress again the intimate connections between economy, culture and ecology. This is not only analytically the case, but also helps us to develop a unified field theory that links economy, rationality and development. For economic decisions are not only or necessarily "maximising" ones; they are also, as we have seen, sociological and cultural and also ecological, often reflecting a deep understanding of climate, animal and plant life, husbandry and man's relationship to natural forces. The recent "culture and development" debate to which we earlier referred reveals this very clearly with its emphasis on indigenous knowledge or what is sometimes called "ethnoscience": the intimate knowledge of a native people of their natural environment, and the expression of this very often in ritual or religious forms. Obviously "development" which disturbs these carefully worked out cultural-ecological relationship is actually anti-development: the destruction in the guise of progress of a long-evolved system of man-nature patterns. A small but perhaps significant footnote to this is that, in the past, economic anthropology had close connections with its cousin, Material Culture

Studies, which for various reasons have now been largely severed. This is a pity, because the links are real and close, and the indigenous tools, utensils, boats, architecture and dress of a people are a sign of the inner workings of their economic-cultural-ecological sensibility.

Finally we can see that even a modest survey of forms of economic activity points beyond itself into areas that we have only touched on, but have had no space to develop. These include the analysis of gender relationships in economic practices and questions of social power which is often embodied in economic forms, and the manifestation of this in patterns of social hierarchy and inequality. Not only is Marxist class analysis a useful tool here, but non-Marxist anthropologists have been led into discussions of such topics as the role of elites and of the connections between factors such as lineages and economic activity. How, for example, the very different Malay and Chinese social structures, one cognatic, the other [patri]unilineal profoundly influences patterns of saving, capital accumulation, entrepreneurship and commercial success. Other questions which have arisen out of debates about monetisation and the penetration of capitalism are now at the cutting edge of social theory. For example, issues of the consumer society, commoditisation and the semiotics of objects—the way in which things have many levels of symbolic importance quite apart from their purely functional utility. Yet other questions have arisen out of advances in ecology, in the political sociology of the State, in economics itself, and in newer fields that have grown up around the edge of economics and business studies—organisational theory for example. Economic anthropology itself will have to move to take account of these developments, and as it does so its capacity for theorising its empirical material (in this case the indigenous economic systems of contemporary Asia) will expand, and as it does so our grasp of the links between economy, ecology, society and culture will deepen, to the lasting benefit of us all.

References

Barth, F. (1970), "Economic Spheres in Darfur," in R. Firth (ed.) *Themes in Economic Anthropology*, London: Tavistock Publications.

Befu, H. (1974), "Gift Giving in a Modernizing Japan," in T.S. and W.P. Lebra (eds.) *Japanese Culture and Behaviour: Selected Readings*, Honolulu: University of Hawaii Press.

Belshaw, C. (1965), *Traditional Exchange and Modern Markets*, Englewood Cliffs: Prentice-Hall.

Bourdieu, P. (1984), *Distinction: A Social Critique of the Judgement of Taste*, Cambridge, Massachusetts: Harvard University Press.

Borgstrom, B.-E. (1983), *Power, Technology and Culture in Nepal and Northern Sweden*, Lund: Lund University Research Policy Institute.

Clammer, J. (ed.) (1978), *The New Economic Anthropology*, London: Macmillan Press.

Clammer, J. (1985), *Anthropology and Political Economy: Theoretical and Asian Perspectives*, London: Macmillan Press.

Clammer, J. (1987), "Incorporation and Assimilation: The Aboriginal Peoples of Malaysia and the Forces of Modernization," *Journal of Social and Economic Studies*, 4. 2.

Condominas, G. (1957), *Nous avons mange la foret*, Paris: Mercure de France.

Cooper, R.G. (1984), *Resource Scarcity and the Hmong Response*, Singapore: Singapore University Press.

Dentan, R.K. (1986), *The Semai: A Non-Violent People of Malaya*, New York: Holt, Rindart and Winston.

Dove, M.R. (ed.) (1988), *The Real and Imagined Role of Culture in Development: Case Studies from Indonesia*, Honolulu: University of Hawaii Press.

Endicott, K.M. (1979), *Batek Negrito Religion: The Worldview and Rituals of a Hunting and Gathering People of Peninsular Malaysia*, Oxford: The Clarendon Press.

Evans, G. (1990), *Lao Peasants Under Socialism*, New Haven: Yale University Press.

Featherstone, M. (1991), *Consumer Culture and Postmodernism*, London: Sage Publications.

Firth, R. (1946), *Malay Fishermen: Their Peasant Economy*, London: Kegan Paul.

Firth, R. (ed.) (1970), *Themes in Economic Anthropology*, London: Tavistock Publications.

Freeman, J.D. (1980), *Iban Agriculture: A Report on the Shifting Cultivation of Hill Rice by the Iban of Sarawak*, New York: AMS Press.

Geddes, W.R. (1976), *Migrants of the Mountains: The Cultural Ecology of the Blue Miao (Hmong Njua) of Thailand*, Oxford: The Clarendon Press.

Geertz, C. (1963), *Peddlers and Princes: Social Change and Economic Modernization in Two Indonesian Towns*, Chicago: University of Chicago Press.

Godelier, M. (1972), *Rationality and Irrationality in Economics*, London: New Left Books.

Hashim, A. (1979), "Land Development Under FELDA: Some Socio-Economic Aspects," in B.A.R. Mokhzani (ed.) *Rural Development in Southeast Asia*, New Delhi: Vikas.

Hoare, P.W.C. (1985), "The Movement of Lahu Hill People Towards A Lowland Lifestyle in North Thailand: A Study of Three Villages," *Contributions to Southeast Asian Ethnography*, 4.

Jaghid, S. and P. Hyer (1979), *Mongolia's Culture and Society*, Boulder, Colorado: Westview Press.

Kahn, J.S. (1980), *Minangkabau Social Formations: Indonesian Peasants and the World Economy*, Cambridge: Cambridge University Press.

Lansing, J.S. (1991), *Priests and Programmers: Technologies of Power in the Engineered Landscape of Bali*, Princeton: Princeton University Press.

Mauss, M. (1954), *The Gift*, London: Cohen and West.

McCloskey, D.N. (1985), *The Rhetoric of Economics*, Madison: University of Wisconsin Press.

Polanyi, K., C.M. Arensgberg and H.W. Pearson (1957), *Trade and Market in the Early Empires*, Glencoe: Free Press.

Sather, C. (1985), "Boat Crews and Fishing Fleets: The Social Organization of Maritime Labour Amongst the Bajau Laut of Southeastern Sabah," *Contributions to Southeast Asian Ethnography*, 4.

Scott, J.C. (1985), *Weapons of the Weak: Everyday Forms of Peasant Resistance*, New Haven: Yale University Press.

Shanin, T. (ed.) (1974), *Peasants and Peasant Societies*, Harmondsworth: Penguin Books.

Sopher, D. (1977), *The Sea Nomads: A Study of the Maritime Boat People of Southeast Asia*, Singapore: National Museum.

UNCRD (1989), *Industrialization and Development: Focus on ASEAN*, Nagoya: United Nations Centre for Regional Development.

Voss, J. (1987), "The Politics of Pork and the Rituals of Rice: Dedistributive Feasting and Commodity Circulation in Northern Luzon, the Philippines," in J. Clammer (ed.) *Beyond the New Economic Anthropology*, London: Macmillan Press.

Weiner, M. (1991), *The Child and the State in India: Child Labour and Education Policy in Comparative Perspective*, Princeton: Princeton University Press.

Wittfogel, K.A. (1973), *Oriental Despotism*, New Haven: Yale University Press.

Chapter 7

RELIGION, VALUES AND SOCIAL CHANGE: WEBER IN SOUTHEAST ASIA

The purpose of this chapter is to examine the relevance, if any, of Max Weber's views for the analysis of religion in Southeast Asia, and in particular for Islam. This is not because Weber had all that much to say very directly about Islam, and certainly not because he had anything much to say about Southeast Asia, references to which hardly appear in his writings. Rather it is because of the use to which some of Weber's ideas have been put in relating religion and economic development, and indeed for many people that it is upon precisely this conjunction that his fame rests. The question here then is to explore the significance of Weber's ideas in the Southeast Asian context, and in particular to examine of seemingly significant paradox: that Islam in Southeast Asia is strongly associated both with economic "underdevelopment" (as in the case of the Malays of Malaysia) and on the other hand with entrepreneurial capitalism (as in the case of the Muslim Indian and Arab trading communities). How is this paradox to be resolved? We shall approach this by way of an examination of the possible significance of Weber's ideas on religion and economic action for Southeast Asian Islam, by exploring the use to which beliefs about what Weber had to say have been utilised in explaining Islam in the region and finally to identify some of the important practical, theoretical and conceptual issues that this debate raises.

Weber's contribution to the sociology of Islam is scattered and incomplete, although fortunately has been drawn together and splendidly analysed by Turner[1] in a work for which all subsequent scholars must remain grateful. This study I will use as something of a base line for examining the very substantial differences between Middle Eastern Islam and the Islam of

---

1 Bryan S. Turner (1974), *Weber and Islam: A Critical Study*, London: Routledge and Kegan Paul.

Southeast Asia, and it was of course to the former, and in particular to the Ottoman tradition, that most of Weber's observations apply. Let us initially then say something about Southeast Asia, its characteristics and geographical distribution.

Islam, despite its contemporary importance as one of the major religions of Southeast Asia, is actually a relatively late arriver, historically speaking. Indeed one should perhaps speak of a process of Islamisation which began in earnest in the 15th century and which is still continuing. For the most part Islam was not successful in penetrating the Buddhist areas of Southeast Asia—and until today very few Muslims are to be found north of the southeastern most part of Thailand. But south of that line—in what are now the six southern provinces of Thailand, Malaysia, Indonesia and the southern Philippines, Islam took root with vigour in a religious soil made up largely of a mixture of animism and Hinduism. Only in Bali did the Hindu cultures stand up successfully against the strongly missionary spirit of Islam, which was brought through trade and culture rather than through military conquest. Islam today is thus largely a phenomenon of the Malay world in Southeast Asia: it has had little impact on the Sinitic, Burmese, Thai or Indochinese cultures of the area, on isolated tribal peoples of Borneo, Peninsular Malaysia or the Philippines or on Christianised Malays of the northern and central Philippines. Historically then it developed as the religion of the coastal, maritime and lowland peoples of peninsular and insular Southeast Asia. Where exceptions to this occur, it is usually found that the Muslim communities are enclaves of people ethnically different from the surrounding majority cultures. This fact has many political and economic consequences, some of which we will discuss in due course. The key ideas to point out here are essentially these: that Islam in Southeast Asia is not indigenous, it exists in a politically, culturally and ethnically pluralistic context and it was grafted onto, rather than absolutely replaced, the existing cultural traditions—a factor which is of great ethnographic significance.

It is against this background then—very different indeed from that of the Middle East and North Africa—that we must explore the possible significance of Weber's ideas. But here we must make a second point: that Weber's own ideas are complex and by no means consistent. Almost always, when anyone begins to talk about "Weber and Asia", they really mean the so-called "Weber thesis", i.e. the expanded form of the famous Protestant Ethic argument about the relationship between Calvinism and the rise of European capitalism. There are two observations to be made about this: first, there is far more in Weber than just the "Weber thesis", and second, even if we do take that "thesis" as the central issue for the analysis of Asian civilisations, there is, as Turner phrases it, both a "strong" form of the thesis—that Protestantism caused capitalism, and a "weak" form—there are indeed connections between religion and economic behaviour, but they are not rigorous or deterministic ones.[2] Proponents of the "strong" version are those who tend to argue that the lack of "development" (in an economic sense) is because of the negative influences of the local religious traditions. A natural corollary of this view would be that the solution to Asian underdevelopment is either a good dose of protestantism or the discovery and enhancement of "Protestant" (i.e. presumably Calvinist) elements within the Asian religions. But it is important to remember three things here: firstly, that the original Protestant Ethic thesis was intended as a limited and historically and geographically specific case study; secondly, that Weber's work on Asian religions was not of the same kind—rather it was part of a broad (and unfinished) comparative sociology of civilisations (within which the role of religion played only a limited part); and thirdly, that Weber's own work on Islam (even that of the Middle East) is incomplete. Here then we shall proceed on two assumptions: first, that any generalisation of the Protestant Ethic thesis should be approached with extreme caution, and second, that there is no need to restrict the "relevance" of Weber to the Protestant Ethic thesis alone; if this were all that Weber had to say, he would merely be a minor and probably now virtually forgotten social historian. In fact, the richness of Weber's thought transcends such limitations.

For Weber the emergence of capitalism required a number preconditions, which Turner lists as rational law, a free labour market, autonomous cities, a money economy and a bourgeois class, which were absent in Islamic society, with its patrimonial political institutions and its "warrior ethic".[3] Indeed in many respects Islam is essentially different from ascetic

---

2 Ibid., pp. 8 ff.

3 Ibid., p. 2.

puritanism, since it does not view morality and the world as opposed to each other, but rather accommodates them. However, since for Weber asceticism is only one component in the emergence of a rational, capitalistic worldview, this alone does not explain the differences: rather the nature of political domination, of bureaucracy and of feudal institutions is primary, not the motivation of individuals. It is thus not Islam and capitalism that are incompatible: it is feudalism and capitalism that exclude each other. We should be aware at the outset then that Weber was not a monocausalist; no one thing determines anything else in his thought; and that values are secondary, in the sense that even if they derive from religion, the expression of those values is conditioned and mediated by social structure and institutions. Weber was thus what today we would call a sociologist of knowledge.

The key to understanding Weber's significance for the study of Southeast Asia then lies in the attempt to explain how the Middle Eastern and Abrahamaic worldview of Islam become accepted into (and modified by) those Southeast Asian cultures into which it penetrated. And within Weber's sociology this would require that attention be paid to processes of power, or of legitimation—legal, traditional and charismatic—which accompanied and made possible this process of accommodation. A political sociology rather than a concern with values lies at the heart of Weber's system. If this is the case then there are two dimensions to be explored: the historical background and the contemporary situation. Let us briefly comment on the first. As we have already noted, the historical, political, cultural and geographical conditions prevailing in the Islamic heartlands of the Middle East are and were very different from those in Southeast Asia. In the 14th and 15th centuries, Southeast Asia was at least as complex as it is now. The northern parts were under the influence of Buddhism, of Hinduism and of Chinese civilisation (although interestingly enough Chinese religion never caught on as a popular phenomenon amongst the indigenous peoples, but was confined in its influence to some court circles, as at Hue in Vietnam). The southern parts were occupied by Malay, proto-Malay and aboriginal peoples, and other than indigenous animism the main religious influence was Hinduism. The origins of Islam lay not in military conquest in the initial stages, but was introduced, in some cases through Southern India, by traders from South Arabia, the Gulf and Persia, who traded, taught, settled and married. The key breakthroughs in this missionary effort were two fold: firstly, when the chiefs and kings were converted, and secondly, when the early trading communities began to develop into genuine cities (even though, as Weber would immediately point out, these cities had a very different social structure from their European counterparts). The pivotal community in this respect was undoubtedly Malacca, which eventually extended its political and commercial suzerainty as far north as southern Thailand, into Sumatra and southwards into Java. The form of "feudalism" which emerged is of great interest—it was based on small, mainly coastal, settlements into which a local sultan collected his followers and not on the European patterns of landed estates; the economic viability rested mainly in the hands of foreign trading minorities (Arabs, Gujeratis and Chinese, amongst others) who were, except for the Chinese, usually Muslims; and it depended for its continuance on control of both overland and oversea trade routes—it was trade dependent. As a consequence, Islam was both a trading ethic and a warrior ethic: the first in the case of the foreign trading communities and the latter in the case of the Sultans and their warriors. Conversion could and did take place either by assimilation to one or the other of these models, or by conquest. Islam in turn (and unlike Hinduism in the region) provided a body of law, a code of conduct, a rationale for political expansionism (i.e. conversion), a rational model of political legitimacy, a distinct way of salvation and means (e.g. Sufism) for satisfying the mystical yearnings of Southeast Asians. Paradoxically then, much of Weber's account of the characteristics of Islam (if not of specific political institutions) applies better to Asia than it does to the Middle East.[4]

This being the case, the Southeast Asian example forces us to closely re-examine the stereotype of the "Weber thesis" as it is often represented: that Protestantism "causes" capitalism, and that non-Protestant religions "cause" underdevelopment. Quite apart from the fact that Weber did not say this, it is not even implied in his comprehensive sociology of civilisations. Indeed, given the methodological principles of Weber's sociol-

---

[4] The literature on the spread of Islam to Southeast Asia is extensive. For comprehensive references on the introduction of Islam to Malacca, see C.H. Wake, *Malacca in the Fifteenth Century: Malay Historical Traditions and the Politics of Islamization* and K.S. Sandhu and P. Wheatley (eds.) (1983), *Melaka: The Transformation of a Malay Capital 1400-1980*, Kuala Lumpur: Oxford University Press.

ogy[5](even if he has not always been consistent in their application himself), it is clear that a theory of causes is not the point at all: rather the concern is with the sociological (including systems of belief) circumstances in which the probabilities of certain courses of motivation and action are enhanced and others are reduced, and of the institutional restraints (in particular political and legal) which operate to constrain, express or channel these actions and motivations. In the light of this, and in view of the fact that Weber himself did not write about Southeast Asia we must look not so much at Weber as at the use to which Weber's thought has been put in that context.

It is unfortunate in this respect that the work of Rodinson—and in particular his *Islam and Capitalism*[6]—also does not extend to Southeast Asia, since there, of course, we find an extended argument on the relationship between the two elements in the title of his book. However, by way of preliminary discussion, an important point can be drawn out of that important if inconclusive work: that in Rodinson's view the influence of Islam on capitalism is minimal.[7] The relationship between Rodinson's thought and that of Weber is thus of great interest. To begin with, Rodinson derives his definition of capitalism very much from Weber: "I propose to call 'capitalistic' the whole of the sector covered by merchant capital and financial capital",[8] and thus includes the commercial and user's capital of the European middle ages and the comparable forms in the Middle East. When to this Rodinson adds Weber's concepts of profit achieved by peaceful exchange and of rationality.[9] In Weber's basic understanding of the term then, capitalism would have existed in the early Islamic Middle East. Why

---

5 Especially as enunciated in Max Weber (1966), *The Theory of Social and Economic Organization*, New York: Free Press.

6 Maxime Rodinson (1974), *Islam and Capitalism*, London: Allen Lane. Original French edition (1966), Paris: Editions du Seuil.

7 I have explored the problem of Rodinson's implications for Southeast Asia in Chapter 9.

8 Rodinson, op. cit., p. 7.

9 Ibid., p. 9. cf. Weber (1958), *The Protestant Ethic and the Spirits of Capitalism*, New York, pp. 17, 19.

it did not develop into the forms known in the advanced industrial questions is another issue, but nevertheless "The merchants of the Muslim Empire conformed perfectly to Weber's criteria for capitalistic activity. They seized any and every opportunity for profit, and calculated their outlays, their encashments and their profits in money terms."[10] The only real advantage of Europe, according to Rodinson's reading of Weber, is that for Weber, European rationalism was less encumbered by the reactionary (non-rational) forces of tradition, magic, religion and morality, but even then Rodinson can find very few constraints on capitalistic rationality in Muslim ideology. Indeed Rodinson is at pains to show that the differences in Muslim and Christian ideology in the Middle Ages were not as marked as many would suppose and that in fact the rationalistic aspects of Muslim thought were very developed and conspicuous: at least as developed as those in Europe (although for reasons of historiography they are not so well known).

Rodinson's view is thus of some interest: that while adopting Weber's view of the definition of capitalism leads him to argue that there was capitalism in the Islamic world, it also leads him to argue that Weber was quite wrong in ascribing the success of European capitalism to the superior development of rationality. The capitalist spirit thus existed amongst Muslims: it was not this spirit, but "social, political and economic conditions that enabled it to develop and, at a certain moment, to take over the whole of society in Europe and North America": "The Europeans, who complained (not without hypocrisy) of the absence of the spirit of enterprise among capital owners in the countries they descended upon and in some cases colonised, failed to see, or chose not to see, that conditions in these countries were such as to break in advance all the springs of the capitalist impulse, and that, furthermore, their own presence and the laws they imposed, although they removed some obstacles, were quick to install others, which were often more effective. If the conditions are provided for a capitalist enterprise to be able to make an interesting profit, for the capitalist to keep this profit and to make it multiply with a certain degree of security, for competition from foreign capitalism to be sustained with a certain minimum degree of likelihood from the start that the native capitalist will not

---

[10] Ibid., p. 30.

be crushed by it—then we see the social obstacles constituted by the traditional mentality and the religious and moral bans gradually fading away, the laws themselves being got around, the success of the first pioneers of the foreign models encouraging others to emulate them, the demon of capitalist profit invincibly laying hold of ever wider sections, and the grip of the system becoming, through its incomparable dynamism, ever more extensive and powerful. This is what we have seen happen in Japan, China and India, and begin to happen in the Muslim world, despite the bigger obstacles introduced there by a stronger European competition, safeguarded by commercial and other treaties imposed by force, rather as in Latin America."[11]

Religion as such then is neutral in the development or otherwise of capitalism, except of course insofar as the religion expresses itself in social, political and economic forms and institutions.

Rodinson's argument clearly has many implications for Southeast Asia, the most obvious of which is that in explaining the "underdevelopment" of some of the Muslim peoples of the region, it is clearly not religion as such that is at fault. The relative underdevelopment of Indonesia, the Philippines and the Malay peoples of Malaysia, for example, cannot be seen purely in this way, but requires a historical and political-economy approach to underdevelopment to expose the real causes—colonialism, commodity prices, social structures, lack of success to educational resources, lack of information and in many cases political powerlessness, government inefficiency and corruption and ecological factors. Yet it is interesting to note that where religious explanations are falling out of favour, genetic ones are creeping in. Persistently there is this unwillingness to look for the causes where they really lay and to shift the blame to rather mysterious and invisible factors.[12]

---

[11] Ibid., pp. 217-218.

[12] Conspicuous amongst these attempts is the book by the current Malaysian Prime Minister Dr Mahathir Mohamad (1970), *The Malay Dilemma*, Singapore: Asia Pacific Press. For discussion of this in the local context, see Chee Heng Leng and Chan Chee Khoon (1984), *Designer Genes: I.Q. Ideology and Biology*, Petaling Jaya: Insan.

Weberian explanations of underdevelopment have then to some extent been argued out of existence, in some cases just gone out of fashion and in yet others have been replaced by rather similar looking theories. But not entirely. One recent attempt to revive the significance of Weber and especially of his theory of rationalisation, is Peacock's *Muslim Puritans*,[13] the very title of which shows the influence of Weber. This book and its argument deserves a fairly close scrutiny. Peacock's basic theses are that the psychological dimensions of Weber's concept of rationalisation have been undervalued at the expense of the political and economic; that the Weberian method of Verstehen (interpretative understanding) is the most appropriate method for cultural analysis; that "The guiding assumption, derived from Weber, is that cultural rationalisation, i.e. reformism—will be reflected in psychological rationalisation and that the exploration of the psychological implications of Weber's theory can best be carried out in an "exotic milieu".[14]

One of the major sources of ethnic identity and ethnic conflict in Southeast Asia is religion. Recent events have shown that Islam, with its combination of activism, missionary spirit, sheer size and numerous links with perceptions of national and cultural affiliations, is becoming once again an ascendant political and sociological force in the region. One welcomes the appearance of any work which treats sympathetically and systematically with contemporary Southeast Asian Islam, and the present volume is an important, although in some ways disappointing, contribution. The author is an anthropologist, well known for his work on Indonesia. One of the hallmarks of the book is its attempt to synthesise the traditional anthropological technique of participant observation and the use of questionnaires and, what must be admitted to be, very simple statistical techniques. A little more sophistication with the latter would have greatly enhanced the value and rigour of the analysis, and would undoubtedly have enabled the authors to explore more fully many of the tantalising correlations that he reveals. A great part of the significance of the book lies in its attempt to explore empirically the well-known "Weber thesis" in its applica-

---

[13] James L. Peacock (1978), *Muslim Puritans: Reformist Psychology in Southeast Asian Islam*, Berkeley: University of California Press.

[14] Ibid., p. 21.

tion to Southeast Asia, an attempt summed up in the volume's opening sentence: "This book's central question is: to what extent and in what sense does cultural change imply psychological rationalisation?"[15]

The solution to this question is pursued through an exploration of the psychological and cultural dimensions of the lives of Muslim reformists (i.e. non-traditionalists crudely put: there is a large definitional problem here) in Indonesia, Singapore and Malaysia. The book is systematically structured: the reformist Muslim communities in the three countries are examined and the psychological and cultural characteristic of the sample are enumerated and summarised, both in relation to the "traditionalists" and to a lesser extent comparatively between the three countries, Singapore reformists are thus seen as much less organised, politicised and institutionalised than their Indonesian counterparts, but still much more so than the traditionalists in either country. Peacock's criteria for estimating these characteristics contains a large number of heterogeneous and undefended items: swaddling and cuddling behaviour, observance of rites of passage, toilet training, language use, degree of social hierarchy, play, circumcision, theology, pilgrimage, schooling, occupations, etc. The resulting account is highly descriptive (despite the statistical basis of the surveys) and startlingly predictable: Weber would no doubt be delighted with the Muslim puritans of regionwide psychological and cultural homogeneity who emerge. We are left in the dark as to exactly why they emerge. Could it be that the answer to this question lies to a great extent outside of psychology, but rather in economics, sociology and politics?

Peacock himself notes in passing, but fails to take up, many of these perspectives he recognises, for instance that there is a relationship between economics and ethnicity. but fails to draw any conclusions from this fact, other than noting that it is so.[16] Of more significance is his unwillingness or inability to develop the vitally important fact that there is a highly complex relationship between Islam and ethnicity. Why is it possible to be able to claim Malay ethnicity in Indonesia without being a Muslim, whereas this is virtually impossible in Malaya or Singapore? Nowhere does the key concept of the *Bumiputera* receive a treatment, or even a mention. Yet in

---

[15] Ibid., p. 1.

[16] Ibid., p. 17.

Malaysia it is precisely the politicisation of the alleged relationship between ethnicity, religion and language that gives Islam its power as a tool in "nation-building", that lies behind the alleged incompatibility of Islam and communism in that country, although the Indonesian experience teaches quite a different story on that point. Why are the Malays in Singapore not politically active in the way in which their Malaysian and Indonesian compatriots are. The answer clearly lies not in Islam itself, nor in the reformists' psyches, but in the quite different political and economic systems in the three states and in the critical factor of their ethnic structure: in Singapore the Malays are a minority, in Malaysia they are virtually so, and are economically underprivileged to boot, whereas in Indonesia, Muslims, and people of Malay stock, are the vast majority and comprise the political and social elite. Such structural factors are altogether absent from Peacock's analysis, although they cannot honestly be left out.

In short, while one would hardly quarrel with the author's useful psychological description of Muslim reformists, the account floats freely in a politico-historical vacuum. One must draw the conclusion that Peacock doesn't think much of history (unlike his mentor, Weber, incidentally, although this fact is often forgotten amongst the ideal typologists): even his use of documentary sources reflects this. His sources on Singapore for instance report data that is variously from fifteen to twenty-five years old, in a country with an extraordinary rapid rate of social change. The pilgrims to Mecca for instance who are reported to be boarding a no-doubt ancient pilgrim-ship actually now make the return trip in the luxury of a Singapore Airlines Jumbo Jet.[17] On the same page a very dated figure of Singapore Muslim divorces is given—actually the rate is lower and declining. One would like to know whether this is amongst Peacock's reformists or his traditionalists. Whichever was the case, the analysis would involve precisely those wider social processes which are missing from what one would hope, from an anthropologist, would be a more holistic picture. Systematic comparison of the three cases presented in the book is actually impossible, since the only continuity that we are given is the very abstract character model.

One welcomes and applauds this book for its attempt to describe the Muslim reformist character in Southeast Asia (although Peacock leaves out

---

[17] Ibid., p. 164.

those areas where Islam is disputed—the southern Philippines and southern Thailand) and for its attempt to explore Weber's seminal idea in a context which Weber himself did not directly examine (although one looks in vain in the bibliography for any mention of Turner's important *Weber and Islam*, a major and significant omission). One regrets the lack of historical, political and economic sensitivity, however, which man the work, and renders it very selective in its interpretation. Is Peacock aware of the massive revival of *dakwah* throughout the region? Of the proliferation of *Tarikats* and other Sufi and mystical organisations? Of the pressure being put by the Indonesian syncretists to have their movements recognised as genuine religions. Some would simply see these as manifestations of a worldwide groundswell of Muslim fundamentalism. But this would not be to explain them, and their vital significance for ethnicity and ethic relations throughout Southeast Asia, and for the relationship of Islam to the other religions.

At the end of the day then, one feels that Peacock has not served Weber too well, especially in the light of Rodinson's comments on rationalisation. Whether or not the study could help us to understand issues of development is also a moot point. This indeed points up a major difficulty: the application of Weber to concrete situations outside of the Calvinist one. The diffuseness in what Weber can really have been said to have meant makes the usefulness of his ideas suspect: this is perhaps one reason why there is a perennial irresolvability about the "Weber thesis"—not only exactly what it is, but what one can do with it likewise. However, in Peacock's work, we have a non-Muslim's view of Weber's relationship to Southeast Asian Islam; we will now turn to a consideration of some Muslim views.

It is significant that a recent survey of contemporary Muslim economic thought does not mention Weber at all: apparently his work is considered to have little significance for the Islamic world.[18] There are interesting exceptions to this "neglect" however, one being the work of S.N.H. Naqvi.[19] Naqvi looks upon Weber with favour, since he sees him as the author of the thesis that "the economic performance of a society cannot be

---

[18] M.N. Siddiqi (1981), *Muslim Economic Thinking: A Survey of Contemporary Literature*, Leicester: The Islamic Foundation.

[19] S.N.H. Naqvi (1981), *Ethics and Economics: An Islamic Synthesis*, Leicester: The Islamic Foundation.

separated from its moral philosophy, which since the dawn of civilisation has proved to be a dominant force in shaping the attitudinal reactions in one society after another."[20] From this, Naqvi derives his thesis that "In the strict Weberian sense, economic behaviour in an Islamic society will transform into effective action only in so far as it is immediately dictated by the ethical norms that Muslim's subscribe to."[21] In the light of this, Naqvi argues that Islam rejects both socialism and capitalism, the latter because "According to Max Weber, the Protestant 'ascetic ethics' not only condoned but glorified a kind of callousness towards society in the name of unlimited accumulation."[22] In fact, for Naqvi "the Weberian equation between Islamic ethical beliefs and economic behaviour must be 'satisfied' before the Islamisation attempts can fructify."[23] Naqvi then ascribes a very central place to what Turner would regard as a simplistic form of the "Weber thesis" and sees the resolution of the problems thrown up by Weber as the first stage in linking an ethical (religious) system to any socio-economic system.

Naqvi thus sees Weber in a very positive light: indeed as posing the central question. S.H. Alatas, in his analysis of the Weber thesis in Southeast Asia, sees the problem somewhat differently.[24] Alatas quite rightly perceives that the "Weber thesis" (which, however, Alatas considers to be clear and well defined) must be distinguished from Weber's general sociology of religion. Alatas goes on to discuss the Calvinist notion of the "calling" and to argue that Weber was attempting a causal explanation of capitalism and then briefly surveys some of the authors who have used the Weber thesis or variants of it, in explaining the relationship between Southeast Asian religions and socio-economic development. Alatas finds that in Islam all the characteristics of the Protestant Ethic, including the calling, are present.

---

[20] Ibid., p. 41.

[21] Ibid., p. 44.

[22] Ibid., p. 75.

[23] Ibid., p. 164.

[24] "The Weber Thesis and Southeast Asia," *Archives de Sociologie des Religions* No. 15, 1963. Reproduced in S.H. Alatas (1972), *Modernization and Social Change*, Sydney: Augus and Robertson, pp. 1-20.

But although Alatas finds the capitalist spirit present amongst the early Muslim traders, he cannot find much of it amongst the Malays of present-day Malaysia. Hence, he argues, since both are of the same religion, it cannot be Islam that is at the root, especially as the Chinese have it too! We are then lamely told that we must look at the cultural and historical factors differentiating these communities and so told that the Weber thesis finds little support from the Southeast Asian evidence. In another paper, Alatas similarly comes to the conclusion that religion and modernisation are independent of one another.[25] Again then the result is that although nothing doctrinal can be found in Islam itself to retard capitalistic development (would it be a bad thing of it did?) the question is left open as to why industrial capitalism was imported from the West and why the local mercantile capitalism did not develop. The fact that Weber himself did not leave the question there—at the "preconditions" seems somehow to continue to escape both his critics and those who would use him to advance their own version of the "Weber thesis".[26]

Let us now attempt to draw some of the elements in this debate together. There can really be no conclusion—no doubt the arguments over what Weber really meant to say, and the validity of his ideas will continue to rage on. But by pinning the issues down to a specific case study some light can be shed on both Weber and the study of Islam in its Southeast Asian manifestations. Firstly, there is both more and less to Weber than many people think. More in the sense that in addition to the "Weber thesis", Weber's thought also focused on patterns of political domination and succession, of legitimation, of the role of the law and on the critique of capitalism as well as the analysis of the preconditions for its emergence. To "apply" Weber to the study of Islam, his work needs to be seen in these broader dimensions, otherwise perpetual entrapment in the toils of the "Weber thesis" will be the result. Less in the sense that Weber was confused and confusing, did not stick consistently to his own methodological principles and was very much a child of his times: his general characterisation of

---

25 "Religion and Modernization in Southeast Asia," *Archives Europeenes de Sociologie* 11, 1970. Also reproduced in ibid., pp. 21-52.

26 For example, George G.C. Mah (1975), "Islam and the Protestant Ethic," *Review of Southeast Asian Studies* vol. 5, nos. 1-4.

Asian civilisations is not significantly different from the very dated views of his chief rival, Marx. But the real significance of Weber perhaps lies precisely in this dialectic between what he said and didn't say where his ideas work in practice and where they don't.

Weber clearly defined the preconditions for the emergence of the modern capitalist world order and in doing so indicated that early Islam contained the seeds of capitalism as much as the European middle ages did. Others who have also studied Islam in this respect have also come to the conclusion that what was significant was not ideological restraints within Islam, but the political and social conditions of patrimonial domination and feudalism, which were overthrown early in Europe, but were never fully overthrown in the Middle East. Where further work needs to be done then is not on Islamic ideology, but in the area of political economy—What, for example, has kept Malay peasants in a state of underdevelopment? Why have Arab and Indian Muslims developed very successful trade networks and business in Southeast Asia, whereas the indigenous Muslim peoples have been less entrepreneurical? Can one speak of a Muslim middle class in modern Singapore? What is the role of the significant Muslim community in Bangkok? and so on. Both structural analysis and detailed ethnography are necessary to answer such questions. Issues which Weber did not concern himself with at all—ethnicity, secularisation, religious revival, colonialism, would need to be introduced into the discussion here in a very central way. What a close reading of Weber certainly does show is that Weber's own analysis tended towards a politico-economic rather than ideational form and that one finds scant support in what Weber actually said, for the common thesis that Malays in Malaysia are economically retarded because of religious factors. Not only is the hunt for varieties of the Protestant Ethic all over Asia fruitless, but in Weberian terms rather pointless: if actors define meaning for themselves, there are numerous ways in which action and ideas can be related to one another, depending on the actors themselves, the religion, the social or political situation, the historical epoch, the purposes and motives of the action and so on.

Weber's methodology then is certainly of tremendous value in the understanding of religion and social organisation, since what it points to is a way of bringing together the structural, processural and subjective levels into a single intelligible whole.

Weber's worth also suggests a research agenda for the study of Southeast Asian Islam: what were the sociological conditions for the historical spread of Islam to Southeast Asia? How and why did it succeed in replacing the established Hindu and animist tradition? Why did Islam not penetrate north into the "Buddhist zone"? What was the nature of feudalism in Southeast Asia? Are Weber's views of the patrimonial nature of Middle Eastern Islam applicable to Southeast Asia? How, and why did capitalism appear in Southeast Asia? What were the relationship between colonial and indigenous capital? What was the nature of early Southeast Asian cities? Of the indigenous State? Partial answers exist for many of these questions, but as yet no real synthesis. Weber's own approach to the comparative study of civilisations shows how this might be done.

To summarise then: Weber had very little to say directly about Islam compared with his other preoccupations and he had nothing to say about Southeast Asia. But as Turner has convincingly shown a great deal of insight can be gained into Islamic civilisation from a Weberian point of view, provided that one goes beyond the "Weber thesis" into the areas of method, of charisma and legitimation, of patrimonialism and feudal social organisation, of law, of rationalisation. This helps to put the whole Protestant ethic question back into its proper perspective—as a localised and historically specific thesis never intended to have universal application. When one turns to the question of Southeast Asian Islam one finds that whereas Weber never did discuss its specific historical or sociological characteristics, his broader approach to the theory of civilisations has considerable validity. In particular perhaps his view of modern civilisation with its provisionality, meaninglessness, pluralism and bureaucratisation defines a model not to be followed and which much of the religious revivalism in Southeast Asia is dedicated to opposing.

Indeed MacRae suggests that the central theme of Weber's thought is that of "the rationalising, secularisation and demythologizing of the human world".[27] If this be so we are faced with an interesting paradox: historically Islam in Southeast Asia was precisely this form of rationalisation in relation to the political and religious systems prevailing before it; but after the advent of colonial capitalism Islam has become (amongst other

[27] Donald MacRae (1979), *Weber*, London: Fontema, p. 29.

things) a major force opposing the desacralising of the world. But as MacRae also points out, Weber was also the key sociologist (excepting Marx, who MacRae doesn't consider to be a sociologist) of the economic order and, his conception of the social sciences was as historical sciences, so Weber could not doubt have dealt with this. A deeper paradox perhaps lies in Weber's own concept of Islam. It is, in his terms, a salvation religion, but yet it has most of the characteristics of the "adoptive religions",[28] such as Confucianism. It may be that Weber's categories were too rigid, but it may also be that Islam itself does not fit well into any of these predetermined modes. Certainly in Southeast Asia it runs across the whole spectrum from orthodox rigidity via Sufi spontaneity to Japanese mysticism. One major point in the analysis should thus be the understanding of these internal variations within what to the outsider may appear a single homogeneous religion.

Above all, what we are essentially arguing here is that the attempt to examine the relevance of Weber for the study of Southeast Asia, tells us more about Weber than it does about that region. In particular it points up the need to bring together his sociology of religion and his political sociology into a single whole. We have seen something of the areas in which Weber is both strong and weak in relation to the analysis of Southeast Asian Islam. Weber's guiding themes—rationalisation, legitimacy, the effects of ideas on economics, the relationship between religious ideas and social stratification and the unique and distinguishing characteristics of the West—set certain parameters to his thought. But implicit in Weber's whole approach is the comparative one, and here perhaps it has its greatest value, especially for the analysis of Asian societies, their unique characteristics and their relationships to the West. Inherent in Weberian sociology is the beginning of the attempt to develop genuinely comparative sociological categories. While Weber directly is of little help in understanding Southeast Asian Islam (he did not discuss the topic) the implications for the analysis of Islam in general, for the socio-political and legal structures of Southeast Asian societies, for the impact of capitalism, for the state, for the nature of traditional domination are enormous, and herein lies Weber's value for the Asian scholar, especially since in defining themselves in rela-

[28] MacRae, ibid., pp. 81-82.

tion to Weber, as we have to some extent seen, many such scholars have been led to a clearer understanding of their own societies and of the role of sociological analysis in understanding them.

Chapter 8

URBANISATION AND SUSTAINABLE DEVELOPMENT IN CONTEMPORARY SOUTHEAST ASIA

At some unknown moment in the mid-1970s the world passed a major turning point in its social, economic and demographic history for there were for the first time more people living in the urban settlements than in rural ones. This trend continues to accelerate with the result that the social landscape of the world is ceasing to be the familiar one of countryside with occasional cities, and is becoming cities with occasional countryside. The trend towards the urbanisation of the world's population is not simply a matter of the concentration of that population: it has consequences which are sociological, ecological and economic; it affects stress levels and the psychological profiles of whole masses of peoples, and it creates the necessity of managing huge urban centres.

In this chapter I will review some of the major problems of over-urbanisation internationally and will attempt to relate these problems to current debates on ecologically sustainable development. I will also suggest some topics for debate in relation to defining alternative ways of solving some of the major problems of over-urbanisation. This in turn may suggest some fresh agendas for the sociology of cities, especially in developing countries.

It should be pointed out at the beginning that urbanisation in itself is not a problem. Human beings have lived in cities for a very long time and there is plenty of experience of urban lifestyles to draw on, and indeed cities have long been seen as the focal points of cultural development in their respective societies: places of artistic production, trade and political sophistication (Fox 1977). Urbanisation becomes a problem only when cities become too big to be socially manageable and when such large cities distort the development of the surrounding countryside or even the whole society itself, by drawing to themselves resources that are needed for more balanced growth nationwide.

Why Does Urbanisation Become a Problem

Urbanisation only becomes a problem when certain conditions are met, and even then may still have many very positive features, including creating a cultural mass in which creativity can flourish, concentration of educational, economic and political resources, wide ranges of choice and variety, etc. But typically urban problems can be grouped into at least fourteen major categories, each of which I will discuss briefly below.

1. The extent, speed and intensity of world urbanisation.
2. Primate cities and their effects.
3. Rural depopulation and effects on hinterlands.
4. Poverty and labour issues, including problems of women and children.
5. Urban lifestyles and economy.
6. Physical infrastructure, e.g. roads, schools, health, water, power and sewage.
7. Housing.
8. Pollution.
9. Land use and values.
10. Crime.
11. Stress and psychological problems.
12. Ethnic conflict.
13. Inequality and class issues.
14. Social patterns and family instability.

The Extent and Spread of World Urbanisation

When urbanisation is contained and when it exists in a balance with the countryside such that over-concentration of population in cities does not occur, adequate supplies of fresh food and drinking water are assured and over-centralisation of functions (administrative, educational, etc.) in the cities is avoided, it clearly has many very positive features. But the major problem of late 20th-century society has been the destruction of this historical balance for a number of reasons: population growth, industrialisation and the concentration of political and commercial functions being amongst the main ones. The observable result has been the explosive growth of cities of a large size, bringing with it all of the characteristic problems of massive population groupings: housing shortages, strain on transportation, etc. The general pattern can be seen in the figures below:

1. *Growth of large cities, 1950-2000*
   Cities with more than 10 million inhabitants:
   1950: 2, i.e. London and New York.
   1975: 7, i.e. London, New York, Los Angeles, Tokyo, Sao Paulo, Shanghai and Mexico City.
   2000: 25, i.e. all of the above, plus Osaka-Kobe, Baghdad, Istanbul, Tehran, New Delhi, Bogota, Karachi, Bangkok, Buenos Aires, Manila, Madras, Cairo, Seoul, Jakarta, Calcutta, Bombay, Rio de Janeiro and Beijing.
   By 2000, the population of Mexico City is expected to reach 31 million, Sao Paulo 26 million, Shanghai 23 million, Beijing 21 million, Bombay 20 million, Calcutta 18 million, Jakarta 18 million, Cairo 13 million and Madras 12 million.
2. *Projected concentration of urban population, 1960-2000*
   By 2000, there will be as many people living in cities of 100,000 people or over to constitute the following pattern:

Table 8.1

Population of Urban Areas	1960	1975	2000	1960	1975	2000
	Millions			Percentage		
1,000,000 plus	285	496	1,285	9.6	13.0	20.5
500,000-1 million	88	181	465	3.0	4.7	7.4
Total Urban	1,003	1,615	3,416	33.9	42.2	54.5
Total Rural	1,959	2,213	2,851	66.1	57.8	45.5

These figures which represent growth of only the very largest cities should be seen in the context of general population growth in "Third World" countries, much of which will, given the structural factors which have promoted the growth of cities, translate into urban population. The following figures are for Asia, but a similar pattern can be seen in Latin America and Africa.

3. *Estimated population growth for selected countries, 1985-1991*

Table 8.2

Country	Growth
Bangladesh	2.65%
Philippines	2.5%
Malaysia	1.9%
Vietnam	2.3%
Indonesia	1.6%
Thailand	1.5%
China	1.4%

Asia's urban population:

Table 8.3

Year	Population
1991	1 billion
2000	1.5 billion
2010	1.8 billion

Source: *UN Prospects of World Urbanisation.*

Growth and concentration of population is a major source of other typical problems which are briefly delineated below.

Primate Cities and their Effects

"Primate city" describes the phenomenon whereby within an individual country, a single city comes to dominate all other urban settlements in terms of size, functions and wealth, and also of problems: pollution, urban poverty and infrastructural problems. A good example of a primate city is Bangkok, now between four and five times the size of its nearest rival, Chiang Mai, and with almost all central government agencies, major businesses, leading educational institutions, sources of artistic and literary production, port facilities and the major airport found in this city. Many other countries which do not have a primate city in the strict sense, do nevertheless experience a similar over-centralisation of functions in a single city (Tokyo, Jakarta, Dhaka, Colombo, for example) often leading to the suggestion that governmental agencies be moved, which occasionally they are (Brasilia being a major example). Primate cities or indeed cities that gather large numbers of functions to themselves create certain characteristic effects: constantly rising population as people are attracted to jobs, real or imagined economic opportunities, educational facilities and the sheer energy and range of possibilities generated by such large urban centres. Rural dwellers are often attracted to such cities where they exchange productive labour in the countryside (with its lack of entertainment, education or health care facilities) for what are often marginalised and uncertain existences in large cities (where in reality access to the supposed benefits of urban life may not be possible due to poverty or other factors).

Rural Depopulation and Effects on Hinterlands

City growth is partly because of natural increase in urban population, but in many cities it is because of in-migration, either directly from the countryside or by way of smaller towns which act as way-stations and in a sense as training grounds for life in really large urban centres. An obvious result of this is the depletion of the rural population and often the relative decline in resources devoted to developing rural life, with the spiraling result that even more rural dwellers are drawn from the decreasingly attractive countryside to the increasingly attractive cities. One of the emerging problems in development studies is the effect of this population movement on long-term sustainable development. Decline of the rural sector means potential problems in the maintaining of adequate food supplies, major changes in the social structure of the entire society, shifts in values and steadily declining ability to draw on the rural sector as a resource (for example of traditional medical practices). The conversion of the countryside into agri-business plantations and to a recreational area for (wealthy) city-dwellers raises serious questions about development alternatives and the relationship of culture to development.

Poverty and Labour Issues

In all developing countries poverty is still a problem very much associated with the countryside, where low incomes, difficulties in raising agricultural productivity, debt-bondage, land-tenure issues and other impediments all conspire towards maintaining very low standards of living for the average farmer and his family. Movement to the city is often seen as a solution to the seemingly eternal round of debt and hard labour associated with rural life. But in reality, as a flood of studies have shown, the move to urban living often does little except exchange one form of poverty for another. Life on the land tends to guarantee (unless catastrophic factors such as rain failure or war intervene) at least a secure minimum standard of living. Free-lance living in the city offers no such guarantees: rather it intensifies risks, poses problems of finding housing and forces the job-seekers to enter a market in which he may be ill-qualified for the formal sector (through lack of education or experience) even if openings exist, and in which the informal sector may already be over-crowded with intense competition in such fields as hawking, driving a pedicab, rag-picking and so forth. Even the criminal informal sector may prove to be already over-crowded (on the concept of the informal sector see Bromley 1979; Rimmer et al 1978).

The economics of poverty may be different in the countryside and the city, but its frequency and intensity are not necessarily any less in the urban setting. Strategies to overcome it are many and varied and much of the literature on rural-urban migration is directly or indirectly concerned with this (e.g. Bromley 1979) and the problem of urban poverty has spawned a large body of theoretical literature (e.g. Thorbet 1987; Gilbert and Gugler 1982). With the slow-down in the economies of the western industrialised countries and Eastern Europe, the questions of urban poverty, homelessness and burgeoning of the informal sector have once again become live issues in the first and second world cities as well as third world ones. Urban poverty also has the quality of greatly changing social relations and relations of production. In the countryside women generally work at farm tasks, and so frequently do children. In cities such structured and seasonal labour is not available and a whole range of often insecure alternatives have to be drawn on—domestic labour, hawking, sewing, prostitution, factory or workshop labour for example, for both women and children. Often no skills are learnt, wage levels are low, there may be little or no health or accident insurance and no immunisation or other protection against abuses (Stanford 1988). Another facet of the urban labour problem is that of foreign migrant labour. Almost any major Asian city now contains large numbers of foreign workers who may be there legally (e.g. maids and construction and industrial workers in Singapore) or illegally (e.g. the large numbers of Iranians and East and Southeast Asians who work illegally in Tokyo and other Japanese cities). Many of these workers also face problems of abuse (inadequate labour laws, human-rights violations, inadequate access to health care, education or other social facilities) and also often poverty.

Urban Lifestyles and Economy

It would be a mistake to view cities only from their underside as it were. Asian cities are not only the site of poverty, they are also the breeding ground of a phenomenon that is beginning to attract a lot of attention: a new middle class. Representatives of this group have become conspicuous in every major Asian city both because of their high social profile as indigenous managers and professionals and because of their consumption habits that are changing the physical faces of the cities in which they live. For example, housing patterns are greatly shaped by the proliferation of condominiums and detached residential dwellings. In many cities such middle-class enclaves have to be "protected" against the poor urban masses without their secured boundaries (many such settlements can be found in Manila for example) and zoning for such residential areas excludes poorer urban dwellers from such areas. This displacement effect can have serious consequences such as in Brasilia where many of the poorer people who actually work in the city are forced to live in shanty settlements on the periphery of the town from where they are forced to take long commutes by bus each day. The urban ecology of cities is a fascinating exercise in social geography since it at once becomes apparent that in many towns the relationship of residential to working areas is very peculiar, forcing huge numbers of people to travel into or out of the city daily to work on often very inadequate transportation systems. Some cities have left basically market forces to determine their ecology (many Indonesian cities for example with their elegant streets of Dutch era bungalows fronting the streets but behind which huddle very densely populated self-planned "urban villages"). Others have gone in for exactly the opposite: well-planned cityscapes with widely available public housing and minimal spontaneous housing activity (as in Singapore of course and to a substantial but lesser extent Hong Kong).

Consumption patterns themselves play a major part in determining this ecology. The proliferation of up-market shopping malls in Bangkok for example is not due to tourism, but to rising incomes and internationalisation of taste on the part of the Thai middle-class. And the existence of markets in all Asian cities and their location and types of products marketed is a major clue to patterns of consumption, the working of the local economy, spatial patterns in the city and lifestyles. Lifestyles interact and their totality makes up the total social structure of the city. And it is often at the point of interaction of different lifestyles that conflict takes place, adding another dimension to the dynamism of city life.

Table 8.4

Percentage of urban population with access to safe drinking water (defined as water in dwelling or within 200 metres from a piped source) and sanitation (defined as a connection to public sewerage or septic tank)

Country	Safe Water	Sanitation
	%	
India	74	74
Philippines	70	35
Thailand	55	80
Indonesia	40	32
Bangladesh	25	20

Note: These are approximate figures. Source: *WHO estimates.*

Physical Infrastructure

Rising population places major strain on physical infrastructure: housing (which will be dealt with separately); transportation; educational, health and other social facilities; supplies of clean water and power (gas or electricity) and disposal of garbage and sewage. In many cities these basic physical facilities are sadly lacking. Access to "clean" water (which is however not necessarily potable, defined as availability of a tap within 200 metres) is frequently inadequate as the figures in Table 8.4 show.

Similar figures could be reproduced for other infrastructural facilities and any acquaintance with most large Asian cities proves that public transportation and often the road systems themselves are not capable of handling the volume of traffic created by the circulation of people. The result is massive traffic jams, very slow average speeds and serious over-crowding on public transport. Even in a city as sophisticated as Tokyo passenger volumes of over 200 per cent of intended capacity are regularly recorded at rush hour on trains and subways. An often deteriorating physical infrastructure accompanies the unplanned and rapid growth in urban populations.

Housing

Housing is obviously a primary element in the physical infrastructure of cities. Yet it too is often amongst the least well provided facilities despite the absolutely basic nature of the need for shelter. Again a range of solutions have been tried: massive public housing schemes as in Singapore and Hong Kong, modest public housing combined with private sector schemes (Malaysia, Japan, increasingly Thailand, India and Indonesia), and very much "self-help" schemes, i.e. slums or shanty-towns, found in most large and many small Asian cities. The provision of shelters and with it other necessary infrastructure is one of the major challenges facing urban planners in cities of developing countries. (RIHED 1982; Murison and Townsend 1979).

Table 8.5

Average number of days per year when 1 cubic metre of air contain particulate matter exceeding 230 micrograms and sulphur dioxide exceeding 150 micrograms.		
City	Particulates	Sulphur Dioxide
Beijing	270	64
Calcutta	264	22
Jakarta	166	-
Bangkok	100	-
Manila	18	30
Note: WHO guideline is 6/6.		

Pollution

Over-population, heavy traffic congestion, cooking, cottage industries and lack of adequate garbage and sewerage disposal create pollution. Breathability of air declines, risks of disease from accumulated rubbish increase and visual and noise pollution become major problems. Table 8.5 indicates some typical situations.

Land Use and Values

Land use is affected in major ways by urbanisation: urban gardens and farms become converted into industrial or residential use; land prices rise; housing typically becomes unaffordable for the poor and even for the middle class; zoning changes the entire ecology of the city (a point discussed above); land values rise along actual or anticipated mass transport routes, paradoxically making it harder for the poor to live near means of public transportation that can move them relatively cheaply to their places of work. Green spaces and recreational areas tend to shrink or to become degraded. The relationship of land use, land values, availability of housing, access to transportation and existence of urban recreational land is an important and neglected area of urban ecology.

Crime

Crime tends to be higher in cities partly simply because there are more people and more opportunities. But these are not the only factors; relative deprivation, unemployment, ethnic rivalries, availability of drugs and firearms and spatial factors (for example, the physical layout of housing estates and streets) all contribute to high incidence of crime in urban areas. In many parts of the world, urban crime is so high that the livability of particular cities or areas within a city is measured principally by the safety factor. Protection against crime, avoidance of certain routes, areas or modes of transportation, become major factors in the structure of everyday life. The whole experience of city living is of course transformed by high crime levels, the excitement and vitality of the city become converted into fear and protective strategies. Commonly Asian cities have major inequalities of wealth, and this visible relative deprivation is itself an encouragement to crime, especially in situations where policing is inadequate or the police themselves are corrupt.

Stress and Psychological Problems

Stress, constant fear, worry and the adopting of protective strategies are some of the consequences of urban crime. But crime is far from being the only source of stress, and an overlooked aspect of urban living in large cities is that it is stressful. Crowding, competition for places in public transport, noise, pollution, economic uncertainties, difficulties over housing, fear of getting lost, are all typical sources of urban stress, which often translates into psychological problems which may go unnoticed as such and if noticed will probably not be diagnosed or treated, especially among the poor.

Ethnic Conflict

A disturbing feature of the modern world in general has been the resurgence of ethnic conflict. The cities have not only not escaped this trend but in many cases have been at the forefront (witness, for example, recent ethnic conflict in Karachi, ethnic or religious violence in Bombay, Calcutta and other Indian cities and the continuing ethnic violence in Colombo and other Sri Lankan towns). The close proximity of members of different ethnic groups (which may have a tradition of rivalry) thrown together by rural-urban migration and often competing for jobs, housing and access to education and other resources tends regrettably to fuel conflict rather than co-operation, although members of the same ethnic group may and do form networks of self-help and mutual assistance (Cohen 1974).

Inequality and Class Issues

The Asian countryside is of course notoriously socially unequal: semi-feudal relations of caste, landlordism and the like often predominate. Such inequalities are often reproduced rather than eliminated in the cities and new inequalities are frequently created. These inequalities may be differences of ethnic status or they may be of class or gender. The gross inequalities of wealth and lifestyle characteristic of cities adds a further dimension. So while the countryside remains unequal, new forms and concentrations of inequality appear in the city where the genesis of new varieties of stratification can actually be seen in progress.

Social Patterns and Family Instability

City life changes social patterns, not only in the generation of new forms of inequality, but in the creation of fresh patterns of gender relationships, parent-child relationships, general generational relationships and new relationships between families and between co-ethnics or co-religionists. One major impact of urbanism that is now documented very well is the creation of family instability, especially amongst low-income and slum-dwelling families. The relationship between urbanism and social change of this kind is an important theme for further research, since the stability of basic social units has a major impact on the social organisation of the city in general.

Traditional Sociological Issues in the Analysis of the Cities and their Limitations and Alternatives

The Dominant Approach

A glance at most major textbooks on the sociology and social geography of contemporary Third World cities (e.g. Drakakis-Smith 1987) reveals that four large issues tend to predominate: migration and its effects; the "informal sector" and its many ramifications; cities and the state and the new international division of labour and the impact of "structural adjustment" policies of such agencies as the World Bank, International Monetary Fund or the Asian Development Bank. These four issues and a constellation of derivative ones (ethnic stratification for example) have come to dominate the field. These are all legitimate issues and they all provide a major part of the context within which the problems discussed above are situated. But at the same time they tend to draw attention away from the key issues of solutions to typical urban problems and the maintaining of sustainable development of which cities have to be a part given the structure of contemporary world societies.

The Wholistic Alternative

These key issues are not only sociological: a wholistic approach is necessary which sees the social, economic, ecological and spatial aspects in relation to one another. The factors to be considered here would include:

1. *Physical and Social Infrastructure.* The provision of physical infrastructure, difficult though it may be in practice, is well understood by urban planners, although imaginative solutions are not always considered. For example, much of the movement of people that takes place daily in large cities would be unnecessary if

jobs and residences were close to each other, even when travel is necessary, staggered working hours would relieve much of the pressure on existing transportation systems. Much unnecessary movement which is expensive, tiring, polluting and creates overcrowding on transport systems which may be half-empty for the rest of the day can be eliminated by more rational zoning. Restricting private transport which clogs roads, creates pollution and often only carries a single passenger per vehicle has also already been attempted in innovative traffic control schemes such as that pioneered in Singapore. Jobs, however, while often stressed by economists, are not the only facilities to which relatively easy access is highly desirable. Schools, markets, hospitals, parks and other places of social interaction are equally important in terms of both availability and access.

It is at this point that physical and social infrastructure intersect: the physical, while it may not determine, certainly profoundly influences, the possibilities of social interaction. And it might well be claimed that social infrastructure should take priority and that it is the job of the physical infrastructure to promote and not to retard meaningful social interaction, access to facilities and the widening of co-operative possibilities. Sustainability does not mean simply economic survival at minimal ecological standards, but rather the expansion of life opportunities, and these of necessity are social.

2. *Transportation and Traffic.* An example of this is transportation. The rapid movement of people is usually seen as a purely logistical problem. In fact it is deeply social: for the traveller the day is structured around the need to be transported: when to travel? by what route? will it be possible to get a seat? is it safe? who will I meet? The economical solution to transport needs is not just a matter of economics. For a city to be tolerable and really inhabitable, access, movement and even escape from the city must be answered. Social patterns—friendships, visiting, shopping, baby-sitting and so forth—are highly dependent on safe, cheap and reliable movement. The social and technological aspects of planning invariably intersect when genuinely sustainable development is involved.

3. *Secondary Cities: Their Role and Development.* An obvious solution to the problem of over-concentration of functions and population in a single city is to decentralise those functions. This can be done by a variety of means: dispersal of governmental agencies, incentives to business and industry to locate or relocate in less crowded and generally less expensive places, development of specialised activities in secondary cities and the creation of attractive living conditions (housing, ease of transport, shopping, etc.) in smaller towns. A variety of schemes have indeed been tried to achieve this. One is the creation of satellite towns away from the main business and administrative districts (e.g. Woodlands New Town in Singapore or Shatin in Hong Kong), each with its own markets, shops, entertainment facilities, and factories and other sources of employment. Another is the development of attractive and self-contained secondary cities at considerable geographical remove from the capital. An example of this is Malaysia, where major secondary cities such as Penang, Ipoh and Johor Baru have become in many ways more attractive living environments than the capital, Kuala Lumpur. Significantly most internal migration in Malaysia is between smaller cities and not from the countryside into the capital.

   Development of secondary cities then allows a large proportion of the population to enjoy the benefits of urban life while simultaneously maintaining the spatial distribution of that population and avoiding the characteristic problems of over-concentration that we discussed earlier. Such decentralisation has also proved to have a range of secondary benefits, not for the cities but for the countryside. These include the slowing or reversing of rural depopulation, the redistribution of jobs, industry and skills to the countryside and the encouragement of agriculture as a way of life and indeed as a profitable service needed by the burgeoning population of the cities. Some countries have formal policies for encouraging big-city dwellers to move to the countryside or to small rural towns and encouraging such small towns to attempt to identify their strengths and to build actively on them (in Japan for example where small rural towns have stopped population outflow by developing themselves as hot spring resorts and centres of organic farming).

Ultimately the sustainability of any society depends on its rural sector: people must eat, there must be adequate supplies of clean air and water and there must be space for recreation. The development of the countryside, usually left out of discussions of urbanisation, actually goes hand-in-hand with the growth of cities. In practice, the two sectors need each other and any really sustainable development must recognise the symbiosis between the two.

4. *Housing and Employment.* Housing and employment are both necessities if sustainable development in and of cities is to take place. Innovative schemes for the provision of low-cost housing exist on the drawing board in almost every university department of architecture, but very few are tried in practice, because of lack of political will, lack of imagination in city planning offices, vested interest amongst contractors and property developers and an unwillingness to trust people to create their own satisfactory housing if given the land and basic resources. Such alternative schemes need both publicity and trying out in practice, since they are often cheap, provide high density housing that also promotes community and avoid the problems of the massive, often high-rise housing developments typically favoured by many governments.

If housing is one basic need, employment is clearly another. The informal sector meets many of these needs in the typical city in a developing country. While some jobs are available in the formal sector, a huge range of services and activities are provided through the informal sector (Rimmer et al 1978). But the existence of a large informal sector poses its own problems: lack of taxability, tendency to degenerate into crime, etc. As with housing, clearly imaginative solutions are needed to create work that is productive and meaningful, and this would include work on developing the urban infrastructure itself, opportunities for migration back to the countryside and adequate educational and training facilities so that migrants themselves and certainly their children can prepare for new forms of employment and higher skilled and more productive forms of labour.

5. *Energy, Waste Disposal and Other Issues.* Our list could be extended indefinitely, but simply to illustrate the range of possibilities, two other related areas are energy and waste disposal. Though seemingly opposites they are actually closely linked. Energy—for cooking, lighting and economic activities—is again a basic need. So is the disposal of waste, domestic and industrial. There exist innovative schemes for converting waste into energy (by burning to produce electricity, by producing gas from biomass or compost and fertilisers from domestic waste for example) and recycling systems are not only now becoming fashionable, but have been in use for generations in any Third World city where almost all "waste" is converted into something useful. The problem with many waste into energy schemes is that they are too small, do not receive financial or research backing and are left largely to individual initiative. Vast resources of energy are actually available and still more energy can be saved by the use of efficient electrical and other appliances. Cities are enormously energy intensive and sustainable development requires that energy be reduced and alternative forms of energy production be found (they already exist in fact) that as far as possible recycle energy rather than deplete non-replaceable sources of fuels and use that energy in efficient and non-polluting ways.

   Recycling, fuel efficiency, conversion of waste into power, rationally designed traffic flow systems and mass transit schemes, reduction of consumption, improved industrial practices, zoning, pollution control technology, tax and other legal constraints on inefficiency and over-consumption are all appropriate measures. There have been success stories: London's air is now very much cleaner than it was when coal was allowed to be used as the main domestic heating fuel, and Tokyo's air has improved mainly because of pollution technology, use by industry conversion of cars and taxis to non-leaded petrols and natural gas and the provision of an efficient mass transit system of electric trains and subways.

Sustainability and the Urban Future

We are clearly living in a world of cities. The issue then is not to do away with cities as in some utopian scenarios, but to make cities livable environments in which human beings can flourish rather then be crushed and to establish a balance between the countryside and the city such that each sustains the other, rather than allowing uncontrolled urbanisation to distort the whole pattern of development in a given country.

Some of the ways in which this might be done have already been suggested: development of secondary cities, creation of rural industries, imaginative urban housing projects, meaningful employment opportunities in towns, long-term planning of education for future employment needs (and for its effects on the demographic transition) and so forth.

Habitable cities do indeed exist, and they should provide models for what is possible and what less habitable cities can do to achieve greater levels of satisfaction for their inhabitants. But the discussion of sustainability also raises some much bigger questions. Amongst these are the following:

1. Are there upper limits to urbanisation? As some cities begin to not only exceed 10 million inhabitants, but to move beyond the 20 million mark, this becomes a real question—both of technological management (water, waste, transport, etc.) and of human scale (stress, social networks, access to employment, etc.). The answer would seem to be that while the technological limits constantly expand, management becomes increasingly difficult to the point where complexity and problems simply outweigh any advantages of sheer size. In human terms the limits may be reached sooner despite the amazing adaptability of people; cities ultimately become both physically and psychologically unhealthy places to live.
2. This poses the question of alternatives. We have suggested some: development of the countryside and smaller towns and decentralisation of functions for example. Other solutions have been found less viable: the outright banning of new migrants to major cities unless they have housing and employment (a solution tried in Jakarta which is technically a "closed" city, but which has not worked because policing is inadequate). City life will always attract people, and so far the best alternative appears to be not the (impossible anyway) abandoning of urbanism as a way of life but the creation of smaller, more livable cities that have a more or-

ganic relationship to their rural hinterland. Given contemporary electronic communications and rail, road and air networks, physical distance from major centres no longer mean isolation.

3. Typically, solutions to urban problems tend to come from planners, who often create even more serious problems than they solve. This raises what are basically political questions. Should central planning or self-help be encouraged? Is it the role of urban politicians not to govern but to empower social groups in their precincts to determine for themselves what kind of urban environment they want? Towards this end should urban social movements be encouraged as being the most effective mechanism through which people can alter their own situation? (Castells 1983; Lowe 1986). On the whole, planning and certainly the over-planning experienced by many urban dwellers has not delivered the promised goods. Total self-help is as likely to produce its own problems. The solution once again would seem to lie in achieving a balance between the need for some kind of central control of functions (e.g. of transportation) shared by all, and autonomy or at least influence on the part of those who live in cities over their own environments (Yeung and McGree 1986).

Achieving a long-term balance between cities and the countryside is likely to be a major part of all and any sustainable solutions. An important aspect of this lies in the decentralisation of industry. Industrialisation, like urbanisation, is an irreversible force, but the level of technology now available does not require the concentration of industry in large urban centres, and successful examples of the establishment of large industrial combines away from cities or of the relocation of industries can be found. In Third World countries transfer of technology should bear this in mind: it is no longer necessary to transfer low level techniques. "Appropriate technology" in such a situation does not mean simple technology but rather socially appropriate technology that is useful, employment creating, non-polluting and does not need a large urban centre to sustain it (very few technologies do). This may be asking a lot in the climate of a basically market-led contemporary world economy, but it is entirely achievable, especially with rational planning and industrial or urban policies on the part of governments. Decentralisation of industry, provided it is accompanied by proper infrastructure, is one of the best ways to lead the dispersal of urban populations.

Some Alternative Scenarios

The sustainability of cities comes about as a result of their being ecologically responsible, economically viable and socially livable. A large body of experience and experiment already exists on how to achieve this sustainability although for the most part only small-scale attempts have been made to convert their wisdom into practice. Examples would be the promotion of food production within urban cities by urban dwellers, amongst many of whom malnutrition occurs more frequently than amongst rural people. Urban agriculture, which uses innovative but simple techniques, raises nutritional status, generates income, diffuses technology and provides employment alternatives and can be done in many cases using very little space (Urban Resource Systems 1986). The promotion of circular migration (the seasonal or cyclical movement of rural individuals into the city for specific activities after which the individuals return to rural employment or are replaced by different individuals) which maintains a flow of workers who do not settle permanently in the urban areas is one way of managing population in-flows. Creative usage of space, assistance with self-help housing, adaptive re-use of decaying but viable inner city housing and/or commercial and industrial properties, development of positive aspects of the informal sector, development of transportation networks, zoning to locate employment (of non-polluting types) and residences close together to avoid unnecessary commuting, sensible distribution of social infrastructure (e.g. hospitals and schools), credit assistance for local economic initiatives and an active concern with raising the quality of life for the poorest urban dwellers are all further examples.

This suggests the need not only for technical solutions but for social ones as well, necessary to make the city responsive to the actual needs of its inhabitants. It requires research into exactly what those needs actually are rather than what planners think they are. Use of internal and external space, utilisation of secondary routes than main thoroughfares, city image, coping mechanisms, etc., all vary with culture and often with social class. Blanket recommendations are accordingly not only impossible to make, but are likely to violate the right of city dwellers of all economic categories to determine their own environments in a democratic manner.

Alienation from the built environment is an increasingly serious problem. A cityscape that is pleasurable psychologically and visually is not just a luxury, but is an important part of satisfaction with urban living, and satisfaction promotes stress reduction and probably reduction in crime and other typical social problems as well. Creation of communities through a necessary mixture of sociological and architectural means becomes a major goal for city planners. Sustainability then ultimately means a rethinking of the complex interrelationships of economic, political, ecological, cultural, social and architectural factors in the make-up of urban settlements. Even history cannot be excluded here since many existing cities have evolved from older ones with their own physical layout and social and cultural patterns. Knowledge exists on all these questions (e.g. Lim 1990), but it requires integration at the intellectual level, active experiment at the practical level and trust in people to find sensible and humane solutions to their own problems at the ethical level (provided that the distortions of over-planning, external political consideration and the desires of developers are actively minimised).

The sustainability of urban settlements is a complex issue, some of the major dimensions of which have been sketched out in this chapter: the problems and their magnitude, the general conditions which they can be solved and some of the solutions which have been suggested. The question is an urgent one as cities rapidly become larger, less manageable, more damaging in their environmental impact and less habitable for those who choose or are forced to live in them. The human and ecological costs of not facing the issues are enormous. Furthermore, I have suggested that the sustainability of cities is a key element in any discussion of development in general, as cities not only become a dominating feature of the world scene, but as this domination creates new relationships between the rural and the urban. The need for imagination and analysis in the creation of solutions to what is increasingly becoming an urban crisis have never been greater.

References

Bromley, R. (1979), *The Urban Informal Sector*, London: Pergamon Press.
Castells, M. (1983), *The City and the Grassroots*, London: Edward Arnold.

Cohen, A. (ed.) (1974), *Urban Ethnicity*, London: Tavistock.

Drakakis-Smith, D. (1978), *The Third World City*, London: Methuen.

Fox, R. (1977), *Urban Anthropology: Cities in their Cultural Settings*, Englewood Cliffs: Prentice-Hall.

Gilbert, A. and J. Gugler (1982), *Cities, Poverty and Development*, Oxford: Oxford University Press.

Lowe, S. (1986), *Urban Social Movements*, London: Macmillan.

Jellinek, L. (1978), "Circular Migration and the Pondok Dwelling System: A Case Study of Ice-cream Traders in Jakarta," in P.J. Rimmer et al (eds.) *Food, Shelter and Transport in Southeast Asia and the Pacific*, Canberra: Australian National University, Research School of Pacific Studies, pp. 135-154.

Lim, William S.W. (1991), *Cities for People*, Singapore: Select Books.

Murison, H. and J. Townsend (1979), *Housing in Third World Countries*, Sydney: Macmillan.

RIHED (1982), *Housing as a Basic Need*, Singapore: Regional Institute for Higher Education and Development.

Rimmer, P.J., D.W. Drakakis-Smith and T.G. McGee (eds.) (1978), *Food, Shelter and Transport in Southeast Asia and the Pacific*, Canberra: Australian National University, Research School of Pacific Studies.

Stanford, P. (ed.) (1988), *Hidden Hands: Child Workers Around the World*, London: Collins.

Thorbeck, S. (1987), *Voices from the City: Women of Bangkok*, London: Zed Books.

Urban Resource System (1986), *City Food: Crop Selection in Third World Cities*, San Francisco: Urban Resource Systems, Inc.

Yeung, Y.M. and T.G. McGee (eds.) (1986), *Community Participation in Delivering Urban Services in Asia*, Ottawa: International Development Research Centre.

Chapter 9
ISLAM AND CAPITALISM IN SOUTHEAST ASIA

The attempt to systematically relate particular systems of religious belief to specific systems of political economy is not a new phenomenon either in the history of sociology[1] or in the comparative study of religions themselves. Equally in the case of the Muslim world in particular there is no shortage of attempts to relate the doctrinal content of Islam to the inhibition of "development" in general and capitalism in particular.[2] It is this area of debate that I wish to concentrate on in this chapter, but from three predefined points of view. The first is to examine the contribution of the distinguished French Islamicist Maxime Rodinson in his book *Islam and Capitalism*[3] as an attempted solution to the general question of "what is the relationship between Islam and the capitalist mode of production?"; the second is to relate our conclusions about Rodinson's argument to Southeast Asia, since his own contribution, like that of almost all other Islamicists, is posed in terms of the Middle East; the third is to try and derive from the foregoing some general conclusions not only about the role of Islam in the development process of the Muslim sectors of Southeast Asia, but about the role of religion, and of religious explanations, in the interpretation of modernisation or the inhibition of modernisation, as a general theoretical problem within sociology.

---

1 The classic instance being Max Weber's *The Protestant Ethic and the Spirit of Capitalism*, New York, 1958.

2 For example, Z.Y. Hershlag, *Introduction to the Economic History of the Middle East*, Leiden, 1964; C. Issawi (ed.) *The Economic History of the Middle East*, Chicago, 1966; A. Bonne, *The State and Economics in the Middle East*, London, 1955.

3 M. Rodinson, *Islam and Capitalism*, London, 1974.

Rodinson's *Islam and Capitalism*

Let us begin therefore with an examination of the thesis of Rodinson's (in many ways seminal) book. Rodinson's book is important for three reasons: firstly, because it attempts to come to terms with the problem of the socio-economic implications of Islam from the point of view of the political economist; secondly, because it addresses itself to the problem raised but not solved by Marx, notably that of characterising the nature and evolution of the modes of socio-economic organisation existing outside of Western Europe (examples of this being the "Asiatic Mode of Production", or the problem of accounting for capitalism in an area like the Middle East, where its nature and context (at least in the past) were radically different from the specific combination of socio-economic factors which Marx saw as being characteristic of western capitalism);[4] and, thirdly, because it fails to resolve satisfactorily the problems (especially the two just mentioned) to which it addresses itself. The reasons for this failure are revealing and will be discussed at some length.

A common characteristic of a great deal of writing on the Middle East is the assumption that the analysis should proceed on the lines of explaining why Islam has inhibited the development of capitalism in the Islamic world. Rodinson's position is slightly different, since it involves the claim that the influence of Islam on socio-economic development is minimal. Thus the relationship between religion and development in general is minimal. This conclusion is arrived at by a combination of two arguments: firstly, that there is nothing in the Quran or Sunnah which can be interpreted as inhibiting the growth of a capitalistic economy either in the past or present; and, secondly, that the forms of embryonic capitalism to be found in the medieval Muslim world were of the same type as those in the medieval European or Christian world, so that despite obvious differences in the subsequent socio-economic development of the two regions, Islam *itself* cannot be isolated as the factor responsible for the inhibition of capitalistic development or "modernisation" in either the past or present of the Muslim world.

---

[4] K. Marx, *Pre-Capitalist Economic Formations*, London, 1964. See also Centre d' Etudes et de Recherches Marxistes, *Sur Les Sociétés Précapitalistes*, preface de Maurice Godelier, Paris, 1970.

Two problems are raised by these arguments: the first is that of the legitimacy of regarding the Muslim world as a unity through space and time; the second is that of Rodinson's definition of capitalism. Since these two points underpin the rest of Rodinson's argument we can fruitfully look at them first before returning to his detailed assertions.

The first problem relates to the extent to which the loosely defined unit of study, notably "Islam", or "Islamic Civilisation" or "The Muslim World" can be regarded as an analytically useful device, given that the spatial range or institutionalised Islam is from the Atlantic coast of Africa to Indonesia and the Philippines, and where its temporal range spans twelve centuries. Within Rodinson's own book the assumption that there *is* such a unit of study is reflected in his willingness to draw examples that support his thesis from almost any period of history or from any geographical location, without any consideration of internal diversity, whether cultural, ethnic, doctrinal or historical, within this "Muslim World". It also allows him to implicitly argue that Islam *essentially* is that form which it takes in the Middle East, and especially in the medieval Middle East. (This argument is of even greater interest when it is remembered that it is being advanced not by a Middle Eastern Islamicist, but by a European one.) Robinson's assumption is clearly of significance for the study of Islam in Southeast Asia. (This point also should not be taken as suggesting that I am denying the perfectly obvious and historically valid point that in many respects Islam has been a major force in homogenising and unifying those cultures which it has influenced. My point is an analytically separate one.)

Rodinson's second general argument is that capitalism was common to both the Muslim and Christian sectors of the medieval world is again based on a further assumption, notably that capitalism itself is not to be found in just the Marxist definition—as a particular historical mode of production characterised by certain determinant relations of production, but is essentially any kind of entrepreneurial economic activity carried on a systematic basis. Again on the basis of this assumption it is possible to discover "capitalistic" activities as being normal practice throughout the Muslim world.

Both these assumptions relate in turn of course to Rodinson's general arguments that: first, Islam in itself cannot therefore be identified as having itself a specific economic role; second, that doctrinally Islam cannot be said to inhibit the growth of the spirit of capitalism; and, third, that as a matter of empirical fact the economic transactions of the Muslim world (and therefore also the social structures related to these economic transactions) were not and are not intrinsically different in kind from those of the Christian world. (The "Christian world" incidentally being another unit comparable with, contemporary with and geographically contiguous with the "Muslim world".) Something more therefore needs to be said about these general arguments before we begin to narrow the debate down to the implications of this for Southeast Asia specifically.

Rodinson breaks his theory up into three essential segments:

Firstly, the theory of the temporal and spatial homogeneity of Islam, which we have already briefly discussed. To this discussion it must however be added that quite what is meant by "Islam" is itself obscure, it being not clear whether, or in what proportions, this entity is a "religion", a cultural system, an ideology, a set of doctrinal prescriptions, or even a non-religious criteria-based categorising of a wide group of societies which fall, however loosely, within a linked cultural tradition.

Secondly, there is the relatively uncontroversial claim that there is nothing in the Quran, Hadith and Sunnah which places Islam in an ideological opposition to capitalism. While this may be true in the strictly doctrinal sense, as we shall later see, this is not necessarily the way in which the doctrine has been interpreted in Southeast Asia. The connection between the written word of the Islamic code of behaviour and belief, and the various cultural contexts into which this is transposed is therefore of critical interest. Rodinson, indeed, goes well beyond simply asserting that there are no inherently anti-capitalistic principles to be found in Islam (in this case conceived of the strict or narrow sense of Quranic doctrine), to attacking Weber for his belief that Islam is fatalistic and irrational. Rodinson here makes two category-mistakes—the first of juxtaposing his doctrinal "evidence" with Weber's *sociological* "evidence", and then supposing that the former refutes the latter; the second of assuming that his own wish to find the Quran rationalistic and economically activist actually commits it to being so. In other words, the *desire* that the Quran be found to have something to say on all matters of importance, including the economic, leads Rodinson to suppose that such evidence does exist there, when it manifestly does not.

Thirdly, there is the claim that Islamic society has always been pervaded by capitalistic activities, and that these are not new, and neither are they to be explained by contact with Christian Europe, or by imagining that Islamic capitalism has necessarily gone through the same stages as European capitalism. Again as we have already suggested this hinges not on the identification of a certain range of entrepreneurial business activities which, as is clearly the case, have long been characteristic of Islamic trading and manufacturing communities, and especially those of the cities, but on the conceptual question of what constitutes the capitalist mode of production. Is it *merely* a confluence of entrepreneurial techniques, or is it in fact to be defined by the co-existence of a complex and specific group of structural factors including relations of production, forms of property and the appropriation of the surplus from the producers? Put in more concrete terms, to what extent can one argue for instance that the Malay sector of the Malaysian economy is or is not "capitalistic" without prior definition of the term? Rodinson's attempted solution to this tension—that in the Islamic world capitalism has always been one mode of production which co-exists with others, only confuses the matter further, especially as in itself the theory of co-existent mode of production does not help us to understand the dynamics or development of any particular society, unless the theory also contains specific advice on how the modes of production succeed one another, or which one dominates, or has the modes articulate with one another, and so on.

There is one final consequence which the acceptance of Rodinson's thesis would force upon us. This is the total rejection of the Weberian argument on the relationship between religious motivation and economic activity. Rodinson's attack on Weber falls into two parts: an attempt to discredit Weber's general thesis by showing that even in respect to the Protestant Ethic, Weber can be refuted on empirical grounds; and the attempt to show that Islam itself (despite obvious examples of doctrine such as the prohibition of usury) is not only neutral in relation to general explanations of socio-economic change, but in fact, if anything, is rather conducive to entrepreneurial activity.

The critique of Weber, in other words, concentrates on three points: the "Protestant Ethic" thesis, Weber's own conception of Islam, and, at least in the case of Islamic situations, the lack of connection between doctrine and secular economic activity. Again, it might be noted that any discussion of the *cultural* features of any of the societies in question is conspicuously absent. This is despite the fact that Rodinson argues at some length that Islam is, if anything, *more* rationalistic even than Christian Calvinism, but that this rationalisation, although ultimately based on revelation, leads less to blind faith than to a reasoned pragmatism, especially in the affairs of the world, and gave rise not only to art, literature and philosophy, but also to a body of law derived from religious first principles. (Unlike in Europe where only Canon law had these characteristics). But what we have already indicated still applies—that whereas Weber is talking not about the rationality of religious beliefs themselves, but about the complex levels of sociological, practical and ideological implications that those beliefs have in relation to their attendant cultures, Rodinson continues to talk essentially about the rationality (including the economic rationality) of *belief.*

Islam and Capitalism in Southeast Asia

The question that arises therefore is that of the application of aspects of this conceptual framework to the situation in those parts of Southeast Asia where Islam is a major religious force: Malaysia, Indonesia, southern Thailand and the southern Philippines in particular, plus the addition of Singapore. There are however essentially two parts of this question to be distinguished—that of the applicability of the framework to Southeast Asia; and of the modifications which a study of the Southeast Asian situation suggests should be made to the framework in the light of the empirical evidence.

If it is the case, as Rodinson argues, that Islam *in itself* is irrelevant to the explanation of the forms of economic development in the different parts of the Muslim world, then where must the explanation be sought? One obvious answer is that it should be sought not only in the variation of socio-cultural modes of organisation that accompany Islam (e.g. Malay, Persian, Egyptian, etc.), but more essentially in the links between each of these cultural agencies and Islam. And since the mode of cultural organisation contains not only the religious, but also the economic spheres of influence in any society, it follows that culture is the mediating factor which attaches, even if indirectly, religion to economics. The key to our problem would therefore seem to lie primarily in the ways in which cultural organisation unites or is believed to unite (or to divide) the secular and religious aspects of social organisation in Islamic countries. This in turn reflects again on the question of the "unity" of Islam, since few scholars would lump together Malay culture and Moroccan culture, although both fall under the general umbrella of Islamic societies.

Some Southeast Asian Examples

Malaysian Islam is quite clearly one of these "variants" of Islam, that is, a culturally conditioned and localised form of the religion. The same is also true of Indonesian, Thai, Filipino and Singaporean Islam, all of which are similarly located within different cultural traditions (and often competing ones), which are internally differentiated by the Islamic practices of different ethnic groups, and which equally contain differing degrees of orthodoxy, modernising influences and so on, as well as different patterns of relationship with pre- or non-Islamic practices such as *keramat* (saint) worship, traditional systems of medical belief (*bomoh*), animism (*kurafat*), life-cycle rituals and customary law (*adat*) in the case of the Malays. The tension between indigenous cultural practices and the possibility of the full realisation of both the letter and the spirit of the *Sharia*, and therefore of the ultimate establishment of Muslim unity, is thus a constant theme within the study of modernist Muslim movements. But the question remains as to whether modern Malay nationalism (not against colonialism, but in the internal sense) can adequately be interpreted as a political movement based on religious motives, or as a form of ethnic nationalism of which religion forms a prop and a justification in the eyes of the believers, the logical outcome of which has been not only UMNO, the political wing of the movement, but the *Bumiputera* concept itself.

The concept of the *Bumiputera* has curiously received very little critical attention, yet it is a concept of great interest since it postulates a notion of identity which merges, and therefore perhaps confuses ethnic, religious and linguistic criteria in the belief that within this particular concept the three criteria are logically related. Therefore, a Chinese in Malaysia can become a Muslim, but not a *Bumiputera*. But an Indonesian Muslim *can* become a *Bumiputera*. Nearly all Malaysians speak *Bahasa Malaysia* (or *Bahasa Melayu*), but this alone, although one of the requirements of *Bu-*

miputera-hood is not enough without the ethnic and religious factors.[5] Similarly, although a Chinese can become a Christian without loosing his Chinese identity, a Malay cannot become a Christian without losing his Malay identity, although he retains his language and ethnicity. But *why* is this the case, especially when it is remembered that it is perfectly possible for an Indonesian to become a Christian without ceasing to be an Indonesian, or even a member of his own more limited ethnic group, and of course that many Malays are of Indonesian origin?

The answer clearly lies not in some special peculiarity of the Malays, but at the level of Malay political culture which seeks to make a seemingly necessary connection between being a Malay and being a Muslim, and them erects a system of economic incentives for these *Bumiputeras*, therefore not only *explicitly* recognising them as an economically backward group, but implicitly recognising that the ethnicity-religion-language formula is therefore deficient in terms of a modernising economy. So to return to our original question. What is the connection between Islam itself and the problem of developing and entrepreneurial capitalistic economy amongst the Malays of Malaysia, an intention quite unequivocally expressed in the Third Malaysia Plan (1976-1980)? And is in fact the construction of an Islamic state (the expressed intention of the Malayan Islamic Party) compatible with the construction of a modern capitalist economy, or do the social tensions of capitalism itself, as a Marxist might argue, sow dissension in the ranks of the *Ummat* (the followers of the prophet) thus preventing the objective of the *Sharia*—the unity of Muslims—from being achieved? Interestingly enough, one of the objectives of the Muslim College established at Klang in 1955 was to prevent the erosion of the

---

5 A clarificatory note is perhaps in order here. The Malaysian Constitutional Law does not define *bumiputera* as such, although it does define who is a Malay, and the "special position of the Malays". The concept of the *bumiputera*, while not therefore constitutionally enshrined, is clearly closely related to the constitutional position of the Malays. In fact, in certain marginal cases, a non-Malay can become a *bumiputera* if he is a member of one of the aboriginal and indigenous groups of peoples (e.g. in East Malaysia). In relation specifically to the language provisions see J.R. Clammer, "Bahasa Malaysia: Its Modernization and Relationship to the Politics of National Unity in Peninsular Malaysia," *Southeast Asian Affairs 1976*, Singapore, 1976.

Muslim religion by the importation of the undesirable aspects of Western civilisation, yet capitalism (there as elsewhere frequently confused with modernisation) was not of course identified as being in itself one of these undesirable aspects.

It is in the context of this consideration that the great weight given to the repudiation of the ideas that the profit motive, and its corollary, saving, is ruled out for a Muslim by the rule of *Riba* (the injunction against usury), by attempting to show that Islam *encourages* the capitalist ethic, provided that the enterprise is not pursued to *excess*. But again a conflict between the competing demands of economic modernism and religious orthodoxy can be seen here, as in the parallel question of whether tithes levied on the Muslim community (*Zakat-Fitrah*) can be used for investment, or only for strictly religious purposes (including the relieving of debt, as defined by the *Sharia*). Strictly speaking, religious support for the idea of the *Bumiputera* as a socio-economic category to whom funds generated from within the Muslim community can be devoted can only be given if it can be shown that the community is faced by a "necessity" (*harus*) which if it does not override, at least liberalises, the strict interpretation of the Quranic injunctions on the concept of Islamic legality (*halal*) as applied to the use of religious funds.

If one is thus faced with the problem of characterising the economic ideology of the Malays in Malaysia, the tension, which may even amount to a contradiction, between the demands of orthodoxy and modernism, must play a central part. Furthermore, if the *bumiputera* concept is to be considered viable it ultimately must be able to be shown that this contradiction *is* resolvable, otherwise Malay society itself will stratify not only into haves and have-nots, but into those who follow the orthodoxy of the *alim ulama*, the religious elite, and those who follow the new orthodoxy of the increasingly secular economic elite. A similar tension can be seen in Indonesia, whether expressed in terms of rivalry for the people's allegiance between the *ulama* and the more secularised intelligentsia, as reflected for instance in the kinds of schooling most favoured,[6] or in more general terms of traditionalism versus modernisation.

---

6 Alfian, "The Ulama in Achenese Society: A Preliminary Observation," *Southeast Asian Journal of Social Science*, Vol. 3, No. 1, 1975.

This latter point is worth briefly pursuing. The recent leadership of Indonesia has had no alternative but to take into account the cultural heterogeneity of the country, even though the majority of the population are Muslims. The constant references to the widely differing examples of modernising processes in Islamic countries, for instance Pakistan, Tunisia and Arabia, and of Turkey in the past speeches of Sukarno for instance thus take on a considerable significance when related to the doctrines of the Indonesian Muslim modernists as concerns the relationships between religion and society. The classical Christian issue—that of the relationship between Church and State—is not at issue here since presumably for the Muslim there is no such separation—Islam comprises both a religious and a civil and political society, so the distinction between the "religious" and the "secular" is redundant. The actual expression of this in Indonesia however has tended to take a very different form from its expression in Malaysia. Thus, for instance, certainly in the past if not in the present, many members of the *Partai Komunis Indonesia* (PKI) were also Muslims, and indeed in the 1920s during the anti-Colonial struggle many members of the *Sarekat Islam* (the *Muslim Association*), the dominant Indonesian political party, turned to Communism as a weapon against the Dutch. One of the anti-Communist members of the *Sarekat Islam* expressed the underlying social theory to this very succinctly when he wrote:

> Individualism, which permits every person to meet his own needs and reap his own fruits without caring for the needs and happiness of others should be changed into socialism which makes the welfare and happiness of everybody dependent on the welfare and happiness of all.[7]

In turn the reform movement generally (*Kaum Muda*) with its stress on education, nationalism and religious and secular modernisation generated a group of ideas, such as those that not Islam itself, but the stress given to the *fiqh* or jurisprudence aspects of the *Shariah* by the traditionalists (*Kaum Tua*), made Islam a break on development; that the idea of *kebangsaan* or nationalism as developed in Indonesia was essentially an Eastern and pro-Muslim movement, and had nothing in common with Western nationalism, and united and did not divide peoples; and that the study of

---

[7] Haji Agus Salim, *Neratja*, October 27, 1921. Quoted in D. Noer, *The Muslim Modernist Movement in Indonesia, 1900-1942*, Kuala Lumpur, 1973.

history rather than of tradition should be the basis for a forward-looking reform movement, on the basis that the principles of Islam are eternal and therefore always modern and compatible with the demands of time and circumstances. Clear examples of these themes for instance can again be found in the speeches of Sukarno where are clearly illustrated the themes that the *Shariah* is divided into sections relating to the purely religious, the worldly-cum-religious and to the purely worldly, and that the traditionalists confuse these three levels; that an Islamic state does not imply theocracy; that the errors of other Muslim nations such as pre-reformed Ottoman Turkey where the idea of *Kismet*, of fatalism and surrender to fate, was deeply embedded by the political structure in the social organism can be avoided rather than imitated; and that much of the teaching of the unreformed Indonesian religious teachers, such as the imposing of *fatwas* or religious prohibitions outlawing (*haram*) the entering of modern secular schools, were based on self-interest or misconceptions of the true relationship of Islam to modernisation.

If one returns for a moment to the Malay world, in the past the same structural tension has tended to express itself less as a conflict between orthodoxy and modernisation, than as an internal conflict between the values of simplicity, hospitality and the futility of excessive striving, and those of industry, frugality, self-reliance and adaptability. An examination of traditional Malay culture (and its oral and written literature) shows both sets of attitudes to be constantly present.[8] And since in the past the futility of

[8] See for e.g. Tham Seong Chee, "Tradition, Values and Society Among the Malays," *Nanyang Quarterly: A Review of Southeast Asian Studies* (1): 4, December 1971. There are some other factors which are also worth mentioning in this context. With the advent of Islam the ruler became "Dzil Allah fil 'alam"—the Shadow of Allah on Earth, Islam thus strengthened the Sultanate, which in turn legitimises the *bumiputera* concept, as a Sultan, or the King, is titular head and defender of both the Islamic religion and the *Adat*. The *Adat* is still a deeply-rooted body of customary law, both in terms of behaviour and institutions, even though it has undergone many modifications in recent years. Also closely linked with this constellation of concepts are those of *Bahasa*, which refers not only to the Malay *language*, but to *manners* as well, and the notion of *Kemelayuan* or "Malayness". In the contemporary period it can often be noted how frequently these ideas are applied to the support of the traditional Malay community conceived of in *rural* terms, as opposed to the destructive and immoral qualities of the urban cultures.

accumulation was underscored for the *ra'ayat* (the common people), not by the depredations of foreigners, but by their feudal relationship to their own aristocracy (*orang atasan* or *bangsawan*), and since Islam entirely lacks the Protestant emphasis on the edifying role of labour *in itself*, there are socio-historical and religious *structural* reasons for the reinforcing of the ambiguity of attitudes in Malay culture. And the attitudes themselves (which have "hardened" into stereotypes) are therefore of less explanatory value than these structural properties of the Malay socio-cultural system when it comes to discussing the reasons for development, or the lack of it, in the economic sphere.

At this point perhaps a useful qualification can be added, notably that perhaps without exception the literature on the "retardation of development" amongst the Malays has assumed that a purely capitalist road to this state of "development" is the only viable one, thus overlooking certain respects in which Malay society suggests its own patterns of modernisation based upon its own structural principles. Additionally there is also the assumption that the idea of "economic rationality" applies only to a system in which entrepreneurship, profit and accumulation are essential elements, an assumption which any acquaintance with economic anthropology shows to be manifestly false. And this belief afflicts not only the sociological analyst, but also the policy-formulating members of the Malay elite, as evidenced by the Third Malaysia Plan, rationalises the need for entrepreneurship on essentially political grounds, i.e. the position of the Malays *vis-à-vis* the other ethnic groups. It is this which explains the continuing influence of the numerous writers who seek either an explanation of the role of "non-economic factors" (i.e. cultural and social structural factors such as the *Adat Perpateh*) in the retardation of Malay economic development[9] or evidence that entrepreneurship has always been an important element in Malay culture.

Some Theoretical Problems

In the light of this, a number of related and interesting theoretical problems emerge. The first of these relates to patterns of causality in explaining

---

9 For example B.K. Parkinson, "Non-Economic Factors in the Economic Retardation of the Rural Malays," *Modern Asian Studies*, Vol. 1, No. 1, 1967.

the relationship between economic and religious factors in any actual situation. If we represent the elements of the situation as follows it can be seen that the issue is to determine both the precise *nature* of each of the relationships and their *extent* or intensity in any given case, given that, structurally speaking, the same *elements* occur in all situations where there is that of religion and the economy. Thus:

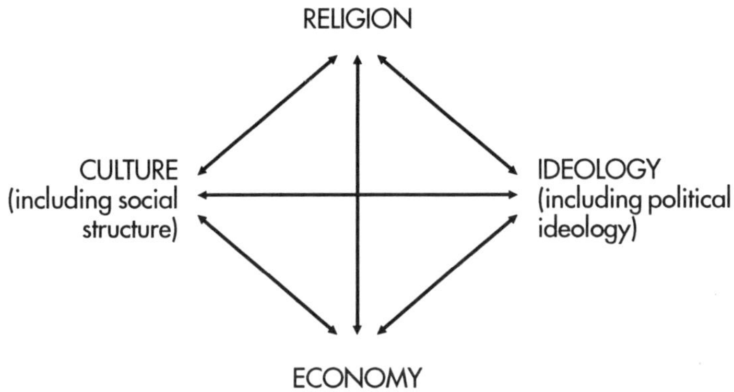

So if, as we have suggested, there is a differential relationship between Religion and Economy in different Islamic societies, then this differential must be explained by reference to either one or both of culture and/or political ideology. For example, the quite different patterns of development in the 19th and 20th centuries in Egypt and Malaysia must be explicable not in terms of religion, since both are Islamic, but by the different cultures and ideologies prevailing in these two states during the defined historical period. Two important aspects of this are the Weber thesis as applied to Islamic societies, and the question not of whether Islam and *capitalism* are compatible, but whether Islam and *communism* are compatible, which is a perfectly valid question given the logical links between capitalism and communism in the works of Marx. This latter question also has important policy implications, a clear example of which is whether or not the Third Malaysia Plan, in openly arguing that it is intended to fight communism with capitalism, is playing directly into the hands of that very communism, by merely hastening the arising of the inherent contradictions of capitalism—the emergence of classes and so on. Finally, there is the general question of whether religion as such has *any* real effect on the development process, or is it merely a perhaps interesting but irrelevant extraneous factor?

Curiously enough (from the point of view of one familiar mainly with Southeast Asian Islam) a great deal of Middle Eastern Islamicist writings in recent years had devoted itself not to the vigorous *denial* of a logical connection between Islam and communism, but to *supporting* the claim that, on the contrary, the two are highly compatible. Let us consider these arguments. These arguments fall into two groups: the first stresses the permanent modernity of Islam and the second stresses what it believes to be the essentially authoritarian character if Islam. Thus, according to the first group of arguments, Islam, outside of certain very basic religious tenets, should be open to *ijtihad*, to continuous innovation. Resistance to *ijtihad* has led Islam to appear unprogressive socially and anti-scientific intellectually. If, on the other hand, the principle of continuous innovation is adopted then Islam seeks to find solutions to problems as they arise, and is always abreast of the times. So if Marxism is a scientific doctrine then Marxism and Islam are compatible in exactly the same way that Islam and natural science are. Islam can thus in the modern era be interpreted in a liberal, democratic and socialistic way, just as in the past, for instance under the Ottoman Empire, it was interpreted as despotic and theocratic. In accepting the advantages of modern science and technology therefore, Islam cannot simultaneously reject the findings of the modern social sciences on the grounds that Islam is self-sufficient in this latter respect. The Muslim Marxist who adopts this group of arguments (and many examples can be found, e.g. in Egypt) thus rejects the idea that Marxism is atheistic, accepts science as a fact of modern life (as against those for instance who have recently claimed that a Muslim cannot accept the theories of Darwin), and rejects political and economic paternalism and elitism (so characteristic of Malay leadership for example) in favour of organisation of the people for the people on a socialist basis (it being no more attractive to be exploited by ones' indigenous bourgeoisie that it is to be exploited by a foreign one). Such an argument thus flatly contradicts the beliefs (for instance of the contemporary Malaysian leadership) that a combination of Islam which is ideologically incompatible with Marxism, and of capitalism, which is economically incompatible with Marxism, are sufficient to defeat the "Communist threat" in Malaysia.

The second group of arguments, invariably put forward by non-Marxist authors, for reasons that will become apparent, is that there is a fundamental *affinity* between Islam and Marxism, both being authoritarian systems of belief and practice. The clearest example of this view is the paper by the historian and political commentator Bernard Lewis entitled "Communism and Islam", and it is upon this that I will concentrate.[10]

Lewis' argument is essentially that there are clear features of Islam and of Islamic society which predispose those who are members of this group of cultures to accept the doctrines of communism. What are these features? Basically there are four:

1. the authoritarianism of Islam and its political tradition;
2. the tradition of governmental paternalism or state-directed economic life;
3. the doctrinal totalitarianism of Islam as a religion; and
4. the existence of collective obligations in Islam.

Added to theses is the fact that, according to Lewis, the Muslim countries tend to be anti-western, partly because of colonialism and partly because of the failure, despite repeated attempts, to introduce the institutions of liberal democracy successfully into these countries. Since this viewpoint happens to coincide with that of the Communist bloc, then at the political level there is a further link between Islam and Communism.

Islam, for Lewis and his colleagues, is thus characterised by a long history of autocracy in the political sphere, and the failure to generate institutions of a genuinely democratic character, whether in the geographical heartlands of Islam or in its furthest flung provinces. When this political characteristic is combined with economic paternalism, with its corollaries of a docile peasantry, bureaucracy, ruling class elitism and concentration of planning and decision making in the centre, together with a "total doc-

---

[10] B. Lewis, "Communism and Islam," *International Affairs*, 30, 1954. Other examples are W.Z. Laqueur, "The Appeal of Communism in the Middle East," *Middle East Journal*, Vol. 9, No. 1, 1955; Nabih Amin Fatris, "The Islamic Community and Communism," in W.Z. Laquer (ed.) *The Middle East in Transition*, New York, 1958.; and K. Cragg, "The Intellectual Impact of Communism upon Contemporary Islam," *Middle East Journal*, Vol. 8, No. 2, 1954.

trine" which contains all answers and an inherent tendency to "collectivism" in Islamic social life, the picture is complete. For Marxism, according to Lewis, possesses precisely the same characteristics. The only real argument that the Muslim can advance against Marxism is that it is atheistic, a "secular heresy", but even this, as we have seen, is disputed by many radical Muslims.

How do we assess this remarkable theory? The first consideration that it raises is the point touched upon earlier in the chapter, notably that of the legitimacy of regarding *either* Islam *or* Marxism from an idealist point of view, as unchanging, static entities, uniform throughout space and time. Lewis' argument is idealist, essentialist and a-historical. Furthermore, Lewis' position leads on directly to another very similar one: that the reason for underdevelopment in Muslim countries lies not in a combination of the historical domination of colonialism and subsequent entrapment in and dependency on an international economic system, but in the structural features of those societies themselves and in the psychology of their peoples. What is not made clear in Lewis' argument is the exact nature of the articulation between Islam as a set of doctrines and beliefs and its manifestation as a specific political tradition.

One solution to this may lie in Weber. Another may be in more closely defining what is meant by, or has in the past been meant by, Islam. Let us take these two themes in reverse order. The "great tradition" of (primarily but by no means only) Western scholarship on Islam, certainly until very recently, may be defined as "Orientalism", which took as its unit of study a defined "civilisation" and proceeded to study that civilisation by way of its archaeology, philology, literature and those aspects of its history which had some bearing on these themes. Combined with this was the view which had developed as a result of centuries of mutual contact in Christian Europe of Islam as fanatical, unprogressive and politically repressive.[11] The Orientalist's approach is thus to seek out the "essence", usually defined in religious terms—Islamic, Christian, Hindu, Confucian and so on—of the civilisation in question, and to take this "essence" the civilisation's main defining characteristic. The historiography of Orientalism, with its emphasis

---

[11] T. Asad, "Two European Images of Non-European Rule," in T. Asad (ed.) *Anthropology and the Colonial Encounter*, London, 1973.

on the "rise and fall" of civilisations is symptomatic of this. But to consider the "essence" of Islamic civilisations (note the plural) to be "Islam" is not only circular, but mystifying. For what *is* the role of religion within a complex social organisation?

The suspicion that all is not well when it comes to answer this question only recently began to occur to even some of the leading Orientalists. Thus, for example, Gibb and Bowen in their *Islamic Society and the West*, when faced with the nature and multiplicity of the social institutions to be found in Muslim countries, revealingly comment:

> The term 'Islamic Society' applied to the social organisation which we are analysing implies that its distinguishing features are related in some way or another to Islam. Yet in those groups or activities which we have been considering up to this point there is little which can be regarded as specifically Islamic; on the contrary, the organisation of village and industrial life belongs rather to a stage of social evolution which finds close parallels in many non-Islamic regions of Europe and Asia; and that of the court and the army, though of a more peculiar type, is based on principles on which such Islamic elements as they display appear to be purely accidental.[12]

So where is Islam? Islam according to this view is the thread which ties the whole edifice together; it not only provides bonds of common sentiment and even language throughout the Muslim world, but also, through its institutional framework, provides a common *organisation*. Social cohesion in Islamic societies is thus maintained through this common allegiance or social cement, however wide the gap for instance between rulers and ruled may actually be. The essentialist conception of Islam is therefore a-historical, idealist, typology-building and stereotypic (and therefore, presumably, false). Indeed since Islam has at various times been used to support quite contrary social and political positions, since it has existed over a long period of time and since it co-exists with various and differing cultures, it must clearly be seen in the contexts of its various social worlds, and not reified

---

[12] H.A.R. Gibb and H. Bowen, *Islamic Society and the West: A Study of the Impact of Western Civilization on Moslem Culture in the Near East*, Pt. 1, 1950, Pt. 2, London, 1957.

into the status of an ideal object. Islam *in itself* therefore cannot be appealed to as legitimising any particular social, political or economic position. (As no more can Christianity be appealed to in the same way.)

If, on the other hand, one turns directly to Weber for enlightenment, the initial problem is in determining exactly what Weber's position is, since it varies in its details from his *Sociology of Religion* to *The Protestant Ethic and the Spirit of Capitalism* and from his detailed studies of individual religions (*The Religion of China*, etc.) to his study of the role of Christianity as opposed to the major Asian religions in understanding the organisation of the medieval City (*The City*). But there are three things we may be sure of. Firstly, that in discussing Protestantism, Weber had in mind not Protestantism in general, but specifically the Calvinistic variety, with its emphasis on predestination, "the calling" and the special role of the "elect" within this framework. Secondly, that although for Weber social action must contain a subjective or meaningful component, he did not argue that belief *causes* action or that ideology *causes* society, since if they are not separate from one another then they are internally related to one another, and do not stand in a relationship of linear causality. Thirdly, in his empirical works on the World Religions, Weber does *not* argue that ideological factors cause, or are prior to, material factors in explanations of social life. He rather examines the question *historically* in an attempt to determine under what conditions (if any) a religious ideology determines secular action, and how this is reflected in the composition of the social groups associated with the religion in question. The simplistic view of the "Weber thesis", that Protestantism is functional for the development of Capitalism, and that the major Asian religions, including Islam, are dysfunctional for the development of Capitalism, is thus a travesty of what Weber actually intended to convey.

The role of *history* for Weber, and this is his point of contact with Marx, is thus primary. This is clearly revealed in his work on the Protestant Ethic, where not only did Weber take as his case study Calvinism, which had flourished centuries before Weber wrote, but where it is also revealed that the idea of a religion possessing a single and unvarying code of ethics across long periods of historical time is rejected. Such ethical ideas, rather, have causal efficacy not in the abstract, but only in the context of particular socio-cultural groups. Or put another way, an ideology is only meaningful when it is socially located within a system of cultural, productive and political values, constraints and structures. A clear example of this is the way in which, at different times and in different places, or contemporaneously, Islam has been used *both* to legitimate *and* to subvert an established social order. Indeed the economically and politically activist aspect of Islam is perhaps more pronounced than in any other major religion, with the possible exception of Christianity.

Given then, that there is no contradiction in Islam, either doctrinally or socially, between religion and trade, why is there an association between Islam and economic backwardness (and, by contrast, between Christianity and economic progress), both historically and in some respects in the modern era? If the solution to this is not to be found in the ethics of Islam, them we could reasonably argue that the roots of the association lie both in the *cultural* configuration of some Islamic societies, and in the failure of the entrepreneurial group to evolve into a *dominant* class, largely as a result of the inability of the merchant class to successfully challenge the political position of the aristocratic-military-bureaucratic class by *not* developing the basis for class political autonomy and organisation.[13] The absence or weakness of an *indigenous* Muslim bourgeoisie throughout Southeast Asia is evidence of this. This argument has important implications, for history: why are Christianity and the spread of Capitalism so closely associated?; for sociology, in weighing the relative importance of religious as opposed to socio-economic factors in explaining development; and for policy; is it the case that for example in Malaysia, Islam is used to explain or justify event, policies and social patterns to which it is in fact unrelated?

The argument also has some important implications for our conception of Capitalism. Capitalism, as we can see, involves a certain version of

---

[13] Note Lacoste's argument on one reason why the merchants could not be considered to be a true bourgeoisie or distinct merchant class in medieval North Africa: "In contradistinction from the true European bourgeoisie, which, despite its wealth, was a class subordinated to the nobility, the merchants in Muslim countries, closely associated with royal power, formed a part of the aristocracy. They formed not a bourgeoisie, but a commercial aristocracy, which often had very strong links with the tribal or military aristocracy". Y. Lacoste, "General characteristics and fundamental structures of medieval North African society," *Economy and Society*, Vol. 3, No. 1, 1974, p. 8.

economic rationality, together with the existence of an entrepreneurial class, a tendency to emphasise individualism, and relative freedom from the bonds of kinship and other traditional agencies of social control. But is this all? A Marxists would surely answer "no", since for Marx, Capitalism, to exist at all, has to possess two essential features: firstly, it must be represented as a unique mode of production containing specific forms of the means and relations of production, including the expropriation of the surplus by the non-producer (i.e. the Capitalist); and secondly, it is *historically specific*, i.e. it is a mode of production which arose at a specific time, in a specific place, and in the context of determinate social relations (i.e. those found during the collapse of West European feudalism under the pressure of a rising bourgeoisie). The existence of entrepreneurial activity in the absence of these other conditions does not therefore (if one follows this argument) define capitalism, but merely indicates the existence of one or more of the features of the developed form of that particular mode of production. Marx's own difficulties in extending his own theory to Asia stem from this, as does his attempt to define another mode of production—the Asiatic Mode—as being typical of, for instance, India and China, where at the time Marx was writing, traditionalism, paternalism and economic involution seemed to rule the day. Therefore, we must ask ourselves, has an indigenous capitalism ever existed in Southeast Asia (or indeed anywhere else in the Muslim world)? If we decide in the negative, then the standard form of the "Islam and Capitalism" argument of course is rendered meaningless. Since we have already cast some doubt on the meaning of "Islam" as a universal term, then the whole debate re-emerges in a rather altered form. Weber himself of course recognised this, although from a non-Marxist point of view, when he asserted that acquisitiveness, frugality and a regard for wealth do not in themselves amount either to capitalism or the capitalist spirit. On the contrary, they are universals. Capitalism as such therefore is a combination of behavioural traits-rationality, the profit motive, etc. together with their institutional expression in a specific historical context. It is presumably the case for Weber that capitalism can take different forms, e.g. the Calvinist variety as opposed to modern monopoly capitalism, in different historical epochs. His definition of capitalism, however, is weaker than Marx's in that it contains a large element of circularity. As Weber puts it:

> Unlimited greed for gain is not in the least identical with capitalism, and still less its spirit. Capitalism may even be identical with the restraint, or at least a rational tempering of this irrational impulse. But capitalism is identical with the pursuit of profit, and forever renewed profit, by means of continuous, rational, capitalistic enterprise.[14]

Conclusion

This chapter has touched on a number of, hopefully, significant points. Amongst the most important of these might be enumerated the following:

1. that *doctrinally* Islam and Capitalism are not incompatible;
2. that *therefore* quite conceivably, Islam and Communism are not incompatible if the logic of the "Islam and Capitalism" argument holds;
3. that neither Islam, Capitalism nor Communism can be regarded in an idealist, a-historical way;
4. that whether or not Islam and particular economic, political and social ideologies are actually related, there are many who wish to assert that they are in fact related;
5. that therefore the connections which exist, or are believed to exist between religion and secular action are mediated by cultural principles;
6. that the nature of the causal process linking religion and secular action is complex, multi-faceted and varies from situation to situation, and involves more general questions of ideology, political organisation and the structural properties of the social system within which the religion is embedded;
7. when authors write about religion as a factor in advancing or retarding social and economic development they are almost invariably talking about the conventional capitalist road to development. To talk about "religion and development" or "religion and modernisation" as a general problem requires detailed disentangling of the terms before any progress is possible; and
8. it is not religious *doctrine* as such which necessarily dictates the relationship between religion and secular action, but the nature of

[14] M. Weber, op. cit., p. 17.

> the intervening agencies, cultural, political, ecological or whatever. In any particular case therefore it is necessary to discover the nature of these agencies and the ways in which they articulate with religion on the one hand, and non-religious economic, social or political processes on the other. These agencies need not of course necessarily be indigenous—they can be and typically are colonial, post-colonial or neo-colonial constructions. Indeed such intrusive factors are often paramount. Additionally, in this particular context, it is worth remembering that Islam, together with the other major religions in Southeast Asia, is itself intrusive, and as such overlays a great deal of the indigenous religious organisation and cultural values, many elements of which still persist. Indeed one might legitimately ask, is there such a thing as Islamic *culture*? One might be very tempted to answer "no", that there is an Islamic religion, and a wide variety of cultures with which it is associated, but that Islamic culture as such does not exist.

Finally the relevance of these theoretical issues to the understanding of concrete cases in Southeast Asia should be fairly clear at a number of levels, including those of understanding religious manifestations themselves; the perception of people, both rulers and ruled, of the role of religion in legitimating particular socio-political policies, such as the *Bumiputera* concept in Malaysia, or rebellion in southern Thailand or the Philippines; the relationships between the major religious traditions in the region and their underlying and possibly even contradictory cultural systems, and finally the nature of the connections, if any, between religion and development throughout the region. Islam itself, because of its prevalence in the subcontinent, because of the large sociological literature connecting it with secular economic activity, and because of the way in which Islam itself is used to justify both conservative and radical social movements provides perhaps the perfect case study. Some of the possibilities sketched, for instance that if Islam is compatible with capitalism, it may logically be compatible with communism, or alternatively that Islam is more suited to communist developments than it is to capitalist developments, may seem very contentious, but they are nevertheless implications which *can* be drawn from the wide-ranging "Islam and Capitalism" debate.

Chapter 10
INTELLECTUALS AND DEVELOPMENT

A recent question in social theory in the West, at least since Marx, has been that of the social position of intellectuals. This question has generally been invested with much greater significance than that of a mere sub-issue in the sociology of the professions. Intellectuals in some cases, despite their inevitably minority status, are even seen as the key to social change (or to the obstruction of social change), depending on whether they are regarded as the avant garde of representatives of the *status quo*, as the force for revolution or as the embodiment of the establishment. This ascription of profound social significance to intellectuals stems not only from their possession of intellectual capital—education, but also from their social location as individuals, or as a class, that dominates the institutions themselves perceived as critical in contemporary knowledge-based societies—the universities and the media. The significance of this social role becomes even more apparent when it is recognised that the intellectuals usually assumed to be the most influential are precisely those with social science or even humanities background rather than those from scientific or technological fields. The *role* of producer and transmitter of knowledge in other words outweighs in many respects the actual knowledge generated and communicated.

This said, a number of significant shifts have occurred, again primarily in western social theory, which have redefined the field of the study of intellectuals in several important new ways. The first of these has been the decline of interest in the class position of intellectuals in its traditional form and a corresponding shift towards one of two positions. First, there is the suggestion that the locus of social power is shifting from "traditional" intellectuals (university-based teachers, independent writers or high-brow journalists) towards managerial elites concentrated in industry, business schools and private or public think-tanks. This position raises the interesting question of the status of managers and those who teach management, especially in the universities, bastions of the "traditional" intellectuals. Second, there is the position associated with the works of Zygmunt Bauman that in the transition to postmodernity, the position of the intellectual is seriously undermined because in the new constitution of society they are no longer needed to play a legitimating role. So marginalisation results (Bauman 1988). When we turn to the analysis of the Asian intellectuals, these themes will prove to be of as much significance as they are in the West.

A second shift, as reflected in a book by Pierre Bourdieu (Bourdieu 1988), has been the application of rigorous sociological methods of investigation to the university system itself, in this case the French system. Bourdieu's attempt to detail not so much the relation of university-based intellectuals to the wider society (which is an interesting subject in a society that takes its intellectuals, or at least the leading ones, very seriously indeed), but the relationship of power, prestige and access to publishers and the media amongst intellectuals—teachers and researchers—in the higher education system both relocates intellectuals on the map of the sociology of the professions, offers a methodology for the investigation of intellectuals and relegitimates the serious study of the university and of the system of universities as a project worthy of pursuit. But while Bourdieu offers a distinct approach of a particular hierarchical system of higher education, others have attempted much more wide ranging critiques of the university system, of the education that it provides and of the ideological currents that have created its contemporary problems. Perhaps the best example of this wider approach, interestingly emanating from a literary intellectual, is Allan Bloom's *The Closing of the American Mind* (Bloom 1988) which traces what the author sees as being the crisis of modern American society to a massive failure in and of higher education. Here, while the analysis encompasses the malaise of an entire society, the problem is seen to lie not so much in the organisation of the university system, but in the content of its teaching and the failure of responsibility of the teachers. The "crisis of the university" is of practical as well as theoretical significance as it is to these citadels of cultural capital that many aspiring intellectuals of the developing world, including Southeast Asia, flock for their advanced education.

The third major theme, thrown up by the massive social transformation in Eastern Europe, has been the role of intellectuals in leading those transformations, since they evidently have had significant influence. If it is the case that in Eastern Europe intellectuals have played a leading part in the reform of state socialism and that the thrust of intellectual developments there has been towards democratisation (not away from it as in Bloom's argument), this suggests an important and positive *political* role for educated elites, a prospect not necessarily attractive to authoritarian regimes wherever they may be found.

The issues in the sociology of intellectuals are then currently very lively, and so indeed raise questions of far reaching significance about the generation and dissemination of knowledge, locations of social power, means of accumulating and manipulating cultural capital and sources of political influence outside of formal political institutions, as well as questions about the nature and role of the higher educational system. But as with so many topics of potentially universal significance, in reality much of the debate has actually only taken place within or about a very limited range of societies: France, the United States and parts of Eastern Europe, especially Poland, and the former Czechoslovakia. Relatively little discussion has taken place on the role of intellectuals in Asian societies and there has been even less debate about the role of universities and the position of intellectuals within them. This chapter will attempt to create at least the framework for a more systematic comparative discussion of intellectuals, by raising a number of questions or issues in which the concerns of western social theory and the contemporary reality of a range of Asian societies can be brought into dialogue in the respect of the position of indigenous intellectuals and the role of universities.

What Then Are the Questions?

One major attraction of the sociological study of intellectuals is that it of necessity raises a host of issues which point both to the heart of contemporary social and cultural theory (for example, the issue of the putative transition to postmodernity) and to the concrete analysis of society. It might be useful to begin by sketching what some of these questions are, or at least some of the ones that I consider to be central since the questions are legion.

The first of these I would see as being the question of class. Traditionally the issue has been stated as the problem of whether intellectuals constitute an autonomous elite (mainly by virtue of their education), or whether, despite any possible privileges (often in the form of cultural capital rather than material benefits) they actually act as journeymen for the *real* elite. To answer such an abstract question two kinds of considerations are involved. The first is again the comparative one. Intellectuals in Vietnam face a situation in which, despite *doi moi* (the Vietnamese version of *perestroika*) since 1989, they still exist in a situation in which a socialist bureaucracy dominates political culture and to a great extent culture in general—including the organs for practicing and disseminating all forms of public culture, such as publishing, the media and the universities. Furthermore, a dominant ideology (a Stalinist form of Marxism filtered through the thoughts of Ho Chi Minh) is still officially in place. Intellectuals in Indonesia face a very different situation: authoritarian leadership, an official ideology (*Pancasila*) sufficiently diffuse to be infinitely interpretable, a state theoretically strong but in practice weakened by its own self-censoring bureaucratic tendencies and the sheer size and social diversity of the country and a higher educational system which, while physically underequipped and often of questionable intellectual quality, is very large, encompasses both state and private institutions and which contains substantial ideological divergence—for example universities based on secular, Christian and Islamic principles. The examples can be multiplied: the point is to indicate the huge range of situations existing in contemporary Asia (see Appendix for a schematic outline). Similarly, within any one country a variety of possibilities exist from outright conformity to the dictates of the state to active dissent. And this way of phrasing it assumes that the state is the organ against or in terms of which the intellectual defines himself. But this may not be conceptually correct: in Japan it is the media rather than the state that is the focus of attention and the source of rewards in a society in which the percentage of highly educated people (at least a basic university degree) is great by both absolute and comparative standards. This suggests that the position of the intellectual is inherently ambiguous, subject to conflicting pressures, demands, reward systems and moral imperatives.

It also suggests, perhaps even more fundamentally, that the question of class itself needs reexamination. In the West, under the influence of sociologists such as Dahrendorf and more latterly Bourdieu, the utility of the concept of class has been questioned in interesting ways. In the work of the former, the notion of *occupation* is seen largely to have replaced that of *class*.

A modern industrial society, and certainly the alleged postmodern or postindustrial society, possesses a huge hierarchy of occupations between which class conflict (as in a Marxist understanding of class) or even competition does not really exist. Individuals often attempt to improve their class position (assuming that they think in *class* terms at all, which is questionable), but this is largely to acquire higher status and/or income. Class solidarity, as a result, has radically weakened, and personal identity is seen much more in occupational terms. Bourdieu adds an interesting dimension to this by suggesting that while there are indeed strata in society (at least in France), these are distinguished less by objective economic markers than by consumption choices or *styles*. Individuals or identical incomes may choose very different patterns of life, and particular patterns of taste, often of some consistency, are established which create symbolic means for social strata to distinguish themselves with (Bourdieu 1984). Intellectuals, whose objective wealth is often modest, do however have access to two major sources of social power: symbolic capital in the form of education, a highly valued social good in most societies and perhaps especially Asian ones; and the ability to define taste themselves. A literary critic, for example, may possess social power not through income, but through the ability to praise and promote or ignore and suppress the literary works of others, and therefore to some extent to create both taste and a market for certain kinds of literary creations rather than others. Editors of journals, publishers, readers and examiners of PhD theses possess a similar role: they are, unwittingly or not, ideologues-creators or at least reproducers of taste, style and correctness. In a sense, the educational system is, as its radical critics such as Ivan Illich have so tellingly suggested, a huge system of ideological reproduction (though that ideology may not be primarily political, but may, as in Japan, be largely cultural). This is so not because it creates knowledge, but because it defines "reality". Inevitably, in both historical and contemporary Asia, the more authoritarian a political regime is, the greater its preoccupation with the control of the educational system.

If the class position of the intellectual is this problematic in the "West"—itself obviously a category requiring some careful deconstruction—it is even more so in Asia, where a huge variety of social systems interact with each other and with the more universalistic forces of modernisation. While it is questionable whether class consciousness is a social reality in most of Asia, perceptions of hierarchy and social ranking most certainly are. But class and hierarchy are not the same as can clearly been seen in for instance India where caste rivals class as the primary means of social classification (cf. Dumont 1980), in Singapore where ethnicity is seen as the primary social form (Clammer 1985), or in Japan where any indigenous concept of class is largely absent, but an intense preoccupation with ranking which has parallels with both the Confucian Literati system of pre-Republican China and with the age-grade systems familiar in many African tribal societies prevails. Where class consciousness does exist, or where social inequalities have been defined in class terms, this is historically often as the result of the importation of Marxism. And where such a consciousness, whatever its exact historical origins, does exist it has to be tied to questions of gender, often to religion, and usually to ethnicity. A sampling of the literature on class in any Southeast Asian country reveals this immediately (for example on Malaysia in S. Husin Ali 1984, Hua 1984). To attempt to locate intellectuals simply in terms of class would thus be very mistaken. They, like any other member of a plural society, exist at the intersection of a complex network of political, religious, economic and social forces which produce not necessarily fragmented identities, but certainly subtle ones. A Malay intellectual in Malaysia shares commonalities with his Chinese counterpart, but yet is also divided by differences that no class identity can conceal; a Javanese Christian while sharing much of his ethnic identity with Muslim Javanese inevitably has a world view that in certain respects must differ.

The general issue of class position can also be expressed in relation to a number of specific socio-cultural fields. For example, in the context of social movements it is always interesting to discover whether intellectuals are really the vanguard and initiators, whether they are comfortable fellow-travellers gaining visibility for their participation in movements which they have had little role in starting, or even whether they are a kind of academic vulture, essentially making a living from picking over the corpse. In literary and artistic fields a parallel concern arises: the critic may indeed be able to criticise, but not to produce. It is again appropriate to ask this question in relation to the field of education: are intellectuals essentially the reproducers of state ideology through their role in the universities and in their position as teachers of what are, whatever their anti-establishment posturings, usually highly standardised syllabi, the more so in the "elite" schools which have a major role in socialising the next generation of establishment leaders and indeed of intellectuals?

But really to get closer to the real role of intellectuals in contemporary societies, a very obvious preliminary question needs to be asked: what exactly is an intellectual anyway? Again if the question is posed in comparative terms an interestingly diverse range of example begins to emerge. In the United States and in Britain intellectuals are essentially university teachers, with the addition of writers of "serious" non-fiction. Journalists in the most high-brow sections of the press might just make it in, but with difficulty. Television or radio commentators, however wide their audiences and authoritative their views, are unlikely to be considered intellectuals. Artists, popular writers and even novelists are not likely to be placed in the intellectual category, and even amongst the professors it is a humanities or social science discipline that is likely to confer the status rather than a scientific, technological or managerial one. But in continental Europe—in France, Germany and Italy for example—the category is rather wider and includes university teachers, serious non-fiction and fiction writers, journalists, media commentators, museum professionals and artists, especially those artists who comment on art as well as produce it. While many of these intellectuals are indigenous many are also minorities ethnically or religiously. Indeed the association between minority or émigré status and intellectually is quite pronounced. This is often because of the social location of particular individuals (Marx for example as a German Jew in England) or because of whole migrations (again typically of German, Austrian or in some cases French—Lévi-Strauss for example—Jews as a result of Nazism) of highly educated communities which then settled in their new host countries. The intellectual history of the West is to a remarkable extent the history of these migrations.

But what about Asia? Here we see some rather different patterns, a few of which we can sketch. In Japan, partly as a result of the very high educational standards of the population as a whole (there are approximately 500 universities) the category of the intellectual is wider than that of Britain or the United States and is in many ways similar to that of France, containing as it does not only university-based writers, but also fiction and non-fiction authors (including poets), media people, museum professionals, professional critics (of art, music, architecture and literature in particular), artists, including those in the performing arts, essayists (who abound) and translators. Many of these categories overlap as a major criterion of intellectuals status is to publish, or at least to comment (on the media for example: "TV intellectuals?" are very common in Japan). Artists who write essays, or actors or theater producers who produce books on their art, or for that matter the art of others or all sorts of social or cultural questions in general, can be considered intellectuals every bit as much as the university teacher. There are also whole groups less visible in other national traditions, for example journalists ("serious" ones who are recognised as authoritative) and translators. In Britain translators are considered a valuable but almost invisible profession, whose names appear in tiny print on the title pages of other people's works. In academe, translation is considered laudatory, but not a major way of contributing to one's professional advancement. But, in Japan, translation, especially with appropriate commentary and annotation, is considered a major scholarly activity. Careers are made by introducing the ideas of significant foreign authors to Japanese audiences. Much French social science writing for example finds its way into Japanese before it does into English, and the shelves of any academic bookstore will be loaded with editions of European classics, of major philosophical, economic and sociological works and of editions of the books of almost any major foreign writer and of many really very minor ones.

There are furthermore, to stick with our Japanese example for a moment, several other distinguishing features of the intellectual landscape. One of these is its relation to the media which also, as we have suggested, constitute part of it. In Britain, for an academic to appear on television too often would be considered an abdication of serious academic status (at least by colleagues envious of the fat fees no doubt being collected!). The occasional appearance, especially by people whose esoteric speciality is suddenly in the news—say Eastern Europe—is quite all right, but frequent visibility is likely to be interpreted at best as the popularisation, at worst as vulgarisation, of the expertise of the intellectual in question. The only major exception to this is appearance on the Open University channel, which is seen of course as simply the classroom writ large. In Japan, however, this attitude does not prevail, partly for the very realistic reason that it is widely recognised that it is the media which creates taste and public opinion rather than the classroom intellectual. He who would be heard needs to publish—and the Japanese are voracious readers—and to appear in the mass media, especially television and the large circulation magazines and newspapers. University people often write for the papers, contribute small essays to magazines and appear on television talk-shows. Some intellectuals achieve substantial prominence by this means, such as the cultural critic Akira Asada whose fairly technical books became bestsellers in the mid-1980s as a result of such exposure, or the feminist sociologist Ueno Chizeko whose public prominence has so far somewhat outstripped her professional advancement in academia. Relationship to the media as well as recognition as a creative artist or teacher of a subject, while not absolutely necessary to achieving intellectual status—a highly regarded position in "Confucian" Japan, is certainly necessary to achieving prominence.

Another distinguishing characteristic of Japanese intellectual life is the reproduction within it of the hierarchical characteristics of Japanese social life in general. Universities are clearly ranked and few are in doubt about the status of any given institution. Rank within the overall intellectual community for any individual is very much a function of the rank of the institution of which one is a member, and is less dependent than it would be in the West on individual achievement. To some extent it is true in any university system, but is probably more pronounced in Japan than in other societies. For example, in Britain it is rare that an entire university has a first-rate reputation—it may be excellent in, say, English studies, but much less good in physics. Students or aspiring faculty members are more likely to choose a university on the basis of the reputation of an individual department than on the overall standing of the university as a whole, although where the two coincide obviously so much the better.

A final factor is the role of émigrés: essentially there are none, or at least very few. With very few exceptions Japanese universities are wholly staffed by Japanese, except in language departments and even there most foreign staff are on contracts or short-term appointments. Very few tenured appointments are held by non-Japanese. Although Japan has historically received influxes of Chinese scholars and Korean craftsmen, in recent times there has been nothing comparable to the migrations of European intellectuals to Britain and the Americas that occurred in the 1930s and 1940s, greatly enriching the quality of mental, literary and scientific life in the recipient societies. Even the present world wide interest in Japan which has brought many foreign students and scholars to study in Japan, has resulted in very few actually staying. The Japanese intellectual community is thus almost wholly indigenous and until recently largely self-reproducing in that few of its apprentice members studied abroad, although this is now changing. Many parallels can be drawn between this aspect of Japan's experience and that of other Asian societies, although the mechanisms are often different. Except for the brief postwar period of the American Occupation, Japan has never been colonised, although it has been a coloniser and echoes of the prewar Japanese education system can still be heard in Taiwan and Korea. This lack of a colonial experience has had profound effects, not only allowing the indigenous social structure to remain intact, but also preventing the flowing in of foreign linguistic and philosophical trends and completely eliminating the idea that the metropolitan centre, the source of credentials and the legitimating fountainhead of intellectual value, was elsewhere. For years for Vietnamese such a centre was France, for Indians or Malaysians Britain, for Filipinos the United States. The dynamics of nationalism have thus taken a rather different form in Japan than in the rest of Southeast Asia (cf. Anderson 1993).

But this simple fact has complex sociological consequences as any student of the area knows—for example on the field of ethnicity. Most Asian societies, often tempted to look upon Japan as insular, might consider that they too have no tradition of the émigré intellectual in recent history: indeed they have often been active in getting rid of the few that they did have. In universities in the huge stretch of continent from Pakistan to China, few foreign faculty will be found. And equally few will be found in publishing, media or non-university-based writing, again with the possible exception of those working in language-related fields. Rather, the émigré intellectual has been excluded by politics (China, Burma), deliberate policy of localisation (Malaysia), very low salaries, (Indonesia, the Philippines), poor infrastructure, by cultural nationalism plus those other factors (India), or by instability and security considerations (Cambodia). For reasons of language and by international standards many university jobs are unattractive and are never advertised abroad. The exceptions—Hong Kong and Singapore—both have colonial histories, use English widely and can offer attractive remuneration packages, but neither give the opportunity for the average expatriate to settle permanently. History intersecting with political culture has determined the fate of possible émigré intellectuals in all these societies.

But of course émigrés do not make an intellectual community: they may fertilise and stimulate it, but it is the indigenous intellectuals who are organic to a society. It is actually their position within the university or media and the relationship of that media and educational sector to the wider society that is actually the key issue. And one of the best questions to ask here is why people choose to become intellectuals, however so defined in their own society. Economic factors generally do not seem to be a major pull, since intellectuals are rarely members of the new rich class that has been attracting so much scholarly and media attention in Asia recently. In fact in relative terms they are probably falling behind economically as academic salaries or income from writing rarely match those available in business. A more important consideration is probably the "freedom factor": that of all possible professions, intellectual work tends to confer the greatest autonomy both mentally, and often, physically. Something like this is suggested by Alvin Gouldner when he makes his distinction between intellectuals in a strict sense and the intelligentsia in a broader sense, the former being critical and emancipatory and the latter problem-solving technocrats (Gouldner 1979). The former seeks freedom as a condition of their work and as a way of life; the latter seeks integration into and rewards from the real power elite.

The "Asian intellectual" (to generalise for a moment) in these respects often faces a complex of ambiguities rather different from those of his European or North American counterpart. To be an intellectual at all is almost certainly to enjoy high status or at least good status, even if material rewards are not so high. But this status may be bought at a certain cost: association with former colonial powers through place of graduate education and mastery of the colonial language; rewards from the state for compliant individuals but surveillance and suspicion for the non-compliant ones; inability to publish locally; restrictions on foreign travel or contact with the international community; and lack of resources (books, research materials, etc.). Intellectual "freedom" is itself a difficult concept to define: mental, subjective freedom can easily coexist with severe restraints on external expression. On the other hand, in those contemporary Asian societies where intellectuals, for example university teachers, are reasonably rewarded materially, have status and have basic freedoms—to read, publish, teach and communicate with the wider world—pressures are of a different kind. They tend to be either in the form of the pressure to be co-opted by the state to work on politically approved topics in methodologically neutral ways; or the pressure to ape the west: to conform one's work to the west, styles and standards set by outsiders. Sometimes of course this is desirable in maintaining standards of scholarship, but it can also cramp styles, suppress publication in local languages and prevent certain subjects from receiving attention at all. Consequently the "emancipatory" intellectual, while less well known, or not known at all, at the international level, may be much more truly "organic" than the cosmopolitan type. It is the latter however who tend to occupy prestigious university positions.

Patterns vary however with the particular system of higher education prevailing. In most Asian societies the most prestigious universities are the state ones. In some the *only* universities are the state ones (Burma, Singapore, Malaysia, Vietnam and effectively China and Hong Kong although in the latter two cases tiny signs of privatisation are evident). Where there is a private university sector (Indonesia, Japan and the Philippines for example), greater plurality is evident in the range of ideological positions, which can certainly encompass religious differences and preferences even if not specifically political ones (and religious choice can of course be a way of making political statements). The Philippines for example has specifically Christian universities as does Japan, which also has Buddhist and Shinto ones. Indonesia has Christian and Islamic universities as well as both public and private secular ones. There are actually two significant issues here. The first is the range of social roles and economic opportunities available to intellectuals and the extent to which the university sector dominates there. The second is the question of the socialisation of intellectuals.

Obviously most intellectuals—high in status but usually low in income—begin as students in the very universities where they later themselves operate professionally. The intellectual teaches these students and also provides a role model which some desire to emulate. But the emulation is not easy as the professionals also exercise a fairly strict gatekeeping role whether in the form of the pre-Republican Chinese bureaucratic entrance examinations or these days in deciding graduate school admissions. Students are themselves a very diverse group, but as in most Asian societies a very privileged category, many of whom will accommodate themselves to the demands of employment and political docility, but amongst whom will always be some who are alienated by the incapacity of the particular political economies of their societies to discuss and satisfy alternative needs. The latter might enter politics, and/or they might take the route of becoming "emancipatory" intellectuals. But to do this often requires at least as much mastery of the appropriate scholarly tradition as does entry to the technological intelligentsia. Lifestyle and political choice in other words rather than technical competence distinguish the intellectuals from the intelligentsia.

Indeed Gouldner's distinction, useful as it is up to a point, may actually create more problems than it solves. Some authors writing about contemporary Asia deny the distinction. Yoshino (1992), writing about Japan for example, prefer the term "educated elites" in suggesting that, at least in the Japanese context and in relation to the generation and reproduction of ideology, businessmen and high-school teachers play at least as important a role as professional writers and university teachers, partly because it is the first two categories that disseminate and institutionalise ideas. Without them the views of the self-styled "intellectuals" go mostly unheard. Put a little differently, a consumption model of ideas is at least as important as a production model, there being in reality of course a continuous feedback loop between them. And if one broadens the idea of a consumption model it soon becomes apparent that, to return to the class issue, most Asian intellectuals do not constitute a class in themselves, but are rather firmly situated at the middle to upper end of the newly emerging middle class in terms of income, lifestyle and consumption behaviour.

If this is so then intellectuals as such are not a "new class", but rather a segment of a much bigger category—that of "professionals". Most of the "new middle class" in say Malaysia or Singapore has a university education, but most translate that education into an occupation outside of education itself. They become a technical intelligentsia rather than intellectuals in the older sense. They may be emancipatory in the sense of liberating themselves from constraints of tradition, in solving the problem of poverty at least for themselves and in forcing some political evolution, but they are clearly not revolutionary or even ideological in orientation.

In the context of the university too objective changes force a re-evaluation of the position of the technical intelligentsia. Analysis of the curriculum and student enrolment figures of universities throughout Asia, in keeping here with the rest of the world, shows a major trend towards business studies and to a lesser extent technology. Pure sciences, social sciences and humanities are beginning to lag increasingly far behind. And where there is substantial student enrollment in the humanities and social sciences (excluding economics which is deliberately often related to or has become institutionally part of business studies), they are often predominantly women who, for other well-known sociological reasons, will not go on to dominating positions in the professions. This trend cannot be ignored, especially when major metropolitan universities such as Oxford which for years fought a rearguard action against the introduction of many aspects of the modern social sciences (sociology for example) have now succumbed totally and are busy creating courses in management studies at all levels.

This has many implications. It expands the intelligentsia and at least relatively speaking marginalises the intellectuals. Those of them who are still worried about their status have to find new symbolic means to struggle against this erosion of their position, one of which is often to become not more "relevant" but more esoteric: to write on subjects and in outlets only accessible to a tiny coterie who are also in the know. Another device is to expand areas in which the traditional intellectuals once held sway. A perfect example of this is the expansion of "cultural studies" out of literary studies and certain fringe areas of mainstream sociology into a major growth industry in which the impression of practicality can be conveniently combined with advanced esotericism. An obviously possible implication is that except as a device for subjective self-reference, the category of "intellectual" be abandoned, since the technical intelligentsia or "educated elite" has expanded to largely displace the traditional intellectuals. Overproduction of graduate degree holders relative to the number of job openings in the universities intensifies this trend: even a would-be "old intellectual" must have a marketable product and be able to market himself.

This fundamental shift also affects the position of the university in society. Universities become more "relevant", more entrepreneurial in seeking funding, students and outlets for their applied research. New kinds of courses have to be devised—engineering with business studies, criminology, nursing, computing and so on—and the links between universities and the society tend to deepen albeit for purely practical reasons. The internal organisation of universities shifts as a consequence: funding and facilities tend to go to the new faculties and the traditional pre-eminence of Arts Faculties disappears in practice if not symbolically, and the style of management within the universities becomes correspondingly more "professional", even if this actually means more bureaucratic and technocratic. The relationship between universities shifts: the old ones may retain symbolic domination, but real social and economic influence begins to shift to the new ones which, if they do not have age on their side, do have modernity, often better buildings and of course innovative courses. These shifts have appeared very conspicuously in Asia. All the newer universities in Malaysia are focused on modern specialities—technology, business or agriculture—and the older ones have been forced to innovate by at least introducing subjects like Japanese studies. In Singapore, the second university is almost exclusively technological and business, with its social science element being in new fields for the country such as mass communications. An effect of all this has not been a decline in employment for traditional intellectuals where numerical position has remained stable, even if one of their functions is now often to teach humanities or social sciences to business or technology students, but a massive increase in employment for teachers of these newer subjects. The social growth of the technological intelligentsia in the university sector throughout Asia is an important phenomenon in its own right, quite apart from its effects on the "old" intellectuals.

The role of the Asian intellectual then needs to be understood in a variety of intersecting contexts. These include class position as members of the new middle class while not necessarily being leaders of that class; close association with the university sector of higher education; relation to the media; political involvement; location within global networks; and position within the general ideology of education prevailing in their society. These last two require some comment. The first might typically refer to two kinds of example, one of which would be membership in the international "college" of scholars in a particular field: membership of international associations, attendance at international conferences, access to journals and resources that circulate globally. Another, and rather different one in its implications would be membership of an international ideological network, for example of Muslim scholars. The first kind of situation has a paradoxical effect. In principle it links Asian scholars to the world community. In practice it can also separate. Foreign journal subscriptions are expensive; attendance at conferences more so. Mastery of a metropolitan (i.e. Western) language is effectively mandatory. A brief review of the contents lists of major Western journals in, say, sociology, reveals that very few of the contributions are from Asia. If Foucault is correct and power is to be defined in terms of the generation and control of information and knowledge, North-South imbalances in "academic power" clearly exist. Southerners go north to graduate school; very few Northerners come south. Domination of patronage and prestige system by the North means that few publishers of journals within Asia are considered truly prestigious; today the major journals in Asian studies are published in England, France or the United States. The second form of international network, unlike the first, has not been extensively studied, but is of great interest since it permits a form of intellectual contact different from and possibly opposed to the more Western collegiate model. And since such networks, often extensive within Asia, are motivated by ideological commitment they tend to have a moral depth absent from the "pure" scholarship of the other kind of international network. But like the first, information, contacts, publications all flow, methodologies are invented and new forms of scholarship pioneered that may be very different from those understood or accepted by conventional academia. The closest parallel in the West, although there too are networks of religious and politically motivated scholars, would probably be feminist scholarship—emancipatory, critical of contemporary paradigms and offering an often radically alternative vision. A counter-hegemony is thus constructed by creating an intellectual model quite at variance with dominant reality assumptions. For this reason such "alternative intellectuals" are actually an avant garde and are far more likely to instigate ideological revolutions than establishment intellectuals who are as likely to reflect trends as to create them and whose largely non-political stance and preoccupation with media exposure (and with publication in "approved" places) render their contribution to radical social change problematic.

Intellectuals, Change and Social Vision

It would be nice to be able to agree with Hans Morgenthau's idea that the intellectual seeks the truth while the politician seeks power. Intellectuals clearly seek power too, although not necessarily in overtly political form, but through the creation and control of knowledge, and often in petty ways to such as through the control of patronage *over* other intellectuals—by opening or restricting access to jobs or publications for example. And here we can refer to the second of the two issues raised above requiring further comment—that the position of intellectuals must be related to the general ideology of education prevailing in a given society. In a single sense this can simply mean the amount of status given to intellectuals. In Japan for example, university teachers enjoy very high status: their position is respected to a far higher degree than in most Western countries where to teach in higher education is just another job distinguishable from others mainly by the relatively large amount of free time associated with it. In a second sense the size of the educational sector becomes a factor. Again in Japan, the "education society" in which almost everyone is in fact committed to the pursuit of some form of learning, produces large numbers of intellectuals associated with the arts, translation, the media and publishing and so forth, who are outside of the universities. Indeed we should perhaps even raise the question of whether all academics are really intellectuals, and the answer may be "no": many are simply reproducers or transmitters of ideas, but play little part in their creation or emancipatory application.

If it is correct that it is the "ideological" intellectuals in Asia today that are likely to have the most interesting ideas: Muslim intellectuals in Malaysia and Indonesia, Buddhist ones in Thailand, liberation theologians in the Philippines, then actually it is this group that should attract our attention, not only because of their empirical interest, but because of their impact on theories of intellectuals and of their position in society. Briefly several points can be made here. Firstly, in the West the intellectual is associated with secularisation, but in Asia, very much to the contrary, the emancipatory intellectual is more likely to be religious, and to be very much concerned with, as his primary interest, the relationship of religion to society, including its economic and political dimensions. Secondly, the primary understanding of the intellectual as the unmasker of distortions, the stripper away of masks and veils, has arguably shifted from the secular academic, more concerned with career and recognition than with truth, to those who do have a world view which at least they themselves consider to be more penetrating, fundamental and consequential than secular alternatives. Rapaport's suggestion that "I believe that the intellectual's class interest is served when the quality of life around him is in harmony with his ideological commitment" (Rapaport 1969) suggests that at least for this variety of intellectual, the establishment of a society in which the ideology becomes the reality is the goal, as with Muslim intellectuals in Malaysia (Jomo and Ahmad 1992). Thirdly, the understanding of the class position of the intellectual changes, as while such intellectuals may be objectively members of the new middle class, their identification is often with the masses and in some cases with the very poorest sections of the masses. This inevitably brings such intellectuals into contact with politics as well as with the production of culture: in fact the line between the two begins to dissolve.

Taken together these three have some interesting theoretical consequences. They suggest something rather different from Gouldner's theory of the rise of intellectuals to class power. Rather Asian emancipatory intellectuals are involved in the kinds of project that undermine the legitimacy of class as a concept, not least because of the incorporation of social justice themes into their vision of society. Indeed the very fact that a vision of society is central, rather than "pure scholarship" is itself of major consequence. This in turn suggests that more careful examination of the actual sociology of intellectuals needs to be undertaken. For while the study of establishment intellectuals places them closer to the conventional sociology of the professions, the analysis of emancipatory intellectuals places them closer to the sociology of social movements. The first category too are less likely to be allies of the working class, while the second are more likely to be. And both need to be set in the context of bigger socio-political trends: the commercialisation of the media, growth of the consumer society, expansion of the strong state and rise of ethnicism, all of which can easily suppress critical intellectual work.

And taken together these issues have implications for the position of the university on the one hand, and the position of "postmodern" intellectuals in general on the other. Bourdieu has argued for the relative autonomy of intellectual practice which in his model really becomes the exercise of symbolic power. This empirical question in his major study of French intellectuals (Bourdieu 1988) is really that of the *strategies* of those who attempt to exercise symbolic power and to use it as a means of symbolic domination (usually over other intellectuals as no one else may be listening!). In Bourdieu's model most of these significant intellectuals are in the universities (or their French equivalents). Others (Regis Debray, for example) have suggested that there is a displacement of intellectual power now occurring from the universities into publishing and the mass media. Those who choose a career in university teaching and research may do so because they are making a lifestyle choice, rather than imagining that they are ideally positioned to exercise social power. It is here that Bauman's thesis is of great relevance. He argued that whatever the general utility of the controversial concept of postmodernism, it does articulate the experience of the intellectuals (Bauman 1988). With the collapse of the global hegemony of the West, the erosion of Enlightenment-thought patterns, the diversity and plurality of the universities, there has been according to Bauman what he calls an implosion, a falling upon oneself, an agonising self-appraisal on the part of intellectuals. This arises both because of these global trends, including the fact that the "other" now speaks very articulately for his own self, and because of a status crisis occasioned by the fact that the demand for the services of intellectuals (for example, by the State) is small. This situation, if one follows Bauman's argument, creates a situation in which those who seek legitimation by the state are thrown into confusion, but for others real intellectual work becomes possible precisely because of the indifference of those who hold political power. The consequence of this is that, under postmodern conditions, the intellectuals have moved from centring themselves in politics to centring themselves in culture. The confusion can only be resolved in this situation of postmodern uncertainties by the intellectuals recognising that they are in Bourdieu's felicitous phrase, the "dominated faction of the dominant class".

But it is unclear how far this interesting thesis applies to situations in contemporary Asia. Establishment intellectuals, including those holding positions of authority in state universities, far from being alienated from the political process, are part of it: consultants, commentators, carriers out of commissioned research, sitters on committees, and even, as in Singapore, actually members of the parliament. To some extent indeed they are expected to legitimate their intellectual activities by practical application. Those in private universities often wish to move to public ones precisely because it puts them closer to the sources of such activity. The emancipatory intellectuals have of course a rather different position and often an ambiguous one. Often marginalised from mainstream university power positions they are nevertheless needed because in a sense *they* legitimate the broader political process, in Malaysia or Indonesia by providing the Muslim element, in the Philippines the Christian element, and so forth. A major theme in the political process becomes that of containing these elements while paying at least symbolic lip-service to their aspirations. The universities too must accommodate these forces and here they become especially interesting from the point of view of organisational analysis, since they are probably amongst the only institutions in modern society that can simultaneously contain and even derive synergy from such potentially contradictory forces.

The Asian intellectual in the post-colonial era faces real and potentially creative challenges, provided that privileged education can be translated into workable visions for society, rather than the aridities of "scholarship" for its own sake. At the very least this chapter has sought to expose some of the complex and fascinating issues in the sociology of Asian intellectuals. The issues are legion, but one thing that does help to unify them is the study of the university as an institution, western in origin, that now with varying degrees of indigenisation forms the pinnacle of the educational system in every Asian country. The university, in providing the setting for intellectual work, itself takes on a crucial role in social change. The Asian university is thus itself the legitimate subject of intellectual analysis, but beyond that lies its role in providing the context for the intellectual ferment out of which creative alternative visions for the future can arise, carried forward by that strange but essential group whose job is to think: the intellectuals themselves.

References

Anderson, B. (1993), *Imagined Communities*, London: Verso.

Bauman, Z. (1988), "Is There a Postmodern Sociology?" *Theory, Culture and Society*, 5, 2-3, pp. 217-237.

Bloom, A. (1988), *The Closing of the American Mind*, New York: Simon and Schuster.

Bourdieu, P. (1984), *Distinction: A Social Critique of the Judgement of Taste*, Cambridge, Massachusetts: Harvard University Press.

Bourdieu, P. (1988), *Homo Academicus*, Cambridge: Polity Press.
Clammer, J. (1985), *Singapore: Ideology, Society and Culture*, Singapore: Chopmen.
Dumont, L. (1980), *Homo Hierarchicus: The Caste System and Its Implications*, Chicago: University of Chicago Press.
Gouldner, A. (1979), *The Future of the Intellectuals and the Rise of the New Class*, New York: Macmillan.
Hua, Wu Yin (1984), *Class and Communalism in Malaysia*, London: Zed Books.
Jomo, K.S. and Ahmad Shabery Cheek (1992), "Malaysia's Islamic Movements," in J.S. Kahn and Francis Loh Kok Wah (eds.) *Fragmented Vision: Culture and Politics in Contemporary Malaysia*, Sydney: Allen Unwin.
Rapaport, A. (1969), "Have the Intellectuals a Class Interest?", in H.P. Dreitel (ed.) *Recent Sociology*, Toronto: The Macmillan Company.
S. Husin Ali (ed.) (1983), *Ethnicity, Class and Development: Malaysia*, Kuala Lumpur: Persatuan Sains Sosial Malaysia.
Yoshino, K. (1992), *Cultural Nationalism in Contemporary Japan*, London: Routledge.

Appendix: Intellectuals in their Social Context: Selected Asian Countries

	Political System	Economy	Official/Dominant Ideology	Higher Education	Level of Pluralism (Religious and Ethnic)	Media: Newspapers, TV, Radio, Publications	Levels of Control and Surveillance of Intellectuals
Vietnam	Socialist	Centrally planned	Marxist	State	Low	State	High
Indonesia	Authoritarian-presidential (Guided Democracy)	Capitalist/ Agricultural	Pancasila	State/Private	High	State/Private	High
China	Socialist	Centrally planned	Marxist	State	Low	State	High
Taiwan	Statist Democracy	Capitalist/ Industrial	Nationalism	State/Private	Low	State/Private	Medium
Singapore	Statist Democracy	State Capitalism	National Ideology	State	High	State	High
Hong Kong	Colonial	Capitalism	Capitalism	State/Private	Low	State/Private	Low
Thailand	Constitutional Monarchy/ Parliamentary	Capitalist/ Agricultural	Buddhism	State/Private	Low	State/Private	Medium
Malaysia	Constitutional Monarchy/ Parliamentary	Capitalist/ Agricultural	Rukunegara/ Islam	State	High	State/Private	Medium
India	Republican Democracy	Capitalist/ Agricultural	Secular Pluralism	State/Private	High	State/Private	Low
Burma	Military Junta	Natural Resource Extraction/ Agricultural	Buddhism	State	Low	State	High
Philippines	Republican Democracy	Capitalist/ Agriculture	Catholicism	State/Private	Low	State/Private	Low
Japan	Constitutional Monarchy/ Parliamentary	Industrial Capitalism	Japanism	State/Private	Low	State/Private	Low

Chapter 11

SCIENTIFIC VALUES AND POLITICAL IDEOLOGY

Singapore is one of the world's smallest states, and also one of the most ethnically plural societies. With a large Chinese (76%) majority, it also has substantial minority communities of Malays (15%) and Indians and a considerable number of smaller groups, including Eurasians, Arabs, Europeans and expatriates of Japanese, Thai, Filipino and many other origins. The management of this pluralism has always been a political and social priority—from the transition to independence of a former colonial society in 1965, through the stresses of high economic growth with its massive attendant social changes during the 1970s and 1980s, to adjustment to the geo-political and intellectual challenges of a new world order in the 1990s. But despite these major shifts both within and without Singapore, the political environment has hardly changed in the three decades since independence. The one-party rule by the People's Action Party (PAP) and an authoritarian and paternalistic style of government combined with close management of virtually every aspect of social life—education, housing, language, religion and even reproduction—and the suppression of social movements not directly sanctioned by the government, have characterised Singapore's political culture for thirty years.

There are clearly many angles from which the immediate history and contemporary society of Singapore could be approached. In this chapter, I intend to concentrate on just one aspect of this small but complex society—the conceptualisation and uses of "race" as a key aspect of the construction of Singaporean political culture. I will argue that there have been shifts in the way in which the notion of race has been defined and used, beginning with its use as part of the "social charter" or founding myth of Singapore as an essentially multiracial society (Benjamin 1976), through a period in which race was seen as the primary mode of social classification in an attempt to create an image of Singapore as a society stratified vertically by races, all equal but different and excluding the possibility of class as a horizontal conceptualisation of stratification based on economic rather than genetic differences from emerging (Clammer 1982), to the present situation which has emerged since the mid-1980s of effectively emphasising Chinese pre-eminence. This last stage utilises pseudo-scientific "data" and argumentation to construct an image of ethnicity rooted in a distinctively Chinese version of racial "reality".

This continuing obsession with race is interesting in that many of the original reasons that might have justified it—the colonial racial division of labour, the pro-communist Chinese "chauvinism" of the 1950s, the race riots of 1950 occasioned by the Maria Hertog affair, ethnic instability in neighbouring Malaysia—have all disappeared. But closer scrutiny reveals that the place of race in the political culture has also shifted—from the ethnic fragility model of the 1960s with the strong state as an answer to the inherent instability of such pluralism, through the depoliticisation of race and its reinvention as a set of cultures, to what Brown (1993) calls the "corporatist" model. By this term, Brown means the restructuring of ethnicity in terms of the primacy of the state (ethnic political loyalties are outlawed), a national community defined by a body of values selectively derived from the already engineered four "recognised" ethnic groups (Chinese, Malay, Indian and Eurasian) to ensure a sanitised group of characteristics that can be enshrined in a national ideology, and the conversion of ethnic communities from primordial cultural groups to the status of interest associations, each charged with the duty of looking after the requirements of it own (racially defined) members (Brown 1993: 21).

This is true, but Brown's analysis overlooks one very important aspect of the contemporary reconstruction of "corporatist ethnicity": the role that biology plays within it. To understand the significance of this, it is necessary to backtrack a little. First, a debate has gone on in Singapore for at least twenty years now of the nature of "Asian values" and the necessity of identifying and strengthening them in order to ward off the baleful influences of the decadent west (Clammer 1981). This has proved difficult to do, both because of the variety of "values" to be found in the numerous national and cultural communities of Asia, their differing religious roots and not infrequent incompatibilities, and because, when defined in abstract terms, they prove to be quite remarkably similar to those of the vilified

West, an embarrassing admission that the then deputy prime minister Goh Keng Swee made in a speech in 1976 (*Straits Times* 1976). This problem, which seems to be a perennial one in Singapore and which has most recently emerged again in debate about the proposed national ideology based on a set of shared values (Clammer 1993). Values by themselves turn out to be very free-floating and hard to root specifically in actual cultures. So how is it to be done? One solution, if values are seen as arising from ethnicity (as they evidently are in Singapore), is to understand ethnicity and hence values as having a biological basis.

Second, the trend in social policy over the last decade has clearly been directed towards the enhancement of Chinese primacy in Singapore—aggressive public promotion of Mandarin, the establishment of Confucianism as a kind of civic religion, population policies aimed at suppressing the birthrate amongst non-Chinese minorities, the establishment of formerly banned economic, academic and tourist links with China and the glorification of traditional Chinese culture (the old Immigration Department building at Empress Palace, one of the few surviving examples of real colonial architecture, having ironically been turned into an officially sponsored gallery of Chinese art, for example). This policy has not gone unnoticed by the other communities and most of the muted opposition to the national ideology has not been directed at its logical and ethnographic absurdities, but at the fact that it actually enshrines "Confucian" (as that term is understood in Singapore) values and as such ones both Chinese and functional to the continuation of PAP political dominance (Brown 1993: 25) rather than ones reflecting the true diversity of the country's ethnic and religious make-up. This needs justification and legitimation, and again one way of doing this is to appeal to characteristics that one community, defined of course as a "race", has and which might provide a basis for social policy.

Third, since the very beginning of racial discourse in post-independence Singapore, there has been a strong tendency to confuse race with ethnicity and both with culture. This has had numerous consequences ranging from the semantic to the very substantial implications for the way in which both cultural politics and political culture are structured. It has led, to take one example, to the identification of race and language. Each "race" (in the Chinese, Malay, Indian, Other or CIMO model) is believed to "have" a language—Mandarin in the case of Chinese, Malay in the case of Malays, Tamil in the case of Indians, and English in the case of Others. But many Chinese speak dialects, many Indians are not Tamils and not everyone with Chinese genes carries Chinese culture. But a Peranakan (Straits-born Chinese) child (i.e. one who is genetically of Chinese descent, but who speaks Malay or English and possesses a culture close to that of the Malays) is forced to take Mandarin in school because he is "Chinese" and the "mother-tongue" of the Chinese (and one of the four official languages of Singapore) is Mandarin. Probably the most common reason for failing to gain admission into the university in Singapore is inadequate grades in the second language (the first in school being English), since that language, although defined as a mother-tongue, may not actually be spoken by anyone in the family of the would-be student.

Fourth, in the earlier days, perception of ethnic identity in Singapore was greatly coloured by the idea of the country as the Israel of Southeast Asia—a tiny country, in the Singapore case with a Chinese majority, surrounded by much larger Muslim majority countries (Brunei, Indonesia and Malaysia). Since the advent of Asean, decades of economic growth, changing politics and the virtual collapse of communist movements throughout Southeast Asia, any real or imagined threat from the neighbours has declined. Instead China has arisen on the northeastern horizon as the great potential market, trading partner and recipient of (largely Singaporean Chinese) investments. And with it has arisen both the pragmatic need to speak Mandarin and understand Chinese culture and the subjective affinity for what is one of the great mother-cultures of Asia and which is no longer seen as politically threatening. These factors, together with the resurgence of overseas Chinese networks worldwide, has made it both possible and desirable to emphasise a Chinese identity on the part of Singaporean Chinese whose previously controlled and sanitised cultural identity created little affinity with "real" Chinese culture. But many Singaporean Chinese are very unclear about what they actually mean by the "Chinese culture" with which they are now so eager to establish links. Many in fact, having been born in Southeast Asia, having been educated in an English-medium educational system and having in many cases a stronger cultural orientation towards Europe or Australia than to the rest of Asia, do not know how to create a "Chinese" identity for themselves. A beginning point obviously is to stress descent—a biological lineage that legitimises an identity in racial terms even if culture is absent.

Finally, the PAP approach to the management of society has been through a variety of means, including the management of culture. One of the easiest means to do this has been through the racialisation of a range of social questions, since the identification of problems through the prism of race allows these same problems to be set in the context of the inherent instability or dangers of ethnic strife argument, forms of which have persisted, or are always recoverable when needed, from pre-independence days. Three examples illustrate this tendency. The first is the use of race as the primary means of social classification. All Singaporeans and permanent residents are required to "have" a race—normally one of the four from the CIMO model—and are also sub-classified by dialect—something which applies mainly to the Chinese. This information is inscribed on the identity card which all adult citizens and permanent residents are required to carry at all times. Two things are worthy of note here. The first is this process of classification itself which privileges race over all alternative forms of social identity. The second is that the nature of the culture identified with each race is already engineered: it is not a spontaneous product, but is highly managed. This applies both to the manifestations of each race or culture: there are distinctively Chinese dances, Malay dances and Indian dances (songs, costumes, languages, cuisines, etc.) predefined as being acceptable, and to the detailed manipulation of elements in these cultures, such as the requirement established in the late 1980s that all Chinese babies should have a *hanyu pinyin* name for purposes of both registration and subsequent schooling and not a "dialect" (meaning all Chinese languages other than Mandarin) or English one.

A second example relates to housing. Analysis of voting trends has shown that constituencies with large minorities (especially Malays) tend to vote against the PAP to a greater extent than Chinese-dominated constituencies. The realisation of this had two main consequences—the absorption of such dangerous constituencies into Group Representation Constituencies in which three constituencies are put together and vote for all three candidates, one of whom must be of a minority race, as a team; and the manipulation of housing. To prevent concentration of ethnic minorities in particular areas, the government-run Housing Development Board (HDB) was forced at the beginning of the 1990s to institute a policy of not allowing the sale or purchase of HDB apartments (in which a figure approaching 90 per cent of the population live) unless a certain ethnic "balance" was maintained. A Malay wishing to move to an area such as Geylang Serai or Bedok which already have substantial Malay populations is, under this policy, banned from buying an apartment there and a potential seller may not sell to such a would-be purchaser. A Malay can however move to a Chinese-dominated area without difficulty and a Chinese of course can move to a Malay district. This policy clearly reduces the housing options of minorities, while leaving the majority population to live where it likes.

The third example, which I will shortly comment on in more detail, is population and the clear determination of the PAP to maintain its own domination by maintaining the current ethnic proportions—to keep a substantial Chinese majority or to even increase the size of that majority through population incentives and immigration while simultaneously depressing the population of the minorities. It is this third example that is the most interesting because it is the one in which explicit use has been made of sociobiology to construct arguments for racial superiority.

These moves, like the national ideology, have not gone unnoticed either by the population or by the regional and international press. Brown (1993: 31) commented on this as follows:

> There are signs that the corporatist management of ethnicity in Singapore has promoted some unease. Having hitherto identified ethnicity in terms of the all-embracing primordial racial affiliations, Singaporeans find it difficult to make the new corporatist distinctions between illegitimate ethnic loyalties, admirable ethnic cultural values and legitimate ethnic interests. This gives rise to confusion in three main areas: first, whether the promotion of Chinese culture indicates a government bias in favour of Chinese interests; second, the problem of distinguishing the meritocratic principle of ethnic neutrality from the principle of ethnic balance; and third, demarcating the line between the ethnic values and interests of which government approves, and the communalism of which it disapproves.

While Brown derives from this the conclusion that this commits the PAP to an interventionist policy in relation to ethnicity rather than the depoliticisation of it, he sees the policies as taking primarily institutional forms—creating interest associations such as Mendaki (Council for Education of Muslim Children) or the Singapore Indian Development Corporation. But underlying this is the discourse of race itself—the background and ideological source for these developments, and it is to this discourse that I will now turn.

Scientism and the Discourse of Race in Contemporary Singapore

Singapore then is, and sees itself as, an ethnically plural society, one moreover in which ethnicity, far from being played down, is constantly reinforced and enhanced through social, political and cultural policy. Racial discourse is a large part of everyday conversation—in relation to the identity of self and others, food and everyday culture, language, as the primary folk explanation of habits and behaviour. Race has become a reality for all Singaporeans: it is the taken-for-granted constitution of society, the basic feature of the social fabric. While some of this sense of the reality of race comes from the immigrant background of almost all Singaporeans, most comes from the deliberate political construction of the ethnic discourse to which we have already referred. In this context concern with identity defined always in racial terms becomes paramount and a chronic state of slightly insecure being. It is against this background, already prepared and engineered, that the attempt to provide a "scientific" basis for identities and differences rooted in race appeared, and to the analysis of which we will now turn.

Here I will take one example of this process for more detailed analysis. In his 1983 National Day speech the then prime minister Lee Kuan Yew revealed figures suggesting that fewer graduate women were marrying than their non-graduate counterparts, and that those who did marry produced less children (1.9 each compared with 3.9). Lee expressed dismay over what he saw as being a trend which, if left unchecked, would inevitably result in the decline of intelligence in the Singapore population as a whole. This was underpinned by a theory of the genetic basis of intelligence and the remarkable assertion that, on the basis of studies of separated twins, it is scientifically known that 80 per cent of intelligence is inherited and only 20 per cent is due to environment (Lee 1983).

The intense public debate that followed, unusual for its intensity in highly controlled Singapore, demonstrated that while a substantial (and largely Chinese) group of the population agreed with Lee, a large number did not. Despite the outcry, a "priority scheme" of tax and educational incentives for university graduates to breed more and corresponding disincentives for non-graduates was instituted in May 1984. Even Lee felt (unusually) obliged to defend his views and he did so with reference to twin studies at the University of Minnesota, to the well-known pro-hereditary psychologist Hans Eysenck and through Eysenck to the now entirely discredited work of Cyril Burt. Criticisms of the work of these individuals was not mentioned and their "findings" were offered (in tandem with quotations from Arthur Jensen and other pro-hereditary theorists) as fact. Local intellectuals, if that word can be used in this context, from the departments of medicine and botany at the National University of Singapore were enrolled to provide popularisations, especially of Eysenck's views, and the press ran detailed expositions by these individuals of their "genes and intelligence" position (Chee and Chan 1984).

Lee's owns views had not substantially changed since 1969 when, in debate about the Abortion Bill then before parliament, be spoke openly about the need to create disincentives to reduce the birthrate of "the irresponsible, the social delinquents" (Lee 1969: 321) and the "physically, intellectually and culturally anemic" (Lee 1969: 323). What had changed between 1969 and 1983 was that Lee had amassed the "scientific" data necessary to present his developed theory, which the graduate women fertility figures gave him the ideal opportunity to do. Intelligence and education go together in Lee's vision, so a meritocratic policy which gives more to those who already have, and which makes it harder for those without ever to gain access or empowerment, is neatly justified on biological grounds.

Here the issue might have remained—a case of classical biological determinism resurfacing in a small Southeast Asian country—except that the question rapidly became a racial one. Most graduates are Chinese, and the offending women who were not marrying and reproducing were also Chinese. Malays produce far fewer graduates than their proportion in the population as a whole. The decline in the fertility of the educated was clearly a Chinese problem. The Malays on the other hand have high fertility rates. No great grasp of statistics is needed to predict that if these patterns continued the size of the Chinese population would be eroded, while that of the minorities (all of which—Malays, Indians and Catholic Eurasians—have high fertility rates) would increase, eventually to the point where Singapore would no longer be Chinese-dominated. In practice then the incentives were aimed at the Chinese, and the disincentives at the minorities, especially the Malays.

When the obviousness of this became incontestable, government ministers began to make statements about the desirability of maintaining the present ethnic balance as the "productivity" of the country might otherwise decline (i.e. the Chinese work harder and are more efficient, while the rest are unproductive). To emphasise this not only were the disincentives, which included a cash grant for low-income (read Malay) couples who undertook voluntary sterilisation, widely publicised as positive choices for the poor, but immigration policy was modified to encourage immigration from what were termed "traditional"sources" (China, Taiwan and Hong Kong) and to make it harder for would-be migrants from "non-traditional" sources, which remarkably included India. Educational criteria for potential migrants were strengthened, Singaporean Chinese who had moved abroad were encouraged to return, a Singapore school was set up in Hong Kong, Chinese professionals from Taiwan and North America were welcomed and permanent resident status (normally difficult to obtain and requiring a substantial period of residence and work in Singapore) was offered to Hong Kong Chinese professionals, entrepreneurs sand skilled workers willing to state a willingness to move to Singapore now or post 1990 without their even having to leave Hong Kong. By a very direct chain of logic, biological determinism leads to enhanced opportunities for Chinese and the diminution of opportunities for others, all based upon the most unstable and controversial "scientific" findings.

Theorising the Debate

Pure political expediency or the cynical manipulation of "knowledge" for creating or maintaining power could of course explain the situation I have been describing. However, here I will argue that there is more to the total picture than just this. To more completely theorise the ways in which the discourse of race is used and constructed it is also necessary to explore some key aspects of history and religion, of concepts of body and gender, and the generation of political ideology in Singapore.

The Chinese community in Singapore is historically entirely of migrant origin. While now a majority of Singaporean Chinese are locally born, this is a fairly recent phenomenon and a high percentage of individuals over the age of fifty-five were born outside of Singapore—in China, Hong Kong or elsewhere in Southeast Asia to parents who in many cases were themselves first-generation migrants from China, mostly from Fujien, Guangdong or Hainan. These migrants were diverse in dialect, occupation, local culture and religious practices, and were initially almost entirely male. The establishment of a stable Chinese community—one with some perception of itself as Chinese rather than of specific regional origins, with a more balanced sex ratio, some form of recognisable family life and descent system and with a sociological network of religious, dialect, locality, occupational and mutual assistance associations—has been a long historical process and also one of the constant political construction of identity (Clammer 1983).

The resulting social arrangements have several main characteristics. The first of these is the existence of a conscious model of Chinese identity which is remarkably essentialist in character, stressing, despite the obvious huge spatial, temporal, economic and cultural range and variety of both China itself and the Chinese diaspora, strong commonalities of race, ideology and sociological characteristics, especially the family system and patrilineal descent. These in practice reinforce each other: descent systems legitimate a sense of common stock and biological community; ideology ("Confucianism") provides a unifying theory; and phenotypical characteristics support the idea of a common descent reflecting a common ideology. Interestingly, "culture" as such plays little role in this model: it is secondary to or derivative from the primary racial, sociological and phenotypical characteristics (Ward 1965).

The "folk" model of Chinese identity has been converted by political means and the management of culture into an official model of race. The achievement of congruence between the folk and the official (CIMO) models is precisely one reason why race, while constantly talked about, is not seen as problematic. It has been almost entirely naturalised. In the CIMO situation all ethnic groups are forced to be alert to their boundaries and to create mechanisms (or the state creates them) for policing and maintaining those boundaries. But if loss of culture is not to lead to loss of ethnicty, some other essentialist mechanism is necessary, and a biological one is the ideal answer, especially as it corresponds closely to the Chinese folk model (common descent, phenotype) on the one hand and on the other is difficult to challenge because the average layperson simply does not command the scientific knowledge required.

Thirdly, in Singapore we see the interesting situation of a majority community obsessed with the "problem" of its identity, a situation created by the structural characteristics of ethnicity in the country. To become ethnically "neutral" (a cosmopolitan or universalist solution) is absolutely not the goal of Singaporean Chinese, nor can it realistically be given the politically driven nature of racial debate. Indeed in the latest phases of ethnic management—the "corporatist" one—it is precisely the sociological structures (clan associations, for example) that are being used to further manage these same groups. Multiple ethnic membership, ambiguity of identity, free choice of membership of a particular group because of subjective affinity or the situational selection of identity for particular strategic purposes, are all absent form the Singaporean Chinese model, even though they may apply to other ethnic groups in the region, in Malaysia for example (Nagata 1974).

Potential threats to this identity have consequently to be carefully managed. Such threats come from several directions—interethnic marriage, religious conversion (especially to Christianity, but also to Islam) and the effects of globalisation. One of the highest rates of interethnic marriage in Singapore involves the Chinese community, but most such marriages are of Chinese females marrying non-Chinese males. Since females are not patrilineally significant the effects of this pattern are minimal on overall sense of identity and common (read "pure") descent. The second threat has been handled by both the political and religious authorities by means of simply detaching religion from ethnicity in the case of the Chinese. For Muslims, Sikhs, Jews, Sri Lankan Buddhists and many Hindus, the connection however is still argued to hold. The third threat, from global culture, travel, foreign television programmes and so forth, has been handled in three ways: by vigorously promoting Chinese culture in Singapore, including art, television dramas, film, dance, sport, theatre, music and literature (in addition to language); by censoring offending foreign media which does not meet local political leaders' expectations; and by promoting the idea (until recently absolutely taboo) of a greater China, but now not based on political hegemony of the People's Republic, but on the international community of Chinese with their links of language and culture, and above all their powerful economic networks.

Whereas the category "Malay" often in practice decomposes into Javanese, Bugis, Minangkabau, etc., the concept of Chinese does not. On the contrary its sub-categories (dialect, locality) coalesce into the more inclusive category of Chinese. The logic of "Malay" or "Indian" is to break down into smaller and actually more culturally relevant units; the logic of "Chinese" is to move towards the more inclusive level of identity. This has promoted an interesting trend—the resinification of many Singaporean Chinese who, having lost language and cultural traits when Chinese chauvinism was out, are now scrambling to reequip themselves now that a distinctively Chinese identity is now very much in.

A strong state, paternalistic managerialism, a high level of bureaucratisation, a wide network of social control mechanisms and a fairly successful attempt to create a monopoly version of "reality" and the control of the means (political, media, education) of its production and reproduction, characterises the political context for the organisation of ethnicity in Singapore. This has produced a system which socially is elitist, heavily prone to seeking technical solutions for human problems, treating the social sciences in a purely instrumental way as a means of sophisticated political market research and which has proved very adept at co-opting the local intellectual community and turning them into social engineers and willing servants of the state ideology. Singapore very much has the air of being a modernist society—one pursuing irrational goals by "rational" means, pervaded with positivism and seeing itself very much in functionalist terms—as a social organism in which each element plays its part.

Positivistic and scientistic viewpoints usually go together. The concept of race in Singapore discourse is essentialistic and denies the possibility of races mutating, having origins in the mixing of earlier populations or as being basically social constructs created politically during the process of state formation. Historically this has clearly happened (the Chinese are not a "race" but a culturally constituted group), and paradoxically is happening in Singapore, where the state is actively engaged in constructing a concept of race, partly by insisting that the concept is not constructed, but is primordial and fundamentally biological. In effect this is an argument for the "purity" of races, or at least for the purity of the Chinese race. The maintaining of purity requires the establishment of difference and social distance. The overarching problem in the management of ethnicity in Singapore is that of maintaining the virtually absolute separation of the races while simultaneously insisting on the organic unity of the nation. One way to do this is to argue for biological difference as the fundamental mechanism of distinction, while requiring allegiance to the unitary state (and not to cultural co-operation between groups) as the principle of unity. This is possible if race is equated with ethnicity and indeed may be logically required if an essentialist and biological definition of race is employed.

Interestingly this possibility is probably only possible in Singapore amongst Chinese. Malays by contrast see identity in terms of religion (Islam) and *adat* or custom and language. In principle it is possible for a non-Malay to *masuk Melayu*—to "enter Malaydom" by religious conversion and adoption of Malay custom. "Race"—phenotypical characteristics, biological origins or descent are irrelevant. It is impossible however to become Chinese by any such process of cultural adoption since "blood"—origins, descent and phenotypical characteristics—exclude this. This has an extremely important sociological consequence. In many migrant societies great attention is paid to the social construction of memory—to inventing a past and creating "traditions" even where they do not objectively exist. In the Singapore case however the opposite tendency is discerned: that of the suppression of memory. Identification with the real China (Malaysia, India and Indonesia) is dangerous as it both creates political identities other than or transcending the Singapore state and it undermines the myth of the homogeneous and separated races by drawing attention to the facts of migration, cultural formation, cultural mixing and ethnogenesis (Clammer 1993b). Mythical history is thus required and so not only do the local cultures need sanitising, but so do these Chinese or other pasts.

Race, Gender and Body

The logic of the Singaporean classificatory system is to create differences: the system creates the Other by its mechanisms of exclusion. The possibility of new identities emerging naturally (for example by intermarriage) is excluded. Groups likes the Peranakans who certainly provided the nucleus of a new ethnicity are formally assimilated to the Chinese category and their culture honoured as something in the past, not as a model for future Singaporean identity. Although discourse about difference is essentially a discourse about race, this logic of difference can easily colonise other areas, especially those that are themselves partly biological. Gender is an obvious example. Sociologically, descent in Chinese societies is patrilineal. This has certain consequences. Firstly, arguments about race can easily be disguised as sociology—race becomes descent expressed as ancestralism. Secondly, the demographic imbalance of Chinese migration to Singapore, Confucian ideology and the experiences of the majority male migrants, has led to a highly gendered view both of the Chinese past and the Singapore present. The experiences of female migrants are only now beginning to be recovered. My contention here is that patrilineality and a racial ideology mutually support each other, through the patriarchal ancestor cult, the surname system and the mechanisms of marriage (Baker 1979).

This issue again raises the question of power. The "common sense" reality of Singaporean racial notions turns out to be highly constructed and highly ideological. Power indeed in Singapore resides not in naked force, but in the ability to create such socio-political constructions and to persuade the population at large to accept them as natural, as fact. Not only then is race to be taken for granted (and if questioned to be concealed behind a fog of pseudo-scientific justifications), but so is gender and so is the gendered and racialised body. So there is Chinese medicine for the Chinese body, Malay magico-religious medical practice for the Malay body, forms of *ayurvedic* medicine for the Indian body. Each, furthermore, has a distinct dietary system associated with it. But each of these racialised systems is subservient to the western or "scientific" medical system which is the final repository of medical truth. Singapore is an extensively medicalised society, but one in which the management of the body is structured in racialised ways, but in which racialisation is subservient to a view of science as the system of ultimate legitimacy. The body moreover is naturalised in ways parallel to that of race. Racial and gender differences (and subsequently inequalities) support each other (Coward 1983) in part by subordinating process (construction) to being (essentialism). In this context, selfhood, the basis of identity, becomes both racialised and scientised.

Chinese medical practice and training in Singapore would provide a very interesting way into the race-body-gender-self nexus if space allowed (e.g. Farquhar 1994). But the broader issue is that the body is a social body as well as a natural one and the Confucian-hierarchical model can be expected to express itself in a model of the corporeal. In this model boundaries have to be created, not only in the traditional ordering of space (for example women as bounded within the house), but now in the creation of biological boundaries invested with social and political significance, and which must be expressed through appropriate (i.e. ethnically) cultural activity and participation in the political rituals of the state (such as National, Day parades with their emphasis on display, marching and gymnastics). The racialised body, created by a process not that much different from the one that Said calls "Orientalism" (Said 1978), becomes part of the larger project of social control and state identity: ideology is created through biology. Interestingly this is reinforced by a mechanism that has not, so far as I am aware, yet been identified as a cultural and social control mechanism in Singapore: the creation of notions of propriety and respectability and their enforcement through legal means. Exposure of the body, unsatisfactory toilet habits, consumption of chewing gum, standards of dress and even acceptable gestures are regulated by law, and infringements not only carry penalties, but are subject to public exposure and shaming in the government-controlled press.

A comment by Anagost (1994: 139) on rituals of public recognition and humiliation in China can be transferred almost exactly to the Singapore case:

> We would therefore be in error if we attempted to understand these rituals of objectification solely in terms of their specified ends—the reformation of behavior. They are also rituals of subjection, of subject making; they produce docile bodies and transform these bodies into signifiers that figure in a master narrative ... These rituals objectify subjects in a way that does not individuate them but causes them to be subsumed within a mass identity, the "people as one," for whom the party becomes the sole authorized voice. If, as Michel de Certeau has suggested, "every power is toponymical and initiates its order of places by naming them," then the power to name, in this sense, is a negation of otherness that appropriates what is the other into the self. To be named

is to be heteronomous; it means to be absorbed into another's reality, to be subject to the rule of the other.

It is precisely this power to name, the mania for rigid classification and categorisation that both gives the political apparatus in Singapore its basic power and which fundamentally characterises its style of operation: the naturalisation of the constructed by the Party, and its delineation of models which are promoted as spontaneously arising from the people (their folk models).

Not to "have" a race in Singapore is to be invisible, since officially this is the primary source of identity. Unwittingly the Singapore authorities seem to understand Foucault very well: that power resides not in force, but in the invisible and silent forms of "knowledge". Alternative narratives of identity have not been permitted to emerge. Power in Singapore is exercised through culture paradoxically to establish a "reality" that is essentially biological: deep racialism. Dispositions in Bourdieu's (1977) sense already present in the Chinese population (i.e. attitudes and inclinations), which were traditionally embodied in certain practices (the ancestor cult, for example), have not been abolished but re-engineered, the old forms taken to contain a new content—the racial policies of the state.

Concluding Thoughts

Singapore's policies towards race are of great interest from a comparative perspective. The idea of "China" is fundamentally cultural, yet Singaporean Chinese identity has been thoroughly racialised, and this racialised identity, politically constructed by way of pseudo-scientific argumentation, has been made in turn the basis of the racialisation of housing, medicine, education and population policies and provides the premises for social work practice, theories of deviance and mental illness, athletic prowess or lack of it, entrepreneurial skills and even driving behaviour. Few, if any areas, of Singapore life escape this pervasive racialisation. The historical decision to make race the basis of all social classifications and to emphasise the construct of race has had many consequences. It makes the strong state apparently necessary as only it can arbitrate between the conflicting interests of these groups founded upon the fundamental premises of difference. It banishes the possibility of large scale ethnic assimilation and the eventual achievement of a "post-ethnic" society based on shared history and common identity. It has "worked" as a model primarily because of government success in establishing the identity of folk models and official ideology. The fragility of the model lies not in racial unrest in this materially successful, tightly controlled and high-growth economy, but in the perceived need to find new legitimations for what looks like an increasingly untenable concept of race in an increasingly global society—hence the appeal to "science".

Finally, the racialisation of Singapore society poses the interesting question of how to locate the place on the political spectrum. Here we have an authoritarian and paternalistic, strongly anti-socialist (although with friendly relations with China, Vietnam and with the former Soviet Union and now its successors), equally strong pro-capitalist, yet in a highly interventionist manner while in theory espousing free-market principles. But yet the system does not seem to qualify for inclusion in the category of the New Right. There are four reasons for this. Firstly, ideologically the PAP has associated its legitimacy with Confucianism—hardly an option that was open to Ronald Reagan or Margaret Thatcher. Secondly, Singapore has not faced the crises of rising unemployment, urban decay, immigration and crime that have tended to precede a turn to the right in North American or European politics. Thirdly, the New Right critique of increasing state intervention is not appropriate in Singapore where the state has always been highly interventionist and managerial.

Finally, the New Right is based on a particular ontology—it is for individualism, authority and the market, and against the liberal concept of the organic society. It is based on methodological individualism expressed in a view of human nature which is reductionist and biologically determinist. In Singapore, we find a society committed to the rejection of individualism, yet also committed to the reductionism and biological determinism of the New Right (Rose, Kamin and Lewontin 1984: 3-15). It is precisely this combination of characteristics that in one sense makes Singapore so interesting, and also so strange and even sinister: the attempt to create a conservative utopia rooted in the racialisation of reality and built not upon science, but pseudo-science—science selected and justified for its political utility in a society in which the elite sees, at least for the masses, biology to be the ultimate reality.

References

Anagost, A. (1994), "The Politicised Body," in A. Zito and T.E. Barlow (eds.) *Body, Subject and Power in China*, Chicago and London: University of Chicago Press.

Baker, H.D.R. (1979), *Chinese Family and Kinship*, London: Macmillan.

Benjamin, G. (1976), "The Cultural Logic of Singapore's 'Multiculturalism'," in R. Hassan (ed.) *Singapore: Society in Transition*, Kuala Lumpur: Oxford University Press.

Bourdieu, P. (1977), *Outline of a Theory of Practice*, Cambridge: Cambridge University Press.

Brown, D. (1993), "The corporatist management of ethnicity in contemporary Singapore," in G. Rodan (ed.) *Singapore Changes Guard: Social, Political and Economic Directions for the 1990s*, New York: St. Martin's Press and Melbourne: Longman Cheshire.

Chee, Heng Leng and Chan Chee Koon (eds.) (1984), *Designer Genes: I.Q., Ideology and Biology*, Petaling Jaya: Institute for Social Analysis.

Clammer, J. (1981), "Asian Values and the Paradoxes of Modernisation in Singapore," in R.E. Vente, R.S. Bhatal and R.M. Nakhooda (eds.) *Cultural Heritage v. Technological Development*, Singapore: Maruzen.

Clammer, J. (1982), "The Institutionalising of Ethnicity: The Culture of Ethnicity in Singapore," *Ethnic and Racial Studies* 5(2).

Clammer, J. (1983), "Chinese Ethnicity and Political Culture in Singapore," in P.L.A. Gosling and L. Lim (eds.) *The Chinese in Southeast Asia*, Singapore: Maruzen.

Clammer, J. (1993a), "Deconstructing Values: The Establishment of a National Ideology and its Implications for Singapore's Political Future," in G. Rodan (ed.) *Singapore Changes Guard: Social, Political and Economic Directions in the 1990s*, New York: St. Martin's Press and Melbourne: Longman Cheshire.

Clammer, J. (1993b), "Le mythe de la race et de la Chine ancienne parmi les Chinios d'outre mer: mémoire, historie, ethnicité," Strates 7, Paris: CNRS.

Coward, R. (1983), *Patriarchal Precedents: Sexuality and Social Relations*, London: Routledge and Boston: Kegal Paul.

Farquhar, J. (1994), "Multiplicity, Point of View and Responsibility in Traditional Chinese Healing," in A. Zito and T.E. Barlow (eds.) *Body, Sub-*

ject and Power in China, Chicago and London: University of Chicago Press.

Lee Kuan Yew (1969), *Abortion Bill, Third Reading: Select Committee Proceedings*, Singapore: Government Printer.

Lee Kuan Yew (1983), "The Education of Women and Patterns of Procreation," *RIHED Bulletin* (August), Singapore: Regional Institute of Higher Education and Development.

Nagata, J. (1974), "What is a Malay?: Situational Selection of Ethnic Identity in a Plural Society," *American Ethnologist* 1(2).

Rose, S., L.J. Kamin and R.C. Lewontin (1984), *Not in Our Genes: Biology, Ideology and Human Nature*, Harmondsworth: Penguin Books.

Said, E. (1978), *Orientalism*, Harmondsworth: Penguin Books.

Straits Times (Singapore) (1976) June 24, p. 5.

Ward, B. (1965), "Varieties of the Conscious Model: The Fishermen of South China," in M. Banton (ed.) *The Relevance of Models for Social Anthropology*, London: Tavistock.

INDEX

ALSO BY PELANDUK PUBLICATIONS

Chinese Beliefs and Practices in Southeast Asia

Studies on the Chinese Religion in Malaysia, Singapore and Indonesia

Edited by Cheu Hock Tong

Chinese religion is a subject that has fascinated sinologists and followers of Chinese beliefs and history—both from the East and the West—through the centuries. Its symbolisms, mysticism and rituals have evoked active interest in scholars worldwide. The study of Chinese religion is both interesting and challenging because of its unique twist: there is no one single system of Chinese belief and religious practice. There are as many facets and shades of Chinese religion as there are Chinese settlements, clans and sub-clans around the world.

This book explores the various aspects of Chinese beliefs and practices in Southeast Asia, with special emphases on Malaysia, Singapore and Indonesia. Since these countries are multi-ethnic and multi-religious in their socio-cultural systems, Chinese religion has evolved in its interaction with other religious traditions such as Islam, Christianity and Buddhism. The studies in this volume reveal some of its current trends and images. They show that the Chinese in this part of Southeast Asia are currently going through three interrelated patterns of development: one based on traditional beliefs, another on a mixture of traditional and non-traditional beliefs, and yet another on non-traditional beliefs.

Since these patterns of development take shape in the same pluralistic socio-cultural systems, wherein the Chinese occupy a differential socio-political status in the hierarchy of ethnic stratifications, they have extensive effects on the directions of change and rates of integration in these countries.

This book provides researchers, students, teachers and general readers with insights into the complex and localised aspects of Chinese religion, a compendium of ethnographic materials and local examples, and information about current images and trends of religious development among the Chinese in Southeast Asia.

ISBN 967 978 452 5
Pelanduk Publications

$29.00